Robert Harley and
the press

Robert Harley and the press

Propaganda and public opinion in the age of Swift and Defoe

J. A. DOWNIE

LECTURER IN ENGLISH LITERATURE
GOLDSMITHS' COLLEGE UNIVERSITY OF LONDON

CAMBRIDGE UNIVERSITY PRESS

CAMBRIDGE

LONDON · NEW YORK · MELBOURNE

Published by the Syndics of the Cambridge University Press
The Pitt Building, Trumpington Street, Cambridge CB2 1RP
Bentley House, 200 Euston Road, London NW1 2DB
32 East 57th Street, New York, NY 10022, USA
296 Beaconsfield Parade, Middle Park, Melbourne 3206, Australia

First published 1979

Printed in Great Britain at the
University Press, Cambridge

Library of Congress Cataloguing in Publication Data
Downie, James Alan, 1951–
Robert Harley and the press.

Includes bibliographical references and index.
1. Oxford, Robert Harley, earl of, 1661–1724.
2. Great Britain – Politics and government – 1702–1714.
3. Great Britain – Politics and government – 1714–1727.
4. Press – Great Britain. 5. Great Britain – Public
opinion. 6. Politics and literature. 7. Defoe,
Daniel, 1661?–1731. 8. Swift, Jonathan, 1667–1745.
I. Title.
DA497.08D68   320.9′41′069   78-67810
ISBN 0 521 22187 0

For my parents

Contents

Preface and Acknowledgements

After the freedom enjoyed by the press on the outbreak of civil war in 1642, the Restoration reimposed censorship with the licensing act of 1662. Until the Glorious Revolution, with one short lapse from 1679 to 1685 (when Charles II attempted to control the press through the exercise of his prerogative), the publication of political literature was regulated by law. Each pamphlet and newspaper had to be licensed by authority, and without this seal of approval it was liable to prosecution. The abandonment of the licensing system in 1695, however, did not inevitably mean that the press had been accepted by government. For Macaulay the rise of a free press was of more importance than the signing of Magna Carta, or the acceptance by William and Mary of the bill of rights. But the end of censorship was due to the fundamental inefficiency with which the licensing system had operated, not to a more enlightened attitude. The press had still to win its freedom, although it had escaped for a time the shackles of restriction.

In the course of the eighteenth century the political press gradually became a permanent feature of English society. Alongside the whims of monarchs, and the decisions of parliaments, there grew up a further power in the state: public opinion. The years after 1695 – the age of men like Swift and Defoe – were crucial in this development. In 1712 legislation relating to the press again entered the statute-books. Significantly it sought to tax the press, not to censor it. By then the ministry had developed its own propaganda machine and propaganda agency, and these, in conjunction with laws regarding seditious libel and treason, were felt to be adequate safeguards. The stamp act was passed while Robert Harley headed the administration as earl of Oxford. It represented the views of the prime minister, and he also organised government propaganda. The purpose of this study is to account for his attitude towards propaganda, public opinion and the press, and to relate his attitudes to the wider aspects of political literature in the age of Swift and Defoe.

Two dissertations, one on Defoe's *Review*, the other on Harley and the press, are the groundwork for the study. The award of the Stott Fellowship of the University of Wales allowed me to rewrite and integrate my theses for publication during two years spent at University College of North Wales, Bangor. I should like to record my gratitude. Too many pamphlets and letters have been examined to permit a full bibliography. The reader is, therefore, directed to the notes and to my theses, should he require information about the evidence on which my conclusions are based.

I should like to thank the duke of Portland, the marquess of Bath and Mr Christopher Harley of Brampton Bryan Hall for permission to use and to quote from the various collections of Harley papers. I am also grateful to the duke of Buccleuch and to the earl of Dartmouth for making papers in their possession available to me. The staffs of the following institutions greatly assisted my endeavours: the British Library; the Bodleian Library; Cambridge University Library; the John Rylands Library, Manchester; Lambeth Palace Library; Leeds University Library; the National Library of Wales, Aberystwyth; Newcastle University Library; Nottingham University Library; University College of North Wales Library, Bangor; the William Salt Library, Stafford; the Public Record Office; Carlisle Record Office; Herefordshire Record Office; Northamptonshire Record Office; Staffordshire Record Office; and Surrey Record Office. The librarians of the Goldsmiths' Library of Economic Literature, and of the Houghton Library, Harvard, were also kind enough to respond to my queries.

Mark N. Brown, Henry Horwitz, Giancarlo Carabelli and Lois Schwoerer provided valuable information on several points. My views on the stamp act owe much to correspondence and conversation with David Foxon. Tom Corns was a constant sounding-board for ideas throughout my time at Bangor. My examiners, Geoffrey Holmes, John Cannon and J. P. Kenyon, provided many insights into the problems at hand. Professor Kenyon also read the whole of the first draft in typescript. Pat Rogers's extensive knowledge of the literature of the eighteenth century was always available to me. His assistance has proved invaluable. Above all Bill Speck, my supervisor at the University of Newcastle upon Tyne, has had more to do with the book as it stands than anyone but myself. He read and commented upon successive versions of thesis and typescript, suggesting additions and pointing out errors and other undesirables. Those that remain are entirely my own.

Finally the physical appearance of *Robert Harley and the press* will perhaps be some compensation to my wife, Keturah, for the time consumed in its preparation, and to my son, Nicholas, who has lived all his six years under its shadow.

Leeds, February 1978   J. A. D.

Author's note

Dates are given in the old style throughout. The year, however, is taken to have begun on 1 January instead of 25 March.

Contemporary spelling and punctuation have been silently modernised in all prose quotations. In quotations from verse, where the sense might be impaired by this practice, contemporary usage has been retained.

Introduction

In 1695, with the expiry of the licensing act, state censorship of the press ceased. The end of the licensing system coincided almost exactly with the passing of the triennial act (in December 1694). From the outset the connection between electoral activity and the rise of a virulent political press can be discerned. During the succeeding twenty years there were ten general elections. This heated the political environment, and contributed enormously to the conflict between whig and tory which characterised, in particular, the years from 1701 to 1715. Daniel Defoe recognised that, with all its advantages, the triennial act had one great drawback: 'the certainty of a new election in three years is an unhappy occasion of keeping alive the divisions and party strife among the people, which otherwise would have died of course'.[1] The combined effect of the triennial act and the abandonment of the licensing system was a tremendous growth in the production of political literature.

Understandably enough, contemporaries were bewildered by the development of a 'fourth estate'. They were astonished by the sheer volume of political propaganda that the party presses managed to turn out. Successive administrations were at a loss when it came to dealing with the problems raised by a free press, and they were reduced to proclaiming impotently against the licentiousness of pamphlets and newspapers. But in the course of the reign of Queen Anne a government press policy began to emerge. Painstakingly, a propaganda machine was assembled by authority. In 1702 all ministerial printed matter was carried by the official newspaper, *The London Gazette*; in 1713 the Oxford ministry boasted five press organs. In addition to the *Gazette*, the *Review* addressed the whigs and the *Examiner* the tories in regular periodical essays. The *Post Boy* was a newspaper with a tory bias. The *Mercator* was devoted to the province of commerce and trade. They were supplemented by a constant flow of carefully-worded counter-propaganda in the form of political pamphlets, released to combat tracts potentially damaging to the image of the ministry if left unanswered.

The impetus for this changed ministerial attitude towards the press came largely from one man – Robert Harley, earl of Oxford and Mortimer, lord treasurer of Great Britain, and prime minister in all but title. He drew up the plans for the propaganda machine, and single-handed, piece by piece, he put it together. In 1704 he projected the first unofficial ministerial press organ, Defoe's *Review*, to 'state facts right',[2] and to counter the influence of the party writers. He recruited many of the most prominent and most effective pamphleteers of his, or indeed of any other age. Jonathan Swift, Daniel Defoe, Charles Davenant, and John Toland, as well as a host of minor propagandists, spent long periods in his employ. Harley purposely instituted contact with the party hacks whose pot-boiling efforts kept the conflict between whig and tory at a constant high temperature.

On the practical level of the publication and distribution of propaganda, Harley owed much to his relationships with Davenant, Defoe and Swift. Davenant, in 1701, supervised Harley's own literary efforts, he saw them through the press, and he arranged for their dispersal in the provinces. Defoe established bases for the regular dissemination of pamphlets and newspapers throughout the British Isles. When his *Remarks on the Letter to the Author of the State-Memorial* was published under Harley's auspices in 1706, over 2,000 copies were dispatched to scores of pre-arranged outlets across the country – a striking comment on the degree of organisation attained while Harley was still only secretary of state.[3] Defoe's tours of the British mainland in Harley's service had been utilised to set up an intelligence network that allowed the extensive display of political views held by the ministers in an attempt to influence public opinion in the widest possible sense. By 1709 the *Review* was being supplied not only to the border counties and to Scotland, but also as far afield as Carrickfergus in Ireland.[4]

On his return to office in 1710 at the head of the ostensibly tory administration, Harley was finally in a position to put into practice the methods and theories for manipulating public opinion through the press that he had formulated in twenty years of practical politics. The recruitment of Jonathan Swift, in many ways the linchpin of Harley's propaganda machine, was equally vital in another sense. Swift's extensive connections with printers, with whom he was forever 'doing business' on the ministry's behalf, effectively complemented Harley's arrangements for the actual composition of political literature. With Swift to organise the printing and publication of propaganda, and with the outlets inaugurated at an earlier stage by Defoe, the Oxford ministry possessed a propaganda machine *and* an agency for the distribution of this propaganda which were the envy of the whigs. Only by 1714, under the inspired leadership of Richard Steele, did the opposition come up with an answer to the ministerial challenge, when the organising skills of Samuel Buckley, editor of *The Daily Courant*, began to combat the efficiency of the ministerial distribution agencies. Harley's press policy had, by then, demonstrated the way in which the dual weapons of propaganda and proscription could be exploited by government. Walpole built on the structure first erected by Harley, and the rise of ministerial acceptance of the 'fourth estate' can be traced back to these beginnings. The origins and development of Harley's policies in relation to the press are the basis of the present study.

Harley, then, is the focus through which propaganda and public opinion in the 'age of Swift and Defoe' are to be examined. His role is absolutely crucial to the rise of a free press in Great Britain. In saying this I do not mean to suggest that there would never have been a free press had it not been for Robert Harley. But it seems clear that, had it not been for Harley, a free press would not have existed in Great Britain as early as it did. After the expiry of the licensing act there were numerous attempts to reinstitute press censorship, and to revive, or modify, the licensing system. The latest was in 1712. In that year Harley chose to tax the press, rather than to muzzle it. Had he reintroduced restrictions, it cannot be judged how soon circumstances would again have proved conducive to their removal. The cause of the liberty of the press would have been set back by several years. Harley proved beyond reasonable doubt that government could survive under the conditions imposed by the existence of a free press. For these reasons his contribution can hardly be overestimated.

The picture would be distorted, however, if Harley's role was to be examined in complete isolation. Attention must be paid, in particular, to whig attempts to manipulate public opinion. Until Richard Steele and Samuel Buckley took charge of whig propaganda in 1713 in response to the terrific ministerial initiative, the chief rival to Harley in the field had been John, Lord Somers of the Junto. He, too, was an innovator. In 1701 he organised a brilliant propaganda campaign to discredit the government, and to force an early general election. Penning pamphlets himself, and commissioning others, Somers instituted a direct appeal to public opinion in a series of seminal publications. *Jura Populi Anglicani* and *The Elector's Right Asserted* indicate, by their very titles, Somers's sophisticated conception of the importance of the opinion of the 'people' in the early eighteenth century.[5]

It is no coincidence that Harley and Somers were often compared by contemporaries. They were bitter rivals. In 1712 the third earl of Shaftesbury, lamenting the whigs' lack of a 'genius' equal to Harley, observed that only Somers had been able to give him a run for his money.[6] By then Somers was too frail to take up the gauntlet finally accepted by Steele. A tolerably satisfactory picture of the political press in the twenty years after the expiry of the licensing act can be drawn by sketching the activities of Harley and Somers, and their methods and achievements will be compared and contrasted more than once in the following analysis. But Somers never attempted to operate a compre-hensive press policy. His approach consisted of supplying pamphlets to meet each separate contingency as it occurred. There are few indications that he devoted time and energy to the development of the techniques of propaganda and counter-propaganda *when in office*. Harley, on the other hand, was always ready to adapt good ideas to his own purposes. Many of the most original notions of Somers can subsequently be seen at work under Harley's auspices. The attitude of the electorate could not be ignored under the triennial system, especially after Somers had deliberately brought public opinion into play in 1701. It had become a force to be reckoned with in British politics.

A vast corpus of tory literature, distinct from whig and Harleyite propaganda, was also published in the early eighteenth century. While it is true that at various times (in 1701, in 1708 and 1709, and from the end of 1710 onwards) it is difficult to distinguish tory propaganda from Harleyite propaganda, Harley did not attempt to control the output from the ranks of tory pamphleteers. The tory party was far more heterogeneous than the whig. There was no coordinating group to assume the mantle of the Junto on the whig side. Harley was the most important organiser in the tory party in many ways, and he was not really a true-blue tory. Similarly, excluding Harley, there was no leading figure to concert tory propaganda. Politicians like Sir Humphry Mackworth planned the publication of series of pamphlets, but he did not control the mass of tory writings in any way. The task was beyond a single man. The tory reaction to the Sacheverell trial is sufficient to illustrate this basic fact. The High Church deluge swamped the handful of pamphlets published in 1710 that can be said to be genuinely Harleyite, and few can be grouped together with any certainty, and attributed to this tory cabal or that (see chapter 5, 'The tory resurrection, 1708–1710').

With these qualifications in mind, any treatment of propaganda and public opinion in the age of Swift and Defoe must be selective. A blanket coverage of every pamphlet debate is clearly impossible, especially if we are to keep the focus of attention on Harley's press policies. Englishmen were proverbially interested in politics. 'Nothing more nearly concerns Englishmen', wrote one pamphleteer of the period, 'than to be well acquainted with the state of their own country from time to time'.[7] Conditions in this, 'the first age of Party',[8] were particularly conducive to the rise of a political press, and everything conspired to assist in its development. Englishmen craved political information. It was not, of course, given impartially. Information meant propaganda. Propaganda was designed to influence electoral opinion. We may call it public opinion. On occasions it really was public opinion. Geoffrey Holmes writes that the franchise was given to 'roughly one in every five adult males in the country'.[9] The ratio of $1:4$ is surprisingly large. W. A. Speck notes 'that the electoral system was more representative in Anne's reign than it had ever been before, or was to be again until well into Victoria's'.[10]

The years from 1701 to 1715 – those in which the press made its most spectacular growth in the public imagination – witnessed the most severe party conflict, as party considerations permeated every feature of English society. Party conflict was to be seen at work not only at the centre of power, but in the constituencies.[11] Party prejudice was given free rein in frequent elections. In addition to local elections, there were seven general elections between 1701 and 1715. Geoffrey Holmes has posed a question peculiarly relevant to the present study. 'Granted that the votes of the electors in these years were immensely influential', he writes, 'how accurately did these votes, and the great political changes they wrought, reflect what we should call the "public opinion" of the day?'[12] The party politicians and their propagandists firmly adhered to a conception of 'the will of the people'.[13] Somers deliberately exploited the phenomenon of opinion 'without doors' – extra-parliamentary viewpoints – against an entrenched tory majority in parliament, and he succeeded in dislodging it. Thirty years before the Excise Crisis the power of 'public opinion' was demonstrated quite conclusively, and this verdict was endorsed in 1710. The Sacheverell affair was another example of *vox populi*. A brief analysis of election results provides proof. As Professor Holmes concludes: 'In the thirty years after 1685...there

was not one Election of the twelve fought in that period which failed
to produce a House of Commons initially at least in tune with the mood
of the nation at the time'.[14]

Political literature reached a very wide audience. Ned Ward claimed
that the *Review* was 'read most by cobblers and by porters'.[15] Undoubtedly this was meant to be derogatory, but Charles Leslie, author of *The
Rehearsal*, painted a graphic picture of the *Review*'s readership:[16]

the greatest part of the people do not read books, most of them cannot read at all. But
they will gather together about one that can read, and listen to an *Observator* or *Review* (as
I have seen them in the streets) where all the principles of rebellion are instilled into them.

Defoe chose to write in a style which was avowedly 'explicit, easy, free
and very plain'. He refused to be bullied by 'those gentlemen who are
critics in style, method, or manner'.[17] His audience, in this way, was
potentially very wide. In 1712 one printed petition against the institution
of a tax on newspapers pointed out that they were bought principally
by 'the poorer sort of people...by reason of [their] cheapness, to divert
themselves, and also to allure therewith their young children, and entice
them to read'.[18] A fanciful picture perhaps, but it has been convincingly
demonstrated that the lower classes would be unable to purchase fiction,
or even the dearer political pamphlets. Instead, as Cesar de Saussure
observed in 1726, shoeblacks pooled resources 'to purchase a newspaper',
while 'workmen habitually begin the day by going to coffee-rooms in
order to read the latest news'.[19]

The question of circulation is a knotty one. If contemporaries believed
that the halfpenny newspapers were bought by the 'poorer sort of
people', the regular periodical essays – Defoe's *Review*, Tutchin's
Observator – were supposedly taken by 'a middle sort of people in our
nation, that take things upon trust; these read the weekly papers, and
oft-times find poison, instead of diversion'.[20] The *Review* and the
Observator were not newspapers. They provided commentary on political
matters already reported elsewhere. The *Review* (like the *Examiner*)
resembled the leading article of the newspaper of today. Tutchin's paper,
on the other hand, was narrated in dialogue between two characters called
the 'Observator' and the 'Countryman'. Two tory papers also used
dialogue, William Pittis's *Heraclitus Ridens* and Charles Leslie's *Rehearsal*
(originally called *The Rehearsal of Observator*). It was a popular format.
Defoe used it in 1705 in the *London Post* in a section called 'Truth and
Honesty', and in 1708, when the fortunes of the *Review* were waning,
'Mr *Review*' held a regular discourse with the 'Mad Man'.

Different papers were directed at different audiences, then, and for this reason their format was not consistent. The provincial clergy and gentry could ignore printed papers altogether. John Dyer's manuscript newsletters catered specifically for their taste, and they were sent all over the kingdom. If they wished, the tory country gentlemen could supplement Dyer with Abel Roper's *Post Boy*, and circulation figures of around 3,000 per issue suggest that many did. Whig sympathisers could read news with a whig bias in George Ridpath's *Flying Post*. Samuel Buckley's *Daily Courant* was also slanted towards the whigs, and even Jacques de Fonvive's *Post Man*, widely considered the most reliable newspaper of its day, revealed a whig inclination, despite being ostensibly impartial. The periodical essayists were in contrast to the news re-porters. They were the genuine propagandists. Defoe and Swift aimed not merely at influencing public opinion, but at uniting party political opinion within parliament.

As this would suggest, Harley was concerned with reaching at least two distinct audiences. First, and, in some instances, foremost, were the MPs themselves. Harley never neglected the potential of printed propaganda to stimulate a united stance in parliament on issues of importance. Swift's *Examiner* essays and his *Conduct of the Allies*, as we shall see, aimed at both the readership 'without doors', and 'within'. But other Harleyite propagandists were concerned more specifically with *public* opinion. The audiences of Swift and Defoe, Mr *Examiner* and Mr *Review*, were vastly different, even though both were employed by Harley.[21] The archetypal tory was a monarchist, and an adherent of the Church of England. He believed in the doctrines of passive obedience and non-resistance despite the Glorious Revolution. As a result of his acceptance of the divine right of kings, he was potentially Jacobite. For eleven of the years between 1701 and 1715 England was at war with France. In many ways the War of the Spanish Succession was also a war for the *English* succession. The archetypal tory lived off rents, and he was suspicious of the monied men of the City. He was xenophobic and isolationist. These factors, when added to his Jacobite inclinations, meant that he was habitually unenthusiastic about the war.

Clearly Defoe, in the *Review*, did not address these men from 1710 onwards. Swift did. Defoe was to cater for the whigs. The archetypal whig sought to curtail the prerogative of the Crown. In religion he was more inclined to champion the cause of the Protestant Dissenters from the Church of England, if he was not actually a dissenter himself. He did not subscribe to the close relationship between Church and State that was such an important feature of the tory creed. Benjamin Hoadly, bishop of Bangor, and no mean political writer himself, provided a clue to the Low Church viewpoint in his sermon on the text: 'My kingdom is not of this world'. Yet the archetypal whig was fiercely anti-Catholic. The act of settlement, in which he firmly believed, entailed the throne in the Protestant line – even though George I was fifty-seventh in strict line of succession. Taking this theory to its logical conclusion, the archetypal whig might have followed John Locke in assuming that, instead of constituting a divine order, monarchy originated as a contract between the king and the people. It was clear that if this was the case, the contract could be dissolved, and the king resisted, if he failed to govern within the bounds of the unwritten 'ancient constitution'.[22]

As a result of his anxiety over the safety of the Protestant Succession the archetypal whig was totally committed to the war on the continent, in all its ramifications, including the Dutch alliance. When the Oxford ministry made determined efforts to make peace with France, it had to contest every inch with the whig opposition. The war was largely financed through the offices of the men of the City. In this way a connection (and one that had basis in fact) was made between the whigs and monied men. It did not take much for the tory propagandists in general, and for Swift in particular, to hint at a conspiracy between the whigs and the stockjobbers who made a killing out of the prolongation of hostilities. 'If you would discover a concealed tory, Jacobite, or Papist', Shaftesbury advised, 'speak but of the Dutch, and you will find him out by his passionate railing'.[23] The archetypes, of course, were greatly exaggerated, although individual whigs and tories can be found to fit the most extreme descriptions. Of more importance to our purposes is the use the party propagandists made of these archetypes. Readers of Dyer's newsletter, or Roper's *Post Boy*, or Swift's *Conduct of the Allies*, genuinely believed that the whigs were the embodiment of republican, atheistical doctrines. On their side, the readers of the *Flying Post* and Steele's *Crisis* evidently felt that the tories were Jacobites and Catholics to a man, just waiting for an opportunity to restore James III and impose Popery on the entire population. Symbols are crucial to successful propaganda.

It is doubtful if Defoe's *Review* ever reached a circulation of 1,000 copies per edition.[24] As Henry Snyder remarks, 'the influence of a newspaper was not necessarily proportionate to its circulation'.[25] The *Review* and the *Observator* were coffee-house journals. A single copy could, of course, be read by more than one person. Coffee-houses placed regular subscriptions to journals for the convenience of their clientele. Addison, by a 'modest computation', estimated that each copy of the *Spectator* was, on average, read by twenty people.[26] On the institution of the stamp act in 1712 the *Spectator* was selling at approximately 2,000 copies per edition. Although the editors believed the pre-tax circulation to have been almost double this figure, it suggests a total readership of not much less than 50,000 people. While Addison's figure does not inspire confidence, the *Review* and the *Observator* in 1705, like the *Tatler* and the *Spectator* at a later date, were 'still the entertainment of most coffee-houses in town'.[27] Even if we accept that the *Review* never really exceeded a figure of 500 an edition (although by 1705, 100 *Reviews* were being sent 'every time' to Defoe's agent in Norwich, John Fransham),[28] it indicates a far from negligible readership. Defoe, naturally enough, was prone to exaggerate his audience. 'There are a hundred thousand people in this kingdom', he wrote in 1706, 'that read a *Review* with some pleasure and application'.[29]

Concrete figures, unfortunately, are hard to come by. For the *Review* we have tentative suggestions for both ends of its long career. One, a 1704 estimate, speaks of 400 per issue, while the records of the stamp duty in 1712 and 1713 reveal a similar circulation of 425 to 500.[30] This makes the assumption, of course, that the returns were reasonably accurate, and that papers distributed without being printed on stamped paper formed an insignificant proportion of each edition. This is purely an assumption. We have no means of testing the hypothesis. In 1712–13 it is almost certain that the *Review* was in an absolute decline.[31] But the reign of Queen Anne was the 'golden age' of the periodical essay. Remarking how *The Rambler* 'grew upon the public estimation', Boswell noted that Johnson's paper had a 'sale' which 'far exceeded that of any other periodical paper since the reign of Queen Anne'.[32] The figures we do have would appear to uphold this reputation of the periodical essay's popularity in the age of Swift and Defoe.

At the beginning of 1695 only one newspaper was being published regularly – the official *London Gazette*. Soon it was supplemented by Roper's *Post Boy*, Ridpath's *Flying Post*, and Fonvive's *Post Man*. All of the newcomers were published three times a week. In 1702 they were joined by the first daily newspaper, the *Daily Courant*, and, in 1706, by the first evening paper, the *Evening Post*. The 1704 estimate of circulation for these newspapers (excluding, of course, the *Evening Post*) appears to be moderate. The *Daily Courant*'s sales figure was put at 800 per issue, the *Flying Post*'s at 400, while their tory rival, the *Post Boy*, enjoyed extensive party readership and sales of 3,000 each edition. The *Post Man* was the most successful with a circulation estimated at 3,800 each weekday edition (Tuesday and Thursday) and 4,000 on Saturdays. The total sales of newspapers at this time was reckoned to be about 44,000 a week. By 1712 this figure had shot up to between 67,000 and 78,000. Of course the circulation suffered a temporary decline on the institution of the stamp duty, but the overall growth is unmistakable. The circulation of none of the papers we are discussing went down until after 1712. The *Post Boy* and the *Post Man* maintained their impressive figures. The whig journals increased their share of the market, the *Daily Courant* by perhaps 100 or 200 an issue, the *Flying Post*, which had assumed the mantle of the principal whig propaganda organ, by about 1,000 per edition.[33]

One reason for the tremendous overall growth in circulation was the success of, first, *The Tatler*, and then *The Spectator*. Despite the whig bias of both journals, they were read, the latter in particular, by more than merely die-hard whigs. Both Steele's estimate of the sale of the *Spectator*, and the records of tax returns indicate a production and distribution of around 2,000 a day, six days a week. On its own, then, the *Spectator* accounted for perhaps 12,000 of the gross increase in circulation from 44,000 to around 70,000. Yet it is evident, nonetheless, that the principal cause of the development of the newspaper industry was political, whether in the wider sense of concern for the state of the nation, and the desire for information, or simply for literature with a more or less blatant political slant. The absence of restrictions permitted the treatment of a wider range of political and religious subjects. Previously newspapers had not been allowed to comment on the news they reported. True, the printing of parliamentary debates was a delicate matter, and was to remain so for many years. But the introduction of periodical essays of the stamp of the *Review* and, later, the *Examiner* encouraged the free discussion in print of important political issues.

The most significant development is perhaps to be seen in the production and publication of pamphlets and poems on affairs of state. In 1710 the Sacheverell trial precipitated a paper war of immense proportions. F. F. Madan's bibliography of Sacheverelliana lists over 500 titles.[34] Twelve years earlier the standing army controversy, for all its nationwide interest, stimulated between forty and fifty publications in two years.[35] Ian Maxted suggests that publishing in the eighteenth century peaked around 1714, at least in terms of the number of individual books published, if not in sales figures.[36] Again the question of circulation is a vexed one. If we can believe Defoe, his satirical poem *The True-Born Englishman* went through nine authorised editions, and twelve 'pirate' editions. He estimated that the pirate editions alone sold 80,000 copies.[37] Defoe is prone to wild exaggeration, but the circulation of the *True-Born Englishman* was hardly negligible. Hard figures are seldom to be found, and when they are it is precisely because they are exceptional. A single edition of Sacheverell's sermon, *In Perils of False Brethren*, ran to 40,000 copies. The total number sold has been estimated at around 100,000.[38] Less sensational, but still out of the ordinary, was Swift's *Conduct of the Allies*. In two months it went through five editions, and sold 11,000 copies.[39]

'Editions' are very often unreliable methods of assessing circulation, and booksellers' claims in this respect should be treated with caution. The influence of a pamphlet or poem was, at best, only tenuously related to its sales. The most famous single pamphlet from 1702 to 1710 was perhaps *The Memorial of the Church of England*. Published in 1705, it caused an unprecedented search for the author or authors, debates in parliament on the question of the danger of the Church of England, queen's addresses, and an extensive paper war. It can also be said to have resulted in Godolphin's commitment to an alliance with the whig rather than the tory party. The first 'edition' of the *Memorial* was a tiny 250 copies. Even then many of this batch were gathered up by government officers without ever being offered for sale (see below, pp. 80–8). The *British Embassaddress's Speech*, on the other hand, was not *published* at all in any strict sense. Swift noted that it was printed on scraps of paper (a number has survived) and 'handed about, but not sold'.[40] Here was propaganda in the most pervasive sense, with no motive of profit at all. It was one of the most interesting features of the whig propaganda campaign of 1713 and 1714, when, as Defoe told Oxford, 'no printer will now print at his own charge, which is the reason the world is over-run with their pamphlets, which they disperse privately two or three editions at a time, and no man stirs a hand to oppose them because they must do it at their own hazard and expense'.[41]

The publishing system was, of course, vastly different from that which obtains today. The book trade was essentially a hand-to-mouth business. Printers could not afford to keep print standing. No-one made a fortune by publishing political literature. If they were lucky, the party hacks managed to break even, and earn a crust. Even newspapers and periodicals could not survive on the profit from their sales alone. 'It is apparent', wrote Defoe in the *Review* in 1705, 'the principal support of all the public papers now on foot depends on advertisements'.[42] In Defoe's own case it was quite obvious to contemporaries that the *Review* was not making a profit. 'He is certainly paid well for his pains by a party', a press spy observed, 'for he bestows a copy which hardly bears the expense of the press'.[43] In fact this was precisely accurate. The *Review*, like most of the party papers, was subsidised by politicians for their own ends, in this case by the government. When Defoe claimed to be writing the paper without making a profit, he was ridiculed by the tories. 'In plain truth', he was presented as confessing, 'you may take it for matter of fact, though you are not to let the Church party know of it, I had a handsome allowance, viz. £100 for the first volume'.[44]

The exception to this rule was the genuine, impartial newspaper. Fonvive was, in a number of ways, the most successful newsman of his day. When Harley offered him the Gazetteership in 1705, Fonvive revealed that he was making a profit of £600 per annum from his *Post Man*.[45] Harley was far from convinced that even this was profit honestly come by. He acknowledged that Fonvive had made 'above £15,000 by news', but he qualified the picture by accusing the author of the *Post Man* of 'cheating the postage', by having his papers sent free of charge with an official frank.[46] The *Gazette* itself, also ostensibly impartial, was 'easily the most widely circulated newspaper in England'.[47] With a press run of between 10,000 and 11,000 copies three times a week (not all of these were actually sold), it made a *gross* profit for the six-month period from 16 November 1705 to 16 May 1706 of £718 14s. 9d.[48]

These were profits that the ordinary periodical and the ordinary scribbler could not hope to match. There were, roughly, three distinct categories of writer in the age of Swift and Defoe. First of all, there was a basic difference between the gentleman-writer who dabbled in political literature, and the men who made, or tried to make their living out of their writings. Swift hobnobbed with the powerful. He refused to take money for his services, but hoped for a bishopric as his reward. Addison actually became secretary of state in the reign of George I. Steele was Gazetteer from 1707 to 1710, commissioner of the stamp office until 1713, and, for a time, an MP. Arthur Maynwaring was the friend of the Marlboroughs, and auditor of the imprest. On the tory side Sir Humphry Mackworth, Anthony Hammond and Henry St John were active politicians virtually throughout the period, Francis Atterbury and Henry Sacheverell were clergymen (as was Benjamin Hoadly), while Matthew Prior was a crucial diplomatic figure in the peace negotiations.

Clearly between propagandists of this kidney and the ordinary party scribbler there was a world of difference. In *The Dunciad* Pope presented a gallery of 'dunces' who, he thought, would be unknown to posterity. He included two of Harley's most prominent writers, John Toland and Daniel Defoe:[49]

> Earless on high, stood un-abash'd Defoe,
> And Tutchin flagrant from the scourge, below:
> There Ridpath, Roper, cudgell'd might ye view...
> Toland and Tindal, prompt at Priests to jeer...

Men no longer lost their ears for publishing seditious libel, and Defoe kept his, but he stood in the pillory on three occasions for *The Shortest Way with the Dissenters*. He relied on Harley for patronage, and to get him out of trouble. Even with his 'quarterly' £100 he was often in debt. He was in at least three different prisons, Newgate, the Fleet and the Queen's Bench, on at least five separate occasions. Without his lucrative subsidy from the government throughout the reign of Queen Anne he would have been in dire straits. As it was he could hardly keep his head above water.

John Tutchin was prosecuted in 1704 for remarks made in his *Observator*. He got off on a technicality. Marlborough threatened to 'find some friend that will break his and the printer's bones'.[50] Even for the protected writer, life could be tough. Lord Haversham was Tutchin's patron. Yet he did meet with violence in 1707 which brought on his death. As Pope suggests, Abel Roper and George Ridpath were repeatedly beaten for their views in their rival newspapers, the *Post Boy* and the *Flying Post*. This was an occupational hazard even for those writers fortunate enough to have backers. Roper was championed by the duke of Leeds, and he was ultimately given a minor position in the office of Secretary St John. Ridpath was supported by the Junto, but forced to go into exile in 1713 after prosecution for the *Flying Post*. He broke bail and escaped to Holland to return on the accession of George I. John Toland was in early trouble on account of his infamous tract, *Christianity Not Mysterious*. Despite the successive (and often concurrent) patronage of the earl of Shaftesbury, the duke of Newcastle, and Robert Harley, in addition to favour at the court of Hanover, Toland was constantly in financial difficulties.

But Defoe, Tutchin, Ridpath, Roper and Toland were hardly typical cases either. We must seek the true hack in the mires of Grub Street, or the metaphorical realm of Dulness. The anonymous world of political literature has been rightly described as a 'subculture'.[51] The murky

depths of this underworld are almost impossible to fathom. The
publication of volumes of undistinguished (and largely undistinguish-
able) political pamphlets, broadsheets and poems by unknown scribblers
supplies a powerful impression that somehow they just materialised of
their own accord. It is tempting to assume that they never were
published in the normal way by real men, and to surrender to Pope's
vision of a subterranean spawning-ground for words possessing the
capacity for independent existence:[52]

> Here she beholds the Chaos dark and deep,
> Where nameless somethings in their causes sleep,
> 'Till genial Jacob, or a warm Third-day
> Call forth each mass, a poem or a play.
> How Hints, like spawn, scarce quick in embryo lie,
> How new-born Nonsense first is taught to cry,
> Maggots half-form'd, in rhyme exactly meet,
> And learn to crawl upon poetic feet.

How else, we ask ourselves, are we to account for the overwhelming
quantity produced in the early eighteenth century? But it will be our task
to attempt to peer behind the mask of the 'underspur leather'. The vast
majority of propagandists had no literary pretensions, but they have their
place in the history of the political literature of the age of Swift and Defoe.

The political pamphlet or the poem on affairs of state could take many
forms. It could be a broadsheet – a folio half-sheet printed on one side
only – or it could be a book of many hundreds of pages, whether in prose
or verse. The hack pamphlet tended to be discursive, but the superior
propagandists, the Swifts and the Defoes, used mock form and the
persona to great effect. False vindications, letters, petitions and secret
histories abounded. They had their genuine counterparts. In the best
specimens of political propaganda, Defoe's *Shortest Way*, for instance,
or Swift's *Conduct of the Allies*, the literary technique is of the highest
standard. Defoe's pamphlet is almost indistinguishable from the genuine
address of a High Church bigot. It is a brilliant exercise in sustained,
total irony, just distinct from actual impersonation. In the case of Swift's
Conduct, we are aware that the views of the narrator are not quite those
of Swift himself. But the dividing-line is a very fine one, and where this
occurs we can never be certain when fiction takes over from fact.

It would not be stretching the evidence to suggest that the political
literature of the reign of Queen Anne laid the groundwork for the prose
fiction of subsequent years. It did this in two quite distinct ways. The

fictional aspects of some political pamphlets are not far removed from genuine fiction. Pope ironically observed that Mrs Manley's *New Atalantis* was being read long after the political contingency it had been designed to meet. He did not approve of the phenomenon, but this does not invalidate the fact.[53] Dela Manley's political allegories have already been examined, quite minutely, as embryonic novels.[54] We know that Defoe and Swift went on to write fiction, and to use other personae in the process. Their technique can hardly have been hindered by the serious adoption of personae for a strictly political end. In the early eighteenth century it is virtually impossible to divorce literary and political considerations. The finest works of literature of the age were often produced with political intentions – *Gulliver's Travels* is far from free of political motivation. Equally significant is the fact that the constant appearance of political literature whetted the contemporary appetite for reading matter. There is evidence of a cult of 'pamphlet readers' who, presumably, would buy and consume each tract as it came onto the bookstalls or was cried by the hawkers. The *Spectator's* popularity was one manifestation of the social need for literature; labouring men pooling their money to buy a newspaper, or going to the coffee-houses to read them before starting the day's work was, of course, another.

The rise of the political press, then, prepared the way for the tremendous growth of the popularity of fiction after the political environment had cooled down after 1715.[55] The septennial act ended the triennial system, and acted as a brake on the party propaganda machines. Political sermons were banned. In the 'golden age' of the periodical, the armoury of literary devices to persuade, cajole, exhort or admonish had been rifled by writers of the calibre of Swift and Defoe in the general cause of propaganda. To say that this was *their* age is, of course, merely a conceit. It would be equally foolish to suggest that all this came about because of one man. But Robert Harley's importance to the literature of the period cannot be denied, and, as a consequence of the complex inter-relationship of literature and politics, his place at the centre of the development is assured.

PART ONE

1689–1708

The propaganda of court and country

At the Revolution, Robert Harley was a Shaftesburian whig of the old school. During the upheaval he raised a troop of horse at his own expense and declared for the Prince of Orange. One of his father's fondest memories was of being 'in arms together for the Gospel and the country'.[1] On 6 April 1689 Harley was elected to parliament for the pocket borough of Tregony in Cornwall. He entered politics on a firm Revolution foot: his relatives and his earliest political associates were recognised to be partisan whigs. In the Convention Parliament he distinguished himself as a radical, speaking against a lenient indemnity bill, and supporting the Sacheverell amendment to the corporation bill, which would have disabled those who had had any part in the surrender of borough charters in the previous reigns from exercising their right to vote for a period of eight years. Harley was 'notable, and made speeches'; clearly 'a dangerous person'.[2] 'It is plain now there is a party setting up to play the old game', he warned his wife, 'the same that was in King Charles's and King James's time'.[3] In the 1690 elections he was branded as a commonwealthman, an anti-monarchist, and he was unseated by malpractice at New Radnor, and by tory electioneering at Tregony.[4] He regained his place in parliament on petition. Just over a month later, on 26 December 1690, he was chosen by the Commons to be a commissioner of public accounts. In eighteen months of political activity as a whig he had risen to a position of acceptance and recognition within the house.

It comes as no surprise, in the light of these facts, that Harley was considered to be a young man of exceptional abilities. But it is astonishing to find him on intimate terms with tory elders of the kidney of Sir Thomas Clarges and Sir Christopher Musgrave a mere two years later. In 1690 they had been labelled Jacobites in a whig election blacklist. The width of the political spectrum divided them from Harley, or so it seemed. By Christmas 1691, however, they, too, were being called commonwealthmen, and Harley was accused of having 'too great a familiarity' with them.[5] This volte-face can be explained partly by the experience of working alongside tories on the commission of public accounts.[6] Harley cooperated wholeheartedly with Clarges, his fellow commissioner, once the initial acrimony had subsided. His activities as commissioner of accounts powerfully influenced his subsequent political career.

But there was a more profound influence on Robert Harley when he entered parliament as a hot whig in his twenty-ninth year. He was imbued with 'country theory'. Harley was the direct heir of a 'country' vision of politics as propounded in the reign of Charles II by the first earl of Shaftesbury.[7] In many ways Shaftesbury was the father of the first whigs. J. G. A. Pocock has described the elements which made up this 'country theory', focusing on the ideas borrowed from James Harrington's *Oceana*, in a perceptive paper on the men he calls 'neo-Harringtonians'. Robert Harley should be included among these. The principal consequence of his belief in Old Whig ideology was a dogmatic view of the relationship between the Crown and parliament, upon which the stability of the 'ancient constitution' depended: 'It was for the Crown to govern, and for Parliament to exercise a jealous surveillance of government; "corruption" would follow if the Crown discovered any means at all of attaching members to it in the pursuit of its business'.[8]

The policies pursued by the embryonic 'country' party in the first half of the 1690s reflected the ideology of the 'neo-Harringtonians'. All attempts at interference in parliamentary affairs were met with place bills designed to prevent pensioner parliaments, and with triennial bills to block standing parliaments. Parliament was there to vet the king's policies, to consent to supply or to withold it, to scrutinise his accounts, and to keep a check on his expenditure. Any indication that the king intended to keep a standing army in peacetime, in breach of the bill of rights, was greeted by the 'country theorists' with stony disapproval. 'The standing army was a bogey intended for country gentlemen, part of a hydra-headed monster called Court Influence or Ministerial Corruption, whose other heads were Placemen, Pensioners, National Debt, Excise, and High Taxation.'[9] And this awareness of the 'court' entailed a notion regarding which party was permitted to assist the Crown in the execution of its office: the tories, the traditional supporters of monarchy, were to fulfil this role; the whigs were to remain in permanent opposition.

Other whigs did not subscribe to Harley's idea of the party's 'country' role: William III was their king – they had supported his banner against James II – they should be his servants. In the reigns of the last two Stuarts a fundamental division arose in the ranks of the whig party, important to the dichotomy between whig and tory which loomed large in the reign of Queen Anne. While some whigs continued to tread the path worn by their earlier counterparts at the time of the exclusion crisis, remaining in permanent opposition, others, epitomised by the Junto, rallied in support of the Crown. The former assumed the name of 'Old Whigs', and they ridiculed the fortune-seeking 'Modern Whigs' who took office after 1688. When the whigs (or a majority of them) began to wear the mantle of a court party, following policies which Harley believed to be working against the national interest; and when the tories (or a number of them) could be seen to be pursuing aims not far removed from his own; then Harley felt no qualms about joining forces with them in the face of his erstwhile allies. It was not he that had made a volte-face, he claimed, but the court whigs who had done so: 'it was their deserting the true interest of their country, and running into and supporting all the mismanagements of [William III's] reign, that made him join with those that were called tories...to rescue the nation from the rapine of that corrupt ministry'.[10]

Corruption was the key word in country dogma. The court was a hot-bed of self-interest, and this inevitably meant that the rights and privileges of the country gentleman were put in jeopardy. Official employment in the government's service, then, was not the primary consideration in the formulation of Harley's political creed. During the 1690s he was approached many times by the court, sometimes to hammer out an agreement with the country opposition on certain issues, occasionally to offer employment in the ministry to a dangerous critic of court policy. He was pressed 'particularly...to be secretary of state'.[11] If Harley had wanted office, he could have accompanied his fellow country party leaders into the ranks of the government at virtually any time in the decade. But it is clear that he wished to rectify existing anomalies in policy from the opposition benches. He was not prepared to be bought off by a place in a ministry which he regarded as corrupt, and supported by incompetent time-servers.

Similarly the mere party label was irrelevant to Harley. What mattered was principle. It was not sufficient to call oneself a whig, if one was pursung policies contrary to the spirit of the first whigs. In office, the whigs notoriously did not make a determined effort to implement the ideas of the party theorists. There was no concerted attempt to ensure free proceedings in parliament. The court whigs, like the tories before them, did their utmost to control parliament through placemen and pensioners. The whig intellectuals joined Harley and Paul Foley in decrying this attitude. The circle which met at the Grecian Coffee-house in Devereux Court retained Old Whig virtues. As John Toland put it: 'Three or four bills in parliament did quite take the scales from my eyes. And who, I pray, would endure to hear any whigs oppose the judge's bill, the triennial bill, the bill for regulating trials in cases of high treason, and such like?'[12]

The Old Whig enclave which patronised the Grecian was important to the publication of country propaganda during the 1690s. During the standing army controversy in 1697 and 1698 public opinion was influenced by the offerings disseminated by the 'neo-Harringtonians'. They admired Roman concepts, and Roman probity, deriving many of their ideas from Machiavelli, through the English Machiavellians, James Harrington, Henry Neville and Algernon Sidney. In fact until his death in 1694 old 'Plato' Neville could be heard at the Grecian. Harley frequented this coffee-house.[13] So did men like John Trenchard, Walter Moyle, Andrew Fletcher and John Toland. Their intellectual mentor was Robert Molesworth, whose *Account of Denmark*, published in December 1693, was soon quoted extensively by his admirers as an example of how 'corruption' could ruin a nation, and lead to the loss of civil liberties. Lord Ashley, who entered the Commons in 1695 as member for Poole, was the patron of many of these young thinkers, John Toland in particular. Ashley, who, in 1698, became the third earl of Shaftesbury, was acquainted with Harley and his family from his early days. As he put it, he had been 'bred almost from [his] infancy to have the highest regard' for the Harleys, whose reputation for probity amongst contemporaries was almost proverbial.[14] First and foremost, the name of the family had to be preserved, its political and moral integrity jealously guarded. Ashley freely acknowledged that, 'in [his] young days', Robert Harley had been his 'guide, and leader in public affairs'.[15] The principles of the Shaftesburian whigs were maintained intact by these whigs of the old school.

In essence, Robert Harley was anti-party. 'At the first Revolution [in 1660], if care had been taken, parties might have been prevented', he admonished the Commons in 1694 on the king's rejection of the place bill, 'and we should have had but one, and that for the good of England'.[16] Harley's vision was of a single-party house of commons, separate from the executive, working for the good of the 'people' – the political nation. The representatives of the privileged few who had property to speak of, and could, therefore, command a voice in the nation's affairs through an 'interest' in the kingdom, were 'physicians of the state'.[17] Parliament was there to protect the liberties and property of the 'people'. It was to act as a check and a balance should the pendulum of power swing too far towards tyranny, or towards democracy. In either case the representatives of the 'people' would be called upon to exercise their skill as 'physicians of the state' to heal the ailing body politic.

Significantly, the formative years of Harley's political career witnessed a resurgence of 'country' ideology after the decade of repression during the 1680s. Such ideas were aired regularly, it seems, at places like the Grecian Coffee-house. In William's reign the delicate country plant was brought to flower. For the whole of the reign of Queen Anne it lay dormant, and the buds it occasionally formed, so carefully tended by Harley in 1705, in 1708, and again in 1710, failed to open. But in the early 1690s the country plant was visibly flourishing, and its nostalgic effect on the maturing mind of Robert Harley should not be under-estimated. He was never captivated by the party system of the early eighteenth century. His was an anachronistic ideology stemming from the political world of his earlier and much younger days.

The emergence of a country party in the 1690s had an important bearing on the development of Harley's thinking about the press. The experience of trying to motivate the notoriously unorganised (and largely unorganisable) body of uncommitted country members to follow a concerted policy of opposition influenced profoundly his positive stance on propaganda and the press. By providing the independent country gentlemen who formed a natural majority in the Commons (but who were normally quiescent in the face of court pressure)[18] with opposition spokesmen ready to turn their vague feelings of unease into eloquent, defined statements of discontent, Harley and the other country leaders hoped to transform them from an amorphous mass into an effective organ of country opposition. In this situation propaganda was of the utmost importance; not only in the form of the printed word, but the written word in personal correspondence, the private word in conversation, and the public word through the medium of oratory in parliament. From the first Harley learned to convince potential sympathisers of the validity of the cause, before embarking on the much more difficult task of winning over the enemy. The initial exercises in the dissemination of the propaganda which was to be such a feature of Harley's dealings with Swift, and fully-fledged expositions of the calibre of *The Examiner* and *The Conduct of the Allies*, took place in the 1690s, and the principal medium was the spoken word. The house of commons resounded to the rhetoric of stirring speakers such as Paul Foley, Clarges and Musgrave. And in private Harley was learning the craft that was to hold him in such good stead when it came to managing men, buttonholing individual members to forward his designs.

In the 1690s, then, propaganda had a decided flavour of court and country. The press was seen as a means of persuading large numbers of men to act in a certain way, whether this was restricted to MPs, or was designed to influence opinion throughout the kingdom. Pamphlets were published by the country opposition before the opening of parliament to pinpoint the line their adherents were to toe. They were also meant to counter the 'scribbling court sycophants'.[19] The press agencies of both sides were rudimentary, and the total number of publications prepared for the beginning of each session before the expiry of the licensing act was tiny. The government made little attempt to exploit the advantages it possessed, and even court pamphlets were often unlicensed, and thus open to prosecution. No-one can be singled out as an example of a man of vision or an innovator. One-off pamphlets were the order of the day.

The most prolific and effective opposition pamphleteer of these years was John Hampden, Harley's uncle. The country content of his propaganda can be readily viewed. He encouraged country gentlemen to unite, and to rally around the popular banner of liberty and property. The Revolution had been undertaken for 'the recovery and security of our rights and liberties, which had been so unjustly invaded'. Hampden emphasised the corruption of parliament by the Crown prior to 1688. This, he constantly repeated, must not be allowed to happen again: 'This is the thing we must always keep in our eye, and steer our whole course by this pole-star'.[20] Hampden's pamphlets were published to explain opposition policy to parliament men, and they usually appeared in November, carefully timed to anticipate the beginning of debates in parliament. *Some Considerations about the most proper way of Raising Money in the present Conjuncture* warned against the dangers of imposing an excise. *Some short Considerations concerning the State of the Nation* was almost a country manifesto for the 1692–3 session: it spelled out the opposition stance on almost every issue likely to be debated. Harley and the other country leaders played variations on the theme expounded by Hampden in their speeches in the ensuing weeks. Hampden also viewed parliament as ' our great state-physician, and, under God, the remedy of all our ills'. 'It is plain', he wrote, 'our government is altogether without settlement; and that whilst the holding of parliaments is precarious, and absolutely depending upon the pleasure of the Crown, there can be no safety for the life, estate or liberty of the English subject'.[21]

As evidence for the production and distribution of these pamphlets is so scanty, it is difficult to judge how far they were designed to influence public opinion, over and above parliamentary opinion. In 1693, however, on the return to court of the earl of Sunderland, the press can be seen distinctly attempting to sway extra-parliamentary views. A determined effort was made to discredit Harley and Foley with their fellow whigs, and to unify the party. *A Dialogue betwixt Whig and Tory*, probably by Ben Overton,[22] criticised the fusion taking place between country whigs and country tories: 'your great Paul Foley turns cadet, and carries arms under the general of the West-Saxons [Sir Edward Seymour]; the two Harleys, father and son, are engineers under the late lieutenant of the ordnance [Musgrave], and bomb any bill which he has once resolved to reduce to ashes'.[23] The hint was that Harley and Foley had become tainted with Jacobitism by joining forces with tories. They were prepared to jeopardise measures 'most necessary to our security', such as recognition of William and Mary as sovereigns *de jure*, for the sake of factious opposition.

The *Dialogue* was part of Sunderland's campaign to construct the government along whig lines. In the summer of 1693 he was reviewing lists of parliament men, and discussing 'the best means of persuading them to be reasonable', with the secretary to the treasury, Henry Guy, and the venal speaker, Sir John Trevor.[24] The sanctity of parliament was blatantly ignored. Somers was also involved in these manoeuvres as the newly-appointed lord keeper. Ben Overton was Sunderland's propagandist. He was warden of the mint.[25] The *Dialogue* drew a precise distinction between whig and tory: one was Williamite, the other Jacobite; there was no middle way! And pains were taken to distribute the pamphlet in the provinces. 'The *Dialogue between Whig and Tory* is with great eagerness dispersed here', one contemporary observer noted, 'and all that's said in it goes for gospel amongst too many. The poison is so taking that I think it needs an antidote'.[26]

The very fact that the *Dialogue* stimulated such a reaction indicates that it was unusual to publish and distribute propaganda along these lines. It was an exceptional attempt to influence public opinion. The country response endorses the assumption. Charlwood Lawton's broadsheet, *A Short State of our Condition, with Relation to the present Parliament*, commonly called the 'Hush-money Paper', caused an outcry. It made open accusations of court bribery of members of the house of commons. Guy was alleged to have 'disposed of no less than £16,000 in three days [in the previous session] when the house was a little out of humour'. Nor had Sunderland's role passed unnoticed. Lawton reminded country gentlemen that William had been invited 'to get or to give us all the laws we wanted; to have made the elections of parliament secure and frequent, trials impartial, the militia our standing force, and the navy our strength'. Pointedly, in view of Sunderland's role as adviser to James II, Lawton wrote: 'I thought we had called him over to call ministers to account, and to have put it out of their power impunibly to abase us hereafter'.[27]

The author of the 'Hush-money Paper' was automatically slurred with the charge of Jacobitism.[28] Both the *Dialogue* and its reply were referred to by name in general histories of the period by contemporaries, a sure indication of their unusual nature. John Oldmixon noted that the 'Hush-money Paper' was published by 'some whigs who out of disgust joined with the tories'.[29] By implication, this involves Harley and Foley, and Harley was a personal friend of Lawton.[30] It is almost certain that the country leaders were privy to the broadsheet's publication. Like Hampden's pamphlets, it served as a country manifesto for the coming sessions. But there was more to it than merely that. 'I once thought to have affixed to this paper a list of those that are in office', Lawton had written, 'which if I had, it would not only have shown how many members are bought off, but would have pointed out many amongst the number of favourites and pensioners, who we expected should rather have been punished'. In addition to distributing their 'antidote' to the *Dialogue* through the provinces, the country leaders appear to have supplemented the printed paper with a manuscript list of pensioners. 'I have the names of all the pensioners', Humphrey Prideaux commented on 11 December 1693, 'I am of the opinion that this discovery will so blast that party that we have no need to fear anything from them this session'. The country party had succeeded in not only countering the court pamphlet, but in assuming the initiative in the propaganda stakes. While the list of pensioners was circulating, official enquiries were being made into the production of the *Dialogue*. As if to illustrate the government's lack of foresight, the printer 'and several hawkers' were arrested for printing and selling the tract without a licence.[31]

This, then, was the state of sophistication attained by the propaganda agencies of court and country on the eve of the expiry of the licensing system. Men like the earl of Portland might urge the case for employing a government propagandist,[32] and Sunderland might make use of Ben Overton, but government exploitation of the press was minimal. In fact authority was more concerned with trying to stem the flow of Jacobite propaganda – the most persistent feature of the printed political literature of these years.[33] All along the line, the anti-court groups were showing the way. The General Election of 1695, the first to experience the effect of the lack of press restrictions, saw a real effort to influence the electorate through propaganda. During the elections, the late marquis of Halifax's *Some Cautions Offered to the Consideration of those who are to Choose Members to Serve in the Ensuing Parliament* was published posthumously as part of the country campaign. Although we have no firm evidence, there are indications that Harley arranged for the appearance of this pamphlet. Someone saw it through the press. Not only was Harley on very intimate terms with Halifax from 1693, but a manuscript copy of *Some Cautions* in the Harley papers seems to have been transcribed directly from the Halifax holograph.[34] Twenty warnings were offered to electors, all concerned with the free proceedings of parliament. Halifax dealt in succession with 'men tied to a party', placemen, pensioners, and, significantly, 'those gentlemen who for reasons best known to themselves thought fit to be against the triennial bill'.[35]

On the meeting of the new parliament Harley was immediately involved with the press. On 26 November 1695 leave was given to Harley and to Edward Clarke to prepare and bring in a 'bill for the regulating of printing and the printing presses'.[36] It is difficult to judge whether or not Harley was genuinely in favour of regulations at this juncture; by 1702, at the latest, he was advising against them (see below, p. 55). The 1695 bill was unsuccessful, but the feeling that censorship was necessary was long-lived. One factor in Harley's changing attitude to propaganda may have been a letter he received from George Ridpath, editor of the *Flying Post*, in this climate of hostility towards the political press. The *Flying Post* had been launched on the expiry of licensing, and it was not without its opponents. Ridpath wrote to Harley on 29 October 1696, presenting his 'rude thoughts against laying down the *Flying Post*'. In his 'Reasons', he outlined a scheme by which the paper 'might become more useful to the government than an *Observator*':[37]

those concerned in the *Flying Post*, being thoroughly well-affected to the government, will very willingly, at any time, insert such brief reflections upon pestilent libels as any employed by the government shall think fit to send them, and, their paper being universally read because of the news, the people would thereby be provided with antidotes against the poison of such libels...

It was sentiments such as these that Harley expressed to Godolphin in 1702 when advocating a 'discreet writer of the government's side'.

It is also at this juncture that we find the earliest evidence of Harley's own efforts at political pamphleteering. Throughout his career, he was prepared to put pen to paper should occasion arise, although he usually chose to work through amanuenses who wrote according to his directions, or with his instructions in mind. Around this time he drafted an answer to *A Way to Secure our Wealth now Money is Scarce. Proposed in a Letter to a Person of Honour*. His holograph, extant in the Harley papers, was also in epistolary form, but it does not appear to have reached a printer. It inveighed against the management of the court party, dominated by this time by the lords of the Junto. 'It would make one mad', he wrote:[38]

I had almost said as mad as your Westminster men, to think what they have us to: that a nation and a city which has stood the shock of fire, plague, foreign wars, home-bred confusions and commotions, I say, to see a flourishing nation in two or three years time despoiled of its strength, and led to the brink of ruin by five or six jugglers.

From his introduction to parliamentary politics, then, Harley's mind turned increasingly to appreciate the importance of propaganda of many kinds. Oratory in parliament and personal intercession with parliament men were two varieties. But the end of censorship brought the press to the forefront. Printed publications could not only influence the close circle of friends surrounding Harley, nor merely the representatives of the 'people' in parliament; they could reach out to the electorate itself. Harley had been aware of the polemical strategy of Hampden's pamphlets, and of Lawton's 'Hush-money Paper', and he had himself attempted to write propaganda with the press in view. Soon the opportunity for experiment came his way. In 1697 the signing of the Peace of Ryswick brought peace and French recognition of the status quo in England. The end of the war precipitated a controversy over the army which had fought the war. William III wished to keep it on foot in case of a renewal of hostilities. The country opposition sought an immediate disbandment. From 1697 a prolonged controversy in print first demonstrated the possibilities of influencing public opinion through the uncensored press. Harley's later press policies owed much to the insight into the manipulation of the electorate gained during the standing army controversy.

On 23 November 1697 Harley arrived in London to find the town in an uproar. 'Everyone is full of the common topic, a standing army', he wrote, 'and it is talked with heats on both sides. A sharp pamphlet is sold publicly called *An Argument* against a standing army'.[39] The conclusion of peace had thrust the standing army issue to the forefront of the confrontation between court and country. The most potent symbol of arbitrary government was being used to incite country gentlemen to demand full redress of grievances against the 'corruption' of the Crown. Parliament men had been arriving for the opening of the session extraordinarily early. Harley had been urged on all sides to return to London with expedition. Country cabals had already commenced when he finally made his appearance, and the day prior to his arrival the controversy in print over a standing army was precipitated by *An Argument showing that a Standing Army is Inconsistent with a Free Government, and Absolutely Destructive to the Constitution of the English Monarchy*.

Harley's complicity in the production of the *Argument* against a standing army can be discounted. 'The *Argument* against a standing army has raised a great heat in the town', Harley informed his father on 27 November, 'there is very little prospect of moderate councils'.[40] If anything, he was critical of the methods employed by his country colleagues. Although the standing army question had united the opposition, great efforts were being made by the court to forestall steps towards disbandment. The affair had been inflamed at an early stage, and almost certainly unnecessarily. A naked confrontation between the king and his people, whatever the circumstances, revived unwelcome memories of the previous reign, and the government of James II. 'I pray God directs concerning the army', Harley remarked after the meeting of parliament, 'to deliver this simple nation from themselves'.[41] He recognised the need for compromise. An open show of strength might impress William III, but it could also push him into implementing more extreme measures to preserve his threatened sovereignty. And once the moves towards meeting force with force had been made, it would be difficult for either side to back down without losing face. The issue of disbandment was a crucial one, but Harley did not want ''41 to come again'.

Harley got his way. The Commons voted to disband all forces raised since 1680. This was a compromise only on the surface. True, the opposition pamphleteers had called for total disbandment, but the tiny army granted by parliament hardly amounted to even a partial victory for William. In 1680 Charles II had had no more than 7,000 men on foot in England. The most vocal opposition spokesmen regarded this small army as sufficient to guard against French aggression once the militia had been reformed. In a reply to the *Argument*, one court writer, probably Lord Somers, had posed the question in terms of compromise. He professed himself 'far from the thought of a standing army': 'The case at present is whether, considering the circumstances that we and our neighbours are now in, it may not be both prudent and necessary for us to keep up a reasonable force from year to year'.[42] Another answer, a broadsheet 'printed by order of the court',[43] listed the troops kept on foot by James II, ready, should the opportunity arise, to invade England or Ireland. In a supposed dialogue concerning the army, the Jacobite was adamant that 'the army must be disbanded... we shall be at more liberty to rise and join the French, who a twelvemonth hence, when the army is entirely scattered, will have a brave opportunity of landing to assist us'.[44]

Accompanying a disbandment bill was a bill to reform the militia. Andrew Fletcher's *Discourse upon Militias* was followed by Toland's *The Militia Reformed: Or, an Easy Scheme of Furnishing England with a Constant Land-Force, capable to prevent or to subdue any Foreign Power, and to Maintain Perpetual Quiet at Home, without endangering the Public Liberty*. Published on 3 February 1698,[45] Toland's pamphlet deliberately pushed the arguments propounded 'by the ingenious author of the unanswerable *Argument* against a standing army'. Now that the Commons had voted in favour of disbandment, the sentiments of Somers's *Balancing-Letter* were no longer relevant. Instead Toland reminded the electorate that 'should those who were for continuing [the army] now oppose the regulating of the militia, they give us a demonstration that either they never thought us in so great danger as they pretended, or that they would have us entirely lost because we refused to be saved after their method, though our own be more effectual and less expensive'.[46] After all, Toland pointed out, 'that a standing army or a militia is of absolute necessity is agreed on every side'.

Toland's model for the projected reorganisation of the militia looked, like Harrington's had done, to the Roman republic for guidance. Only 'freemen' would be capable of serving in the militia, and the similarities between Toland's scheme and Harrington's 'model for the commonwealth of *Oceana*' are apparent in this division into freemen and servants. 'By freemen I understand men of property, or persons that are able to live of themselves', Toland postulated, 'and those who cannot subsist in this independence, I call servants'. Harking back to the mythical Anglo-Saxon ancient constitution, the *Militia Reformed* concluded by extolling the virtues of the 'wapentake': 'that this was our own original constitution in the Saxon time, none can be ignorant who is ever so little versed in our ancient customs and writings'.[47] No wonder, then, that one court pamphleteer scoffed at such pretensions: 'when he has done his best, his militia will prove a guard only fit to defend his common-wealths of *Oceana* and *Utopia*, where alone, I fancy, he will be fit to govern'.[48]

Somers appears to have been behind the court propaganda campaign, writing the *Balancing-Letter* himself, arranging the printing of *A List of King James's Irish and Popish Forces in France*, ready (*when called for*), which was a specific reply to the *Argument* against a standing army, and organising a renewed offensive in parliament. Prompted by the king, a new, resolute court party brought up the question of the number of troops once more on 8 January 1698. Harley shrewdly headed off the attack by adhering firmly to the former vote of the house on the issue, and insisting that any further debate should be qualified accordingly.[49] In the belief that the initial vote for disbandment 'was the effect of the gentlemen's first heat and aversion to a standing army',[50] pressure was applied to the fickle country backbenchers. It required all Harley's skill to prevent the court breaking through the Commons's resolution. Propaganda was of the first importance during these weeks. Five days after the publication of the *Militia Reformed*, Harley, supported by Musgrave, proposed a three-shilling land tax to be used for disbanding the army.[51] The opposition had triumphed.

In the division over the question of recommitment, it was noticeable that both John Methuen, chancellor of Ireland, and Robert Molesworth forsook the court to vote with Harley and his friends. In fact Methuen was suspected of leaking information to Harley about the resolution of the whig Rose club to press for recommitment.[52] When the timing of Toland's pamphlet is taken into consideration, it seems probable that in January 1698 the anti-army opposition was concerting policy, and directing the publication and distribution of propaganda. Harley is strongly believed to have directed the publication,[53] although Ashley is, no doubt, the man to whom Toland is referring in the opening address: 'The following discourse (most noble Lord) begun at your request, *and finished within the short time you prescribed*, is now made a present to the world; which, if the favour deserves any return, is obliged to your Lordship for the publication'.[54] The character of the *Militia Reformed* is clear: it was designed to meet a specific contingency. The campaign for disbandment was losing ground. The required message had to be pressed home through the dissemination of more anti-army propaganda. Toland's pamphlet was the last important opposition statement during the 1697–8 session.

Who directed the country opposition propaganda campaign? John Trenchard is usually considered to be the author of many of the anti-army pamphlets, from the *Argument* against a standing army itself, through the *Letter to the Author of the Balancing-Letter*, to the *Short History of Standing Armies in England*. Yet Trenchard never put pen to paper himself. He preferred to dictate to an amanuensis.[55] Walter Moyle is credited with joint-authorship of the *Argument*, but not of the *Letter*, nor the *History*, nor even of the second part of the *Argument* itself.[56] Presumably there were other assistants. Narcissus Luttrell noted that the anti-army pamphlets were written by a 'club' of gentlemen. He mentioned by name Edmund Waller, MP for Agmondesham, and one Littlebury, 'who carried [the *Argument*] to the press'.[57] Clearly the contemporary rumour implicating Waller was widespread. Both Bonet and L'Hermitage, the resident envoys in London of the courts of Brandenburg and Holland respectively, reported the story of how Waller had sued for the king's protection.[58] Other men, such as John Toland, were accused of authorship as a search was mounted for those responsible for the production of seditious libel (as the *Argument* was judged). That Toland was actively involved in the production of anti-army tracts we have already noted. But so was Robert Harley.

John Trenchard was the opposition *chef de propagande* during the standing army controversy. His role can be documented. He coordinated the writing, printing and publishing of all the important contributions. Harley was the opposition leader in parliament. But their roles merged from time to time. Although he was probably not privy to the publication of the *Argument* against a standing army, he actually provided assistance and information when Trenchard was working on the *Short History of Standing Armies in England*. Forwarding a list of nine queries about the armies of Charles II and James II, Trenchard assured Harley that 'these things are absolutely necessary to my purpose, and I don't know where to get them unless from you'. 'I humbly thank you for the paper you sent me', he subsequently reiterated, 'but what I most want is a list of the army we now have. I therefore desire that you will correct and fill up the list I have sent you for I find there are several mistakes'.[59] Contact between the two men was extensive and prolonged. Trenchard sent Harley his proposals for disbanding the army, believing his 'method' would 'more certainly disband the army than the method proposed'. 'If you are leisure either this night or tomorrow morning', he wrote on another occasion, 'I will wait upon you to discourse upon these heads'.[60]

Harley almost certainly learnt a lot about the press from his association with Trenchard. Trenchard did not do all the work himself. He made use of others. The similarity between this system and the one which finally evolved under Harley does not have to be stressed. More importantly, perhaps, Trenchard's propaganda demonstrated that public opinion could be influenced by the press. In 1697 and 1698 it was not only opinion inside parliament which mattered, but extra-parliamentary viewpoints. The disbandment issue was one which could actually be used to change the face of parliament. By the terms of the triennial act, there had to be a general election in 1698. The anti-army pamphleteers, therefore, were aiming not merely at persuading their representatives in parliament to vote for disbandment, they were also attempting to pander to the desires of the electorate to secure an electoral victory. It was clearly to the advantage of country gentlemen not to maintain an army. No army, less taxation. The equation was not a complex one, and the country propagandists hammered out the solution in their pamphlets. 'The truth is', wrote one court observer in explanation of country success at the polls, 'people are so galled with taxes that they kick and wince at every one'.[61]

Both sides recognised the importance of public opinion in the General Election of 1698. It had been the prime cause of the deluge of anti-army tracts, and the court had not been slow to respond to the country challenge. Daniel Defoe, in particular, produced a number of pamphlets seeking to prove that, in itself, a standing army was not destructive to the English constitution. According to Bonet, his *Argument showing that a Standing Army, with Consent of Parliament, is not Inconsistent with a Free Government*, published early in 1698, 'plait fort à cette cour, qu'elle à été bien reçuë'.[62] In later years Defoe claimed to have been the personal friend of William III, and to have travelled 'to every nook and corner of [England] upon public affairs when I had the honour to serve his late majesty'.[63] He has been described as 'King William's pamphleteer',[64] but the available evidence is confusing and inconclusive. In 1697, however, he did become accountant to the commissioners of the glass duty. He had previously been manager-trustee of the royal lotteries of October 1695 and March 1696. This after he had failed in 1692 to the tune of £17,000!

If Defoe was William III's personal apologist, what was his relationship with Somers, who coordinated court propaganda? Were their roles integrated, or was Defoe the lone wolf he so often was? Somers certainly hired other writers to produce propaganda to his requirements. One was Sir Richard Blackmore, whose *History of the Late Parliament* was a prominent feature of the court campaign on the opening of the new parliament in December 1698. In 1701 James Drake explained that it had been written 'to flatter the ambition and serve the interests of one great courtier...who then thought it as much for his turn to exalt and magnify the honour and power of a house of commons, as he has done since to depress and decry it'.[65] Somers's activities in relation to the press and the manipulation of public opinion did not fail to attract attention. He was, however, always on the defensive, after Trenchard had pre-empted the controversy in print with his *Argument* against a standing army. The *Short History of Standing Armies in England* served much the same purpose in 1698. The court publications far outnumbered those of the opposition, but they did not outweigh their arguments. Even a court supporter wrote to his father on 17 December 1698: 'Of the many pamphlets mentioned in the advertisements there are very few worth sending. That about the *History of the Standing Armies* is one of the best'.[66]

This should not obscure the spirit with which Somers fought on the court's behalf. One broadsheet divided the candidates into 'Courtiers, so called', and the 'New Country-Party, so called',[67] in a vain attempt to invalidate the opposition claim that the contest was between court and country. Toland had already warned that the names of whig and tory were 'now of a very doubtful signification'. The *Militia Reformed* postulated that 'a true patriot can be of no faction'. There were 'apostate' and 'adhering' whigs. Such labels meant nothing: 'such distinctions as these of whig and tory cannot miss being often made with a great deal of partiality and injustice; for, according to your predominant passion, he's a whig whom you love, and he that you hate's a tory; and so, on the contrary, as you happen to be engaged in either party'.[68] The country party retained the initiative during the elections. Toland published Ashley's (now earl of Shaftesbury) *The Danger of Mercenary Parliaments* 'with his Lordship's privity'.[69] It was a powerful indictment of corruption, and it advised strongly against electing 'such persons who are now possessed of any places and preferments depending upon the gift and pleasure of the court'.[70] A court reply appeared, almost inevitably, on 21 July,[71] but it was insufficient to halt the flood of country pamphlets on the importance of free parliamentary proceedings in 'a house of commons chosen truly by the people, incapable of pension and place'.[72] One pamphlet took up the hint of the 'Hush-money Paper', and published a list of those with places at court so that electors might be warned against voting for such disreputable characters![73] With a wonderful touch of understatement, James Vernon, the secretary of state, observed that 'there seems to arise a strange spirit of distinguishing between the court and the country party, and visibly discovers itself in several elections'.[74] The available evidence points to the triumph of the propaganda of the opposition.

Things were very similar during the build-up to the meeting of the new parliament. Both sides had each new member under scrutiny,[75] but Harley believed that 'any alteration' would 'proceed' not from the new members, 'but from the change of opinions in some of the old'.[76] The standing army issue was still an emotive one. Despite the resolutions of the previous session the army had not been disbanded. The country opposition, in the closing weeks of the old parliament, had failed to appropriate revenue for the task of paying off the regiments. Trenchard was cooperating with Harley in the compilation of *A Short History of Standing Armies in England* which contained estimates of the army of Charles II in 1680 and, by comparison, that of William III in 1698. The latter outnumbered the former by 59,969 to 17,750.[77] Harley had supplied Trenchard with much of the information for these exaggerated figures.[78] Simultaneously a printed list 'of all the land forces now in England' was circulated by the opposition,[79] while Anthony Hammond prepared the way for the speakership contest by publishing *Some Considerations upon the Choice of a Speaker*.[80] Once again the court pamphleteers were left to pick up the pieces.

Although the opposition did not carry the speakership contest,[81] the country leaders dominated the Commons over the question of disbandment. On 16 December 1698 Harley proposed that the army in England in 1699 should total no more than 7,000 men. The vagueness of the establishment of Charles II necessitated the naming of an exact number of troops. A further resolution insisted that these should consist of only 'his majesty's natural born subjects', excluding, in this way, the king's crack regiment of Dutch guards. Although an extra 12,000 men were stipulated for service in Ireland, the controversy over a standing army had been decisively settled in favour of disbandment. The paper war gradually died down. With a general election perhaps three years away printed propaganda was of less importance. The men inside parliament had made up their minds. At this time no-one thought of exploiting public opinion as a weapon with which to embarrass a parliamentary majority. There was, for the present, little need to appeal to the electorate. Neither Trenchard nor Somers used the lull to organise permanent agencies for the production and dispersal of propaganda. Occasional offerings were still the only manifestation of insight into the use of the press as a means of channelling public opinion.

Harley had not been the driving-force behind the dissemination of anti-army propaganda. It would be unwise to make such an assertion. The Grecian Coffee-house was the centre for the distribution of these pamphlets, and it appears that Trenchard was the coordinator. But Harley had been involved in the production, and he had gained in experience accordingly. His relationship with Trenchard was only part of his association with the anti-army writers. We cannot exclude him from active collaboration in the formulation of some anti-army tracts – broadsheet lists of forces and compilations of anti-army debates.[82] But more important to the development of his press policies was his cultivation of individual propagandists like John Toland. In 1699 Toland embarked upon a project for the republication of Harrington's works with Harley's encouragement.[83] By 1701 he was writing pamphlets matching Harley's personal propaganda requirements. At various times throughout his life he was in Harley's employ. That Toland was 'Mr. Harley's creature' was well known.[84] 'I passed for Mr. Harley's friend when he was opposed by the court', Toland remarked, and he reminded Harley in 1711 how their 'familiarity commenced, founded upon the same love of letters and liberty...many years ago'.[85]

Toland was an Irish deist and commonwealthman. In 1696 he created a furore with his book, *Christianity Not Mysterious*. To help him, whig friends such as Edward Clarke and John Freke, intimates of Locke, endeavoured to secure his appointment as secretary to John Methuen, chancellor of Ireland. He crossed over to Dublin, acting outrageously with the trappings of an office not yet his, and making 'visits in form...to all the ministers and persons in any considerable post'.[86] When the Irish realised who this strange man was, he was forced to flee to England to escape the consequences of *Christianity Not Mysterious*. He arrived in England in the autumn of 1697.[87] Harley was informed of his flight.[88]

In London Toland moved within the circle of commonwealthmen at the Grecian, apparently severing his former connections with the court whigs. He was a malcontent, and it was in this condition that he came to the notice of Lord Ashley.

Toland became acquainted with Harley either through the offices of Ashley or of Methuen. Unfortunately we cannot be certain when the contact was made. Toland's edition of Harrington's works went to press on 11 July 1699.[89] Earlier that year Secretary Vernon had warned the earl of Portland about Toland, that 'noted Socinian and no less an incendiary'. He advised keeping a check on Toland's movements. He was reputed to be in Holland on the pretence of 'printing some book'. Although Vernon assumed that it would 'be no very good piece', it was presumably the edition of Harrington.[90] Toland produced the *Militia Reformed* for the opposition cause during the standing army controversy, as well as seeing Shaftesbury's *Danger of Mercenary Parliaments* through the press during the elections. Harley patronised this writer, finding his abilities as a propagandist of more relevance than his morals. He was to prove a key figure in the production of Harleyite propaganda in 1701.

A second recruit during the years of court and country was Charles Davenant. Davenant was a budding economist, the author of several interesting but dry tracts on the ways and means of raising supply for the war with France. He, too, was on terms with the anti-army pamphleteers.[91] In 1698 he was elected to parliament. His *Essay upon Trade*, published around the turn of the year 1698–9, was admired by the Harley camp. Harley sent his father a copy in the hope that it would afford the old gentleman 'some diversion to hear it read'.[92] Davenant's next pamphlet was of much more significance. His *Discourse upon Grants and Resumptions* played a crucial part in the country propaganda campaign leading up to the confrontation between king and parliament in April 1700 over the vexed question of the Irish forfeitures.

This issue was in essence an extension of the standing army controversy. The question was one of taxation. William III had made lavish grants of the forfeited rebels' estates in Ireland to his Dutch favourites. The country opposition wanted to put the revenue of these lands to the use of the public, thus cutting taxation. On 19 April 1699 seven commissioners were chosen by ballot to look into the matter. John Trenchard was one of the men named. Davenant was soon at work 'to prepare the town to give the report of our Irish commissioners a kind reception'. Propaganda was being used to influence public opinion in advance. In this case of perhaps more significance was the attempt to

persuade *parliament men* in advance of their consideration of the report
of the commission. Propaganda was designed to prejudice their
judgment.[93]

Davenant openly acknowledged his connections with the country
leaders – 'the Old Whigs (who are now turned tories)' – and it is almost
certain that both Trenchard and Harley were privy to the publication
of Davenant's *Discourse*. Oldmixon noted that he had been 'employed
to write a book...to prepare the way for resuming his Majesty's grants
in Ireland'.[94] The *Discourse* is a fine example of concerted opposition
propaganda. Under the thin guise of various ill-fortuned historical
characters the Junto, Portland, Sunderland, and the king's other
favourites were subjected to a swingeing indictment. Davenant directed
the dark threat of impeachment at the king's servants: 'When the people
of England desire an act of resumption, the work must begin with
impeaching corrupt ministers'.[95] In this way, Davenant implied, quite
openly, that the opposition represented the 'people', and that the
country leaders were acting on the wishes and desires of the electorate.

The precedent had been set for aligning the actions of MPs with the
views of the electorate. In many ways it was to prove a dangerous step.
Somers was to exploit the relationship brilliantly in 1701 by insinuating
that the men in parliament were out of tune with national feelings.
Davenant had tried to suggest the opposite. Harley was running the
house of commons. By 1699 the court managers had lost all semblance
of control. 'Mr Harley now manages the whole business of the supply',
one placeman noted,[96] while Vernon agreed that Harley could give 'what
turn he pleased to the taxes'.[97] The report of the Irish forfeitures
commission led to the introduction of a bill to resume the land grants.
William, unable to strike a bargain with the opposition,[98] engendered
a confrontation between Lords and Commons. Conferences between the
two houses failed to reach a settlement. When the Commons heard the
rumour that the Lords had thrown out the Irish bill, they locked their
doors, and proposed a declaratory vote relating to the army, which had
not been fully disbanded. Events were moving towards open hostilities
when the Lords gave way. On 11 April 1700 the king gave his reluctant
consent to the bill for resuming the forfeitures. Harley had been leader
throughout.

April 1700 was the zenith of the conflict between court and country
in the reign of William III. The country party had won. Somers was
dismissed in the same month. He was the last court whig to hold office.
Harley assured Vernon that the king 'now had a better opportunity to

make himself easy than had offered itself these ten years'.[99] Throughout the summer the country leaders were planning an alternative administration. Added incentive was provided by the death on 31 July of the duke of Gloucester. He had been Princess Anne the heir-apparent's only living child, and second in line to the throne. A solution had to be found to the problem of the succession. The price William had to pay for a settlement in the Protestant line was further clauses reducing his prerogative in the form of a place bill and a judge's bill. In 1701 politics and propaganda gradually reorientated around the poles of whig and tory.

Davenant's association with Harley continued, and flourished. Secret treaties had been concluded between William III and Louis XIV of France catering for the partition of the Spanish Empire on the death of the childless Charles II. In his will, however, Charles proposed to leave the Empire intact to the Bourbons. The partition treaties, which had been negotiated and signed without the consent of parliament, were rendered meaningless when Louis accepted Charles's offer. On 22 August 1700 Vernon observed that Davenant was 'preparing a book against the Spanish treaty'. 'We shall have many records brought', he pertinently observed, 'to prove that treaties are not to be made without the consent of parliament'.[100] As authorities for his assertions, in his *Essays upon I. The Balance of Power. II. The Right of Making War, Peace, and Alliances. III. Universal Monarchy*, Davenant appended records containing 'many precedents', which, he claimed, had been 'carefully examined by the author at the Tower'.[101] In a letter to Harley dated 19 September 1700, however, Davenant assured him that: 'your man has delivered me the records, of which about two months hence you will find I have made a plentiful use. The work goes on vigorously, but is infinitely of more labour than I expected'.[102] Once more we have evidence of Harley actively assisting the production of country propaganda, this time on behalf of Charles Davenant.

Davenant's *Essays* were not published in 1700. The reason lies in the changed attitude of William III to the country leaders after the death of the duke of Gloucester. When the country party was transformed into a court party, the paradox was sufficient to nullify propaganda which exploited the division between court and country. The passing of the bill of settlement necessitated a new parliament. The publication of the *Essays* was held over until after the general election. It was not the only preparation made against the opening of the new parliament in February

1701. Harley became speaker of the house of commons, and he could now be recognised as the driving force behind the production and dissemination of *ministerial* propaganda, in collaboration with Davenant and Toland. He had witnessed the usefulness of the press in the long and bitter struggle between court and country, and he had made contacts that would prove invaluable during the exigencies of 1701. Harley, it is clear, was no longer content to leave the direction and organisation of political propaganda to others such as Trenchard. He had his own brand to sell, his own ideology to follow, and a gradual divergence can be discerned between his views and those of Trenchard and Shaftesbury. These features serve to distinguish Harleyite propaganda from the writings of tories and whigs in 1701. He attempted to control events in parliament through the press. And, when Somers mounted a campaign to discredit the men in parliament, Harley extended his plans to the electorate, producing counter-propaganda to block whig endeavours to influence public opinion. From now on, his role can be fully documented, as he fought to gain control of an unrivalled medium for the manipulation of men.

2

The paper war of 1701

In 1700 William III rejected the leaders of the court whigs, Somers, Halifax, Orford and Wharton – the group known collectively as the Junto – apparently once and for all. In the autumn of the same year negotiations were on foot between the king and the most prominent members of the opposition in both houses of parliament regarding the succession. As well as Harley, who led the Commons in most things, the talks involved the earl of Rochester and Lord Godolphin (among others). Parliament was dissolved, elections took place, and preparations were made against the opening of the new parliament in February 1701. Harley was elected speaker, supported by both the court party and the country opposition. He was opposed only by those whigs irreconcilable to him, and outside the control of the court. A whig party again existed at the centre of power as a separate entity which could not be classified as either court or country. The New Country Party was now working alongside the permanent courtiers. The whigs could hardly claim to be the country opposition. They were no longer members of the court party. By the end of 1701 the realignment was virtually complete, as political terminology returned to the previous dichotomy between whig and tory in trying to establish accurate terms of reference.

Accompanying the political transformation, contributing greatly to it, and generally symptomatic of a period of flux, was a paper war which was by far the most extensive and the most general since the lifting of censorship. Harley was responsible for many of the 'country' offerings, as he fought to prevent a reorientation around the poles of whig and tory, either indirectly, by commissioning pamphlets and providing hints and suggestions, or directly, by taking up the pen himself. Charles Davenant acted as Harley's agent, making arrangements with the printers, and distributing pamphlets in the provinces. On the whig side Somers played what would appear to have been a similar role, concerting propaganda with Halifax, Edward Clarke and John Freke – the whig 'college' which Harley believed to be responsible for the campaign to discredit the house of commons. A principal weapon in the whig armoury was the connection with Jacob Tonson, 'genial Jacob' of Pope's poem,[1] the leading publisher of his generation. His services no doubt greatly assisted the distribution of whig propaganda.

Outside these relatively organised propaganda agencies were the pamphleteering activities of individual whigs and tories. Defoe claimed to be working on direct orders from William III after the publication of his *True-Born Englishman*, which reputedly sold 80,000 copies on the streets. Certainly a link with Somers cannot be proved, but even the relationship with the king stands on conflicting evidence. According to Defoe, this poem was 'the occasion of my being known to his majesty'. He was subsequently 'received by him...employed, and...above my capacity of deserving, rewarded'.[2] All this, of course, casts a strange light on Defoe's actions during the standing army controversy. Was he writing to orders, and, if he was, to whose? On the tory (or country) side, several pamphlets were written by Anthony Hammond, such as *Considerations upon Corrupt Elections of Members to Serve in Parliament*,[3] and by Sir Humphry Mackworth, whose *Vindication of the Rights of the Commons of England*, it seems, stimulated a response from the pen of Somers himself. It was impossible for *chefs de propagande* like Harley and Somers to control the massive output from independent men like these.

Both men realised a considerable advance in propaganda techniques during the exigencies of the paper war, Somers instituting a direct, emotive appeal to the electorate. Public opinion emerged as a weapon that could be wielded against the establishment. This culminated in *ad hominem* attacks by Somers on Harley, and by Harley on Somers, as each man acknowledged the leadership of the other in the production of propaganda. Harley was convinced that Somers personally had taken charge of the whig campaign to undermine the credibility of the house of commons chosen early in the year. Harley's opinions and activities can be documented. Somers's role can merely be asserted on the grounds of widespread and sustained circumstantial evidence. Between them, they engendered and nourished the paper war which was to prove to be seminal in the rise of paper wars in the reign of Queen Anne.

In preparation for the meeting of parliament on 10 February 1701, John Toland published *The Art of Governing by Parties*. The timing was similar to that of the country 'manifestos' of John Hampden, and so was the intent: to pave the way for the parliamentary debates. Of more interest are the arguments propounded by Toland. Passages echo *The Danger of Mercenary Parliaments*,[4] while others anticipate the arguments of Simon Clement's *Faults on Both Sides* and Harley's own 'Plain English' in exposing court methods to divide and rule. Parties were traced back to their origins in the reign of Charles II, but it was post-Revolution politics which most concerned Toland:[5]

The king fell in heartily with the public interest, his new ministers served him faithfully for a considerable time, and all our affairs took a better face both at home and abroad, by land and sea. But see the instability of human councils. Some of those surly whigs grew by degrees the most pliant gentlemen imaginable. They could think no revenue too great for the king, nor would suffer his prerogative to be lessened. They were on frivolous pretences for keeping up a standing army to our further peril and charge. They filled all places in their disposal with their own creatures, combined together for their own impunity, whoever found fault with their conduct they represented him as an enemy to the government, and even opposed the best of laws, lest the tories, as they said, should partake of the benefit. Surely these gentlemen, if it were in their power, would not suffer the sun to shine on any but themselves and their faction. But as this language, this partiality, this conduct, were directly contrary to the principles and practices of the whigs (and the tories themselves will do justice to the Old Whigs) so these apostates were abandoned by their former friends, and left to the support of their own interest, which appeared to be so very little with any party, that the king did wisely cashier them.

In terms peculiarly like those Clement was to use ten years later, Toland traced the whig split to its cause. In retrospect Toland approved Harley's stand against the Junto whigs, 'the sense he then had of our corrupt ministry', and he thanked him 'for the strenuous efforts he made to dissolve it'.[6] Contemporaries felt that Harley was involved in the publication of the *Art of Governing by Parties*. 'I could almost swear it was revised by him', one wrote, 'and that the report Toland gave out himself, that Harley was his friend, was true'.[7]

Toland had found new friends. As Shaftesbury recognised, his former protégé was meeting encouragement from men in high places.[8] 1701, moreover, saw the parting of the ways as far as Harley and Shaftesbury were concerned. The latter could no longer tolerate cooperation with tory elements when whigs (albeit Junto whigs) were in danger of being impeached for their services when at court. He had been against the dissolution of parliament, and he did not like the change of government.[9] When Toland blatantly indicted the Junto in the *Art of Governing by Parties* for failing in their patriotic duties, he was adhering to Harleyite precepts. He had not altered his attitude perceptibly in the two years since Harley had sponsored his edition of Harrington. But Shaftesbury had. On 4 March 1700 Shaftesbury sent Benjamin Furly a copy of Toland's pamphlet 'from the author'.[10] The divergence between Toland's views on the new parliament and those of Shaftesbury is marked.

Toland's pamphlet was more than simply a rehearsal of the wrongs perpetrated by the court since the Revolution. It was pertinent to the new parliament, to the new arrangement between the king and his people (in the form of the country party), and to the impending bill of settlement. 'The only remedy against all the mischief of parties', Toland concluded, 'is a parliament equally constituted':[11]

If this parliament be of that healing disposition which all true patriots most heartily desire, something may be offered that may not be altogether impracticable nor unsatisfactory towards abolishing these fatal distinctions of whig and tory, and making us at least bear with one another in religion, where we cannot agree.

The Art of Governing by Parties was designed to prepare the ground for parliamentary approval of the bill of settlement. A pattern relating to the production of country propaganda can be seen emerging, and Harley appears to have been at the bottom of it. Toland timed the publication of his next pamphlet, *Limitations for the Next Foreign Successor, or the New Saxon Race*, to coincide with the first vote of the Commons upon the question of the Protestant succession on 3 March 1701.[12] When the act was passed, he produced *Anglia Libera: Or the Limitation and Succession of the Crown of England explained and asserted; As grounded on his Majesty's Speech; the Proceedings in Parliament; the Desires of the People; the Safety of our Religion; the Nature of our Constitution; the Balance of Europe; and the Rights of all Mankind.* Once again, with affairs settled in parliament, propaganda was supplied to those 'without doors'. The electorate was not allowed to remain in a state of ignorance. Public opinion was considered to be of sufficient importance to warrant explanation of proceedings in parliament.

But Toland, and his patrons, took things further than merely this. Harley was surely one of 'quelques personnes des premiers dans le gouvernement' reported to have commissioned *Anglia Libera*.[13] The pamphlet was presented to Sophia, dowager-duchess of Hanover, by Toland in person. He accompanied the official mission of the earl of Macclesfield which was to report the enactment of the bill of succession. One cynical writer (quite possibly Somers himself) wanted to know[14]

Whether Mr Harley has not made choice of a very proper envoy, in sending Toland to notify the good old Princess that she owes her Crown to the speaker? And whether, hereafter, if she finds herself obliged to make the one her treasurer for his honesty, she must not make the other archbishop for his religion?

Even men in official circles like George Stepney made sinister reference to the 'deceitful message' from Harley to Sophia conveyed by Toland.[15] And after the official notification to the court at Hanover of the decision of the English parliament, came the unofficial supply of information for popular digestion. Toland told Shaftesbury that *Anglia Libera* was being translated 'as fast as may be' into French and Dutch. 'They have already put me in all their *Gazettes* for writing it', he boasted, 'and look on me so far to be a sort of ambassador from the people, that whether I will or no they seriously advise me what to do and say at Hanover'.[16]

Toland was not Harley's only propagandist, which was just as well. Prone to megolamania, Toland quickly and easily persuaded himself that he should become a man of political consequence, and stand for parliament. He rekindled his whig zeal in anticipation of an early general election. After the passage of the act of settlement things did not go well for Harley in parliament. A witch-hunt for the whig lords led to the impeachment of Somers, Halifax, Orford and Portland for their parts in the signing of the secret partition treaties. As Sunderland remarked: 'had they left alone Lord Portland and the civil list, they might have hanged the other three in a garret'.[17] Not content with letting whig blood, the country backbenchers sought to purge the king himself. They deducted £100,000 from his civil list. This was enough to convince him that he had made a wrong turn. True, his alliance with the opposition leaders had secured the passage of the bill of settlement, but at the price of clauses reducing royal prerogative. The end of the parliamentary session in June led to the dismissal of the impeachments by the house of lords. By November, after the death of James II in exile at St Germain and the recognition of his son as James III by Louis XIV, William was ready to reappoint the Junto. As he told Harley on the dissolution of parliament for the second time within a year: 'Mr Speaker, your project of the succession has done me no good'.[18]

The deadlock between the two houses of parliament which characterised the last month of the short life of the 1701 parliament led to printed justifications of conduct. Both houses reprinted their journals, while respective apologists explained proceedings. Both sides appealed to public opinion. In May, at the height of the backbench reprisals, Defoe's famous 'Legion-Letter' was presented to Harley as speaker of the house of commons. It purported to express the desires of the electorate. 'Two hundred thousand Englishmen' *commanded* Harley to deliver their memorial to their representatives in parliament. The country weapon was turned against its maker, and a precedent was set for similar addresses from electoral boroughs throughout the reign of Queen Anne, whenever they felt themselves dissatisfied with the votes of their representatives. The country propagandists had previously pretended to speak for the electorate. Davenant's *Discourse* had played on the fact that it was 'the people of England' who desired to resume the Irish forfeitures. The image had been invoked, and the spectre of public opinion proceeded to haunt Harley and the other country leaders for the rest of William's reign and beyond.

Five freeholders of Kent had been imprisoned when they tried to lobby their MPs to express unease at the international situation, and parliamentary attitudes towards the aggression of Louis XIV. The Kentish Petition, as it came to be known, was almost certainly concerted by the whigs. It was anything but a spontaneous outburst of public feeling. The whigs saw public opinion as a means to combat the threats of impeachment hanging over their leaders. Defoe's 'Legion-Letter' was similarly planned. It called for the release of the Kentish Petitioners, and for preparations for renewed war with France over the Spanish Empire. Public opinion was being used to exert pressure on a house of commons in which the whigs were heavily outnumbered. As one observer noted, 'whether there be more signs of Legion without doors, or within, is a question'.[19] Could the 'Legion-Letter' really claim to be the view of the entire electorate? Clearly not, but that was what it insinuated in offering to append the signatures of two hundred thousand Englishmen.

After the prorogation of parliament the whigs continued to appeal to public opinion. In August Defoe published a biased *History of the Kentish Petition*, while *Jura Populi Anglicani: Or, the Subject's Right of Petitioning Set Forth* was only the most influential of several pamphlets preaching the rights of the people. It is usually attributed to Somers himself, and it was a savage attack on the 'new ministry', and on Harley in particular. The old charge of toryism was levelled against the apostate whigs. 'Is not Robert Harley a ring-leader in this tory party', the author of *Jura Populi Anglicani* demanded, 'Whatever difference might formerly have been between them, it will, upon a fair examination, appear that now there is a great agreement in their principles'. The whigs pressed for a total acceptance of party labels. He who was not with them, was against them. Harley voted with tories: by association, he was a tory. 'Whatever matter was offered [during the last session] that seemed to have the least tendency to war', the point was driven home, 'was violently opposed by the speaker, Musgrave, Seymour, Shower, Finch, Howe, Harcourt, and all those who were entirely in the interest of that party'.[20]

This *ad hominem* attack was supported by two principal sorts of publication. Somers appears to have been behind both. 'The parties are every day writing and printing against one another with great bitterness', James Vernon told Shrewsbury at the beginning of September 1701, 'and the chiefs seem to have a hand in it'.[21] The first continued to assert the rights of the electorate. The pretence of pamphlets such as *The Elector's Right Asserted: with the Advices and Charges Of Several Counties, Cities, and Boroughs in England to their Respective Members of Parliament* was that the country backbenchers had completely ignored the wishes of their constituents once elected. It sought in fact to invalidate the decisions of parliament men who acted contrary to their brief. If Somers himself was not responsible for this pamphlet, it certainly came out of his stable. It denied vehemently that it was[22]

the law and custom...of an English parliament that, as soon as ever the members were chosen, they were then left to the absolute freedom of their own wills, to act without control, and though they are abusively called the people's servants, yet really and in truth they instantly, upon the sealing of the indentures of their elections, become their masters.

The claim that the country party represented the people was in this way thrown back in the teeth of the country backbenchers. It was for this reason and no other, it was ingeniously claimed, that the Kentish Petition and the 'Legion-Letter' had been delivered to the Commons. The *Elector's Right Asserted* concluded with lists of addresses and petitions from electors to their representatives in parliament. It was a seminal pamphlet. Others, like *A Letter from Some Electors to One of their Representatives in Parliament, Showing the Electors's Sentiments touching the Matters in dispute between the Lord and Commons the last Session of Parliament, in Relation to the Impeachments. And giving Some Advice to their Member How to demean himself in Parliament for the future*, were of the same stamp.

The second type of whig propaganda was the publication of sets of punchy queries, disputing the integrity of the new ministry, the leading members of the Commons, and generally allowing full rein to scandal and malice. The advantage of lists of political aphorisms is readily apparent. Where a polemical pamphlet had to be read fairly closely, the vehicle of queries was designed to satisfy the most basic literary requirements of propaganda. It stated nakedly an accusation or a rumour, whether or not it was based on a solid foundation in fact. Libel abounded. Open insinuations of bribery were employed in explanation of supposed ministerial tardiness to make preparations for a renewal of hostilities with France. *Some Queries, which may deserve Consideration*, the broadsheet which sparked off the publication of rival lists of questions, asked: 'If it be not necessary to enquire on what occasion a million Louis d'Ors have come into England since the death of the King of Spain, that so, according to the event of the enquiry, somebody may be thanked, or may be hanged?' The country response, *Some Queries which deserve no Consideration, answered paragraph by paragraph, only to satisfy the ridiculous enquiries of the trifling Peer that made 'em Public*, indicated quite clearly where it was felt blame lay for the libel – with Somers and his colleagues.

Annotations on Harley's own copy of *Some Queries* refer to 'the peer that queries'.[23] He, too, was aware of the author, and as he directed his attack in print at Somers, we would probably be justified in discerning his hand. Late in August Henry St John reported that the speaker 'had a paper ready for the press'.[24] Vernon similarly wrote of a pamphlet 'said to be written by the speaker':[25]

It sets forth all their resolutions in relation to foreign affairs, and the king's answers approving of them, with a comment upon them, to show what prudent steps were made by the house [of commons], and how rash others were that would have had an immediate declaration of war, without giving time either to ourselves or our neighbours to be in a posture for it.

Although Vernon spoke of a 'vindication' of the Commons, it is on this evidence, it seems, that *A Justification of the Proceedings Of the Honourable the House of Commons, In the Last Session of Parliament* has been attributed to Harley.[26] The discovery that at this time Harley was writing pamphlets in collaboration with Charles Davenant adds weight to the assumption.[27]

Davenant's *Essays* were finally published on 15 March 1701. As Frank Ellis remarks, 'publication was again perfectly timed to produce the maximum propaganda effect'.[28] Davenant's pamphlet had been held in abeyance, ready for the revelation of the existence of secret partition treaties, while Toland's tracts on parties and on the bill of settlement were being utilised. This would appear to suggest a guiding hand, and, if so, that hand was almost certainly Harley's. On 14 March the Lords sent a message to the Commons concerning the illegal treaties. The following day Davenant's *Essays* appeared, 'conserté avec ceux de son partÿ'.[29] His next effort was *The True Picture of a Modern Whig*, published on 29 August when the whig propaganda campaign was being launched.[30] It was heavily Harleyite, and, as Caroline Robbins remarks, it was 'probably inspired by Harley'.[31]

In the *True Picture*, Davenant distinguished between the Old Whigs who were famous for their probity, and the unscrupulous, fortune-seeking Modern Whigs. The parallel with Toland's description of the whig split in the *Art of Governing by Parties* need hardly be mentioned. Davenant caricatured and lampooned the archetypal Modern Whig as Tom Double. The connection between whigs of the kidney of Somers, who had amassed a pile of wealth, not to mention a peerage, since the Revolution, and the fictional Tom Double was easily drawn. 'I can name you fifty of your friends who have got. . . fortunes since the Revolution, and from poor beginnings', Tom Double admitted, 'In describing myself, I have drawn most of their pictures, and there are few of 'em that do not resemble me in some of my features. Look generally into their origins, and you will find 'em full as mean as mine'.[32] The *True Picture* was a useful counter to the charges of apostasy that were being levelled against Harley and his Old Whig colleagues in *Jura Populi Anglicani*. 'Prithee friend Whiglove', Double advised his companion, 'leave off calling thyself an Old Whig, it will do thee hurt with the party. We reckon those men our worst of enemies. . . [they] think us the very rogues we know ourselves to be, they have quitted our side, and vote every day with Seymour, Musgrave and Jack Howe'. By offering an alternative interpretation of the allegations made by the author of *Jura Populi Anglicani*, whether or not it was Somers himself, Davenant sought to draw the sting of his attack.

Frank Ellis observes that the *True Picture of a Modern Whig* is 'a very different kind of work from Davenant's earlier compilations of precedents and statistics'. This, Ellis surmises, was due to the 'wit and humour' of the earl of Peterborough.[33] The use of mock form and personae are considerable advances in the employment and appreciation of propaganda techniques, it is true, but there is evidence to suggest that they had emanated not from the witty Peterborough, but from the more down-to-earth Harley. The paper war had witnessed a proliferation of false vindications such as *The True Patriot Vindicated*, a covert attack on

Rochester. But on at least two occasions Harley himself decided to employ mock form. In response to *Some Queries, which may deserve Consideration*, Harley impersonated two hot whigs and sometime acquaintances, Edward Clarke, MP for Taunton, and Junto spokesman in the Commons since the standing army controversy, and John Freke, a lawyer and secretary, to all intents and purposes, of the whig 'college' thought to be directing the production and dissemination of whig propaganda during the paper war. *The Taunton-Dean Letter, from E.C. to J.F. at the Grecian Coffee-house*, dated 3 September 1701, ironically exposed the tactics and motives of the whigs in pressing for an early dissolution of parliament.

Similarities can be noted between the arguments of the *True Picture* and those of the *Taunton-Dean Letter*. Whiglove had expressed doubts about Tom Double's optimism that the whigs would 'be able to bully the court into a dissolution'. 'Who knows', Double had replied, 'if we make a great deal of noise...we may fright 'em to it'.[34] Like Tom Double, E.C. was afraid that the country party would 'never leave off looking into our mysteries, and examining accounts, to the ruin of many honest godly people'. Harley's holograph draft of the *Taunton-Dean* broadsheet, preserved in the Portland papers, supplied the mock answer. Until a dissolution could be secured, 'the power of parliaments must be retrenched, and their sitting quietly to do the nation's business must be prevented, otherwise it will be impossible to carry on our designs, or secure what we have got'. Edward Clarke and John Freke were archetypal Modern Whigs. Harley highlighted the aims of their press campaign:

Your contrivance of *Legion* was a noble work, and though it was sealed up in the house, you printed, and we dispersed it successfully. The style is suited to the people, who we would be glad to inflame, and there are not only reflections on particular persons, but you touch the main point against the authority of parliaments. The *Queries* do the same. The authors of *Jura Populi* have done well, they overturn the power of the Commons to commit, and thereby make them useless, and also show they are not the representatives of the people.

Here, in a nutshell, Harley listed, in mock form, the tactics of the whig propaganda drive, and their motives in appealing to public opinion. The Commons were 'not the representatives of the people', who the whigs 'would be glad to inflame'. A minority 'within doors', they were trying to make up the deficiency by drumming up extra-parliamentary power. They had to secure a dissolution, and to do this they had to sway public opinion. Not only did Harley discern their motives, he recognised the men behind the policy. E.C. proposed the production of propaganda along the usual lines, to be considered by 'my Lord Somers, and my Lord Halifax, in conjunction with yourself, Jacob Tonson, and two or three more of the ablest politicians of our party'.

Appended to the *Taunton-Dean Letter* was a list of 28 queries supposedly written at Exeter. They were country counter-queries to the original whig *Queries*. On 7 September Davenant wrote to Harley: 'I beg you would be pleased either to send me the queries, or, which I had rather, let me know when I may wait upon you for 'em'.[35] But the publication of the *Taunton-Dean Letter*, the first pamphlet for which we have documentary proof that Harley was responsible, was merely the prelude to his second, more extensive printed attack on the whigs, and on Somers in particular. On the back of a letter from William Bromley, dated 20 September 1701, Harley sketched out his satire. The phrases he used ('we went always upon persons, and not things'; 'how shall you dissolve this parliament but by exposing persons, and how shall we expose parliaments but by dissolving them') found their way into *A Letter from the Grecian Coffee-house, In Answer to The Taunton-Dean Letter. To which is added, A Paper of Queries Sent from Worcester*. On 6 October Harley forwarded his lampoon to Davenant, writing: 'The enclosed are but poor and confused materials, you are desired to alter, transpose, leave out, or burn them. They are all yours'.[36]

Confused, or not, Harley's ideas in the *Letter from the Grecian Coffee-house* were made public. The ultimate sentence of the *Taunton-Dean Letter* set the scene for a bitter assault on Somers's political morality. 'It is reported here that one of our noble friends grows cool in the cause'. E.C. had concluded, 'and I have letters hinting at some such thing, at which we are all very much alarmed. Pray let me know the truth by your next'. J.F. opened the *Letter from the Grecian Coffee-house* by supplying 'an answer at large' to E.C.'s pretended letter of 3 September. 'As I told you in my last', he wrote, 'I have communicated it to our noble friend to keep him in heart, and flatter him that he heads our party, who, you know, are all heads when we please'. 'Our noble friend' was, of course, Lord Somers, and the longer second pamphlet was an *exposé* of the Junto whig. According to J.F. (and the real-life John Freke would be in a position to know the truth about Somers), Somers had stolen books when he was a student at Oxford. He had sent a commission down to try rioters at Worcester while he was lord chancellor purely because a ballad had been published there making fun of this piece of scandal. Moreover he had imprisoned Charles Blount, author of a pamphlet called *King William and Queen Mary Conquerors* (1693), and had kept him in confinement while he lay with his wife, Elizabeth Fanshawe Blount. Finally Harley quoted the Commons's journals concerning a breach of parliamentary privilege of which Somers had been guilty in 1679, and for which he had been arrested by the serjeant at arms. 'Our noble friend...was fine and warm the last day [of the previous session] in the house of lords when he began the cry, *withdraw, withdraw, clear the house, clear, clear the house*, after his majesty had come in with his robes and crown', J.F. concluded, 'this was a noble, undaunted stroke, after huffing the Commons'. Two of the 33 *Worcester Queries* were levelled specifically at Somers. Significantly they are the only two extant in Harley's hand:[37]

XXII. Whether a man from £200 or £300 a year practice and estate, and no gentleman, might not be contented with £6,000 a year, and a title, without setting the nation in a flame?

XXXIII. If the proverb be true, *save a thief from the gallows, he will hang you if he can*; by the same rule, save a man's father from the pillory, and the son will endeavour to ruin you and your family. Are not both these equally grateful?

Davenant, as far as we can gather, took charge of the publication of Harley's pamphlets, and he was also instrumental in arranging for their dispersal both in London and in the provinces. Although details are missing, it is evident that country gentlemen were encouraged to have them sent from London to give away to influential electors. There was a promotion campaign in the metropolis itself. This much is clear from Davenant's letter of 6 October to Thomas Coke:[38]

There are some papers come out lately, which have been taken very much in town. The authors are unknown, but their performance has met with a general approbation. Your friends here have thought you will not take it amiss to be put to a guinea charge. I have therefore undertaken to send you forty of one sort of the papers, and eighteen of the other to give away among your acquaintances. They will be as antidotes against the poison that is spread about by the other side, who spare no cost to scatter their libels upon the parliament round the kingdom.

As for so many other particulars of the paper war of 1701, we are forced to seek information about the whig campaign from the writings of their adversaries. From Harley's reaction to the whig challenge we are able to deduce Somers's involvement, and from Davenant we learn that, as is to be expected, the dissemination of whig propaganda was heavily subsidised by the lords of the Junto.

We have no means of estimating the extent of the arrangements for the distribution of Harleyite propaganda in the provinces. We do not know how many Thomas Cokes there were, or how many pamphlets were dispatched to country sympathisers. But the numbers conveyed to Coke seem fairly large. Forty broadsheet *Taunton-Dean Letters* multiplied by the mass of country MPs would amount to quite a formidable barrage of counter-propaganda, but this would be simply an hypothesis. Yet we now know that Harley was fully aware of the need for 'antidotes' to the 'poison' that the whigs were injecting into the body politic. In collaboration with Davenant he had succeeded in printing broadsheets and pamphlets to answer the charges of the whigs. He tried to control the situation by regulating the flow of country writings. He sought to direct the campaign against a dissolution by regular contributions of Harleyite propaganda. The *Letter from the Grecian Coffee-house* boldly enumerated the intentions of the whigs:[39]

I. This parliament is to be dissolved.
II. No parliament must sit quietly, or be suffered to examine miscarriages.
III. The nation must be made weary of parliaments...
IV. Moderation must be avoided, let both sides be exasperated.

Harley similarly provided the obvious outcome if such policies were to be carried through. 'All this will tend to the impunity of our friends', wrote J.F., 'and by keeping up parties, preserve us in power (whatever our reputation be) which...nothing else will do...we must be for humbling the house of commons, unless we could hope to see our power flourish there once more'.

The whigs appealed to public opinion to secure a dissolution, and to defend themselves from reprisals. They put up a smokescreen to obscure their real motives for upholding the rights of the electorate. Harley was sufficiently impressed by their tactics to produce counter-propaganda. For the first time the boot was on the other foot. It was the country party which was reduced to the defensive. Somers and his henchmen had launched an effective challenge, and Harley could only attempt to respond to it. He arranged for the production of country propaganda at the beginning of the 1701 parliament; in the autumn of the same year he was defending the very existence of that parliament in print. He had surrendered the initiative to the whigs. His reaction to the challenge was striking. The opinion of the electorate mattered. If the whigs managed to force a dissolution, it would be the voice of the 'people' that would be heard on the issues of the previous parliament. Somers, moreover, had pre-empted the election campaign by publishing spurious views of individual electors. This was no mean innovation.

The system founded by Harley in 1701 was essentially the same as the set-up which organised the dispersal of the propaganda of Defoe and Swift under the auspices of Harley in the reign of Queen Anne. At this time, of course, it was all rather hand-to-mouth. Harley himself wrote the pamphlets (excluding the *True Picture*), Davenant corrected them, arranged for them to be printed, and relied on friends and contacts in the provinces to distribute them. But large oaks from little acorns grow, and it was the establishment of centres for the dissemination of propaganda, plus agreements with printers, that facilitated the control of the press by the Oxford ministry. Another parallel can be drawn between Swift's propaganda for the government after 1710, and Davenant's writings on Harley's behalf in 1701. Davenant pointedly distinguished between Old Whigs and Modern Whigs. Swift shared Harley's country prejudices, while retaining his essential whiggery. In effect he, too, was attacking *Modern Whigs* in *The Examiner* and the *Conduct of the Allies* in censuring the role of the Junto under the Marlboroughs, while Davenant came up with *Sir Thomas Double at Court and in Great Preferments*. Both men assumed the support of the country gentlemen, and were reluctant to apply to these men the blanket labels of whig and tory.

Davenant wrote a second part of the *True Picture* in 1701. *Tom Double Returned Out of the Country* was published early in 1702. For some weeks Davenant had been preparing 'a full vindication' of his conduct 'from all the aspersions of the libellers'.[40] At the end of September he had been found in the company of Anthony Hammond, John Tredenham, and M. Poussin, the French secretary, when news came through that Poussin had been expelled from England. This earned Davenant the unwelcome distinction of 'Poussineer' – a term that was applied liberally to the leading members of the country party during the election campaign in November and December 1701. Harley was involved in the genesis of the second part of the *True Picture of a Modern Whig*. 'What you gave me in charge went last night to the press, and will be public tomorrow', Davenant wrote to Harley on 26 December, 'I have put a stop upon what was crossed out'.[41] Clearly by the end of 1701 Davenant was shouldering a heavy burden of responsibility for the production of Harleyite propaganda. After wishing the speaker 'a happier Christmas ...than can possibly be expected by me', Davenant continued, in his letter to Harley:

I beg you will send to Mr Winnington for his papers, for I am at a full stand without them. I would likewise borrow your printed account of the Irish forfeitures, for mine is lost. If you have a brief account of the English grants it would be of use to me. I likewise want my Lord Orford's contingent accounts, which I beg you to lend me.

Harley's active involvement in the production of printed propaganda at the turn of the year 1701–2 explains his unenthusiastic response to a suggestion that press regulations should be reimposed. Despite the electioneering of the Junto, and the influence of the king, Harley was again elected speaker of the house of commons in the new parliament. He was immediately sent the draft of a bill relating to the suppression of the political press by an Archbishop Tenison who was clearly horrified at the dimensions of the paper war of 1701. Harley's equivocations serve to document his awareness of the potential of propaganda to achieve political ends. The Junto had provided the test-case over the change of ministry and the dissolution of parliament. Harley's answer was not simply to muzzle a means of influencing public opinion, but to devote more energy to the development of the press as a political weapon. 'I have no doubt but there are sufficient authorities given by the laws in being for the suppressing [of seditious libel]', he wrote to Tenison, 'whenever it shall be thought fit to put those laws in execution'. He merely suggested that the archbishop, if he thought it necessary, might introduce a bill into the Lords, as was his prerogative.[42]

In the final analysis, however, Harley's propaganda in 1701 must be judged by its success or failure. It did not prevent the dissolution of parliament. His agency for the dissemination of counter-propaganda was not sufficiently developed to combat the influence of the whig campaign. And while Harley's preparations for the opening of parliament in February and March 1701 did actively assist the passage of the bill of settlement, Toland's plea for the abolition of parties fell on deaf ears. When the whigs urged the total adoption of party distinctions, Harley's advocacy of 'one party, and that for the good of England' was insufficient as an emotive slogan (see above, p. 22). Partisans are always more enthusiastic than moderates, even though it is possible to be passionately moderate. The political dichotomy was settling down once more around the poles of whig and tory, as Harley's narrow victory in the speakership contest in December 1701 made evident.

But increasingly in the course of the year Harley displayed a heightening awareness of the value of printed propaganda, and a shape can be discerned to his developing press policy. He no longer thought in terms of presenting irrefutable facts for the edification of parliament men to assist them in making up their minds. He appealed to a wider audience in the country at large. Electoral opinion had to be taken into consideration, and by making light of whig propaganda Harley was endeavouring to make light of their arguments. By mocking their validity he was hoping to take the edge off their writings in the process of exposing their methods and their motives. In this way he was attempting to turn public opinion against his adversaries, not by discursive argument, but by satire. He even appears to have wished, naively perhaps, to stimulate divisions by insinuation in the ranks of his opponents. 'Those that herd with us are naturally selfish, peevish, narrow-spirited, ill-natured, conceited...envious at any abilities in others, loving to find fault'.[43] The picture J.F. painted of the average whig accords well with the character given Tom Double by Davenant. 'If you talk or think of the public good', Whiglove was warned, 'you will never become a right Modern Whig'.[44] Pamphlets such as these were designed to convince the country gentlemen that they had been right all along in their suspicions that the Modern Whigs were rogues.

J.F. put forward the view that the country party was 'satisfied with the strength of their cabal, and their interest with the people'. But, he continued, 'we shall lie and rail them out of that'.[45] This, of course, was precisely what the whig propaganda campaign, marshalled by Somers, succeeded in doing in 1701. It was a tremendous feat. A programme had been put together for the manipulation of public opinion which, in the space of a year, resulted in a complete transformation of government and a second general election. But Somers neglected to build on these triumphs. In March 1702 William III died. The accession of Queen Anne was favourable to Harley and his allies. The whigs were refused office, and, as James O. Richards remarks, 'linking any whig leader to whig propaganda in 1702 is extremely tenuous at best'.[46] It was left to Harley to organise ministerial propaganda. One of the first suggestions he made to lord treasurer Godolphin concerned the press. He intended to adopt and adapt the innovations in propaganda techniques resulting from the paper war. Somers's ideas can be seen at work under Harley, as his relationships with Charles Davenant and John Toland proved to be prototypes of the deeper associations he was to forge with Daniel Defoe and Jonathan Swift. It took considerably longer for the whigs to employ full-time propagandists. The outcome of the paper war, for Harley, was an idea. Under the triumvirate he tried to put that idea into practice.

3

Harley and Defoe

In the first years of the reign of Queen Anne the relations of Robert Harley, lord treasurer Godolphin, and Marlborough, the captain-general, were so intimate that contemporaries referred to them as a triumvirate. In retrospect Harley emphasised that until Anne's accession he had had 'no habits' with Marlborough,[1] but he had been in prolonged contact with Godolphin for some time. In 1705 he was to write of the 'seven years' he had enjoyed the lord treasurer's 'friendship' and 'protection' dating back, presumably, to around 1698.[2] Harley and Godolphin had cooperated over the act of settlement in particular. On William's death Godolphin consulted the speaker on the queen's first speech to parliament. He asked Harley 'to make a draft of it yourself, and appoint us to come to your house tomorrow night to see it'. 'I agree entirely', he added, 'the best way will be to go on...as if no occasion of interruption had happened'.[3] The principal feeling is one of continuity from the country cabals of the last years of the reign of William III, and this has an important bearing on the development of ministerial press policy. The triumvirate did not suddenly spring to life on the accession of Queen Anne; it was inherited from the era of her predecessor.[4]

From the outset, then, Harley was in a position to direct affairs relating to the press. On 28 March 1702 the queen issued a proclamation 'for restraining the spreading [of] false news, and printing and publishing of irreligious and seditious papers and libels'. This was the official response to the challenge posed by a free press. But Harley quickly came to realise that party conflict was too virulent to permit the suppression of party propaganda without repressive legislation. This he did not want. He was never in favour of harsh proscriptive measures, and at no time in his career did he attempt to stifle the press through censorship. Instead, with the events of 1701 as a guide, he was beginning to appreciate the full potential of a government propaganda machine.

Previously, like the whigs, he had thought only in terms of ad hoc publications. Now his thoughts focused on the periodical as a format which would allow a continuous presentation of official propaganda for public digestion. Even if it had had an efficient editor, the *London Gazette*, 'published by authority', was hardly the required vehicle.

Clearly, Harley had discussed the matter with Godolphin on former occasions when he wrote to him on 9 August 1702 to express his opinion on the outcome of the elections to Queen Anne's first parliament. His thoughts turned on more than merely the composition of the new house of commons:[5]

As near as I can guess...though there are many violent whigs left out, yet those who come in their places will be for moderate and safe counsels, unless deceived by the artifice of some few hot men, whom I hope the government will take care to prevent, by applying proper antidotes...

I cannot but, upon this occasion, again take the liberty to offer to your lordship that it will be of great service to have some discreet writer of the government's side, if it were only to state facts right, for the generality err for want of knowledge, being imposed upon by the stories raised by ill-designing men.

The character of the propaganda envisaged by Harley is important. Again we find the idea of 'antidote', of counter-propaganda. The cultivation of favourable public opinion was felt to be desirable, if not essential, to the well-being of the government.

Of equal interest is the audience at which Harley was aiming. He was not primarily concerned with the die-hard whigs in opposition to the ministry, but with the independent country gentlemen. Even confining ourselves to parliament men, Harley wished to prevent the new men from being 'deceived' by the extreme ideas of the backbenchers who had jeopardised the 1701 parliament. He was less worried about the 'violent whigs' who had been left out. This overwhelming preoccupation with country tories is significant. War with France had recently been declared. Many country tories retained the doubts that Harley had once shared over the wisdom of renewed hostilities, particularly relating to land warfare on the continent. Now that Harley accepted the conflict as inevitable, he was faced with the task of providing sufficient reason for the policies of the new government. Although he consistently looked for an early settlement, Harley wished to persuade public opinion to endorse the decisions of the ministry, and to embrace the war whole-heartedly. He sought national solidarity in the national interest.

A permanent press organ presenting the ministerial view was, to

Harley, of vital importance in this constant fight for the approval of public opinion. No post-Revolution administration had even thought of establishing a full-time propaganda weapon, let alone had founded one. On Saturday 19 February 1704 a new periodical made its appearance in London. Its full title was *A Weekly Review of the Affairs of France: Purged from the Errors and Partiality of News-writers and Petty-Statesmen of all Sides*. Today we usually refer to it as Defoe's *Review*. The opening paragraph echoed Harley's words to Godolphin:[6]

This paper is the foundation of a very large and useful design, which...may contribute to setting the affairs of Europe in a clearer light, and to prevent the various uncertain accounts, and the partial reflections of the street scribblers...which have at least this effect, that people are possessed with wrong notions of things.

The growing obsession with the views of the 'people' is once more apparent. Information was essential for them to reach the required opinion. But now an organ for the dissemination of government propaganda was in existence. Harley's idea was finally being given practical application. The gestation had been long and uncomfortable, but the *Review* had been born.

There are two principal reasons for the long lapse of eighteen months between Harley's suggestion to Godolphin and the actual inauguration of the *Review*. The first was simply the lord treasurer's extremely unenthusiastic response to Harley's scheme. Despite the impression given by successive commentators on the history of the press when quoting Harley's well-known words, Godolphin was anything but encouraging. He was notoriously unimaginative when it came to influencing people or events. Oldmixon, who derived his information from Arthur Maynwaring, observed that 'the earl of Godolphin had the last contempt for pamphlets and always despised the press'.[7] Responsibility for the press officially fell within the jurisdiction of the secretaries of state, so Godolphin simply replied to Harley's prompting: 'I thank you for your hint of appointing somebody to write for us. I have spoken of it to Lord Nottingham, who has promised to take care of it. *Indeed it is his business*'.[8] There is no evidence to suggest that Nottingham, 'Harley's bitterest foe',[9] acted on the advice.

The second reason for the delay in the establishment of a press organ is the lack of a suitable writer to act as editor. Despite the assertions of some scholars that Harley 'almost certainly' had Daniel Defoe in mind as the 'discreet writer' he wished to enlist in the struggle with the parties, the evidence does not bear out the assumption.[10] For one thing Defoe had embarrassed Harley with the 'Legion-Letter' just over a year before. He had followed this with his *History of the Kentish Petition*, which Harley attacked in print as 'full of lies and romantic stories'.[11] It seems unlikely that Defoe could simply change sides, and find a welcome awaiting him from the man who had borne the brunt of his propaganda. Of more immediate significance is the fact that the 'discreet writer' to whom Harley *was* referring was William Paterson. 'This morning I received a letter from Mr Paterson', Harley's letter of 9 August to Godolphin continued, 'I believe his circumstances are very difficult at present, and he as unwilling to let it be known. Her majesty's bounty to him would, I believe, be seasonable, and quicken his diligence to serve her'. The sequence of correspondence between Harley and Godolphin in August 1702 refers persistently to William Paterson, a writer who had received assistance from Harley in the past.[12] Paterson met the lord treasurer, who treated him 'very favourably'.[13] Godolphin felt, however, that Paterson's role was not that of propagandist: 'the most that can be made of him will be by his correspondence and the intelligence he may give'.[14] Godolphin was not prepared to sanction the setting up of a permanent, unofficial press organ.

Defoe's name crops up in conjunction with Harley at this time because, strange as it might appear on first consideration, he did approach the speaker in 1702 through the offices of William Paterson. The details are missing, but Paterson offered Harley Defoe's 'acknowledgements'. Although he knew him 'only by character', it seems he received 'hopes' of Harley's favour.[15] This is scarcely as surprising, for the speaker was hardly likely to have missed an opportunity to neutralise the pen of the 'Author of the *True-Born Englishman*' (as Defoe liked to style himself). In 1702, two months after the death of his benefactor, William III, Defoe was in the custody of the Fleet Prison – the debtor's gaol.[16] It was this, no doubt, which prompted him to approach Harley. He was prepared to sacrifice his integrity as a writer to secure financial relief. As Arthur Secord suggested, more reasonably, 'Defoe and Harley had been approaching some kind of an understanding before *The Shortest Way* appeared'.[17]

After Godolphin's rebuff to Harley's suggestion about the press, there are no indications that positive steps were taken to employ government propagandists. Paterson was relegated to the more mundane position (in the eighteenth century) of an intelligence agent. Davenant, Harley's collaborator in 1701, was hoping to return to the political career he had pursued briefly in the 1690s, and he was not prepared to dirty his hands with ink any longer. Toland was still in Hanover. Harley's plans were left in abeyance. But a more promising situation arose after Defoe published *The Shortest Way with the Dissenters* in December 1702, just when the storm was brewing in parliament over occasional conformity. The pamphlet angered High Churchmen everywhere. Defoe had tried to perpetrate a hoax, representing the views of the narrator of the *Shortest Way* as genuine, when he advocated hanging Dissenting preachers, and confining their congregations to the galleys. If we can believe contemporary rumour, most people missed the subtle ironic stance adopted by Defoe, and accepted the impersonation. When the joke was discovered tempers raged. 'I had last night some talk with the speaker', Godolphin informed Nottingham on 14 December, 'and he has had a mind to speak to you about a book lately come out called *The Shortest Way with the Dissenters*. He seemed to think it absolutely necessary to the service of the government that your lordship should endeavour to discover who was the author of it'.[18]

We are left to ponder the ingenuousness of Harley's insistence that Defoe should be 'discovered'. In exactly what sense did he feel it to be 'absolutely necessary to the service of the government'? The wheels he set in motion ultimately resulted in the projection of Defoe's *Review*. Despite the moves made by Nottingham to round up suspects, Defoe escaped and fled. He went into hiding, evading for five months all ministerial attempts to secure his apprehension. On 3 January 1703 Nottingham issued a warrant for Defoe's arrest, and the *Gazette* announced a reward of £50 for information leading to his detention. On 24 February he was indicted (in his absence) before the justices of oyer and terminer for writing and publishing a seditious libel. The following day the Commons ordered the offending tract to be burned at the hands of the common hangman. On 27 February the queen's speech called for 'further laws for restraining the great licence, which is assumed, of publishing and spreading scandalous pamphlets and libels', and it urged MPs, 'as far as the present laws will extend', to do 'your duty in your respective stations, to prevent and punish such pernicious practices'.[19] The only official answer to the problem was the threat that press regulations would be instituted. Nottingham's vision stretched no farther than that.

Paradoxically, Harley managed to exploit this situation to gain Godolphin's approbation of Defoe's employment in the government's service. Defoe was finally apprehended in May 1703. A week following his arrest Harley received a letter from Defoe to William Paterson, which implored Paterson to intervene with the speaker on his behalf.[20] Harley did nothing until after Defoe's trial. Defoe had angered too many powerful men to save him. He was given an exemplary punishment, and Nottingham encouraged him to indict others to save himself from the pillory. The secretary was convinced that the whig lords of the Junto had been behind the publication of the *Shortest Way*. Aided and abetted by Buckingham, lord privy seal, Nottingham interrogated Defoe in Newgate. He urged him to reveal 'the set of men' with whom he used to 'concert matters of this nature'.[21] Godolphin, and even Queen Anne herself, expressed great interest in the outcome of the questioning, but Defoe stayed silent.[22] With all attempts to persuade him to cooperate at an end, and with the pillory and virtual imprisonment at her majesty's pleasure awaiting him, Defoe received a message from Harley.[23]

The approach was unofficial. Harley needed to exercise caution. Godolphin had still to be convinced that Defoe should be employed by the government. Harley played on the possibility of utilising Defoe in Scotland in an intelligence network which was being established there. 'I thank you for your hints about Scotland', Godolphin wrote on 13 August 1703, 'Defoe would be the properest person in the world for that transaction, but I doubt the rigour of his punishment the other day [in the pillory] will have made it scarcely practicable to engage him'.[24] Yet the lord treasurer urged Harley to maintain his interest in Defoe. 'If you have any means of sounding him', he continued, 'I wish you would try it, it must be done by you'. Harley hardly needed pushing. With Godolphin's sanction, and with no chance of interference from either of the secretaries of state, he was in a position to make more concrete proposals both to Defoe and to Godolphin. He told the lord treasurer that Defoe's morale was poor, that he blamed Nottingham and Buckingham for his callous treatment, and not the queen. Leaving Godolphin with the final responsibility for employing Defoe, Harley carefully led the lord treasurer to believe that there was 'a private attempt among his friends to raise the 200 marks for his fine':[25]

He is a very capable man, and if his fine be satisfied without any other knowledge but that he alone be acquainted with it that it is the queen's bounty to him, and grace, he may do service, and this may perhaps engage him better than any after rewards, and keep him more under the power of an obligation. This is entirely submitted to your lordship's judgment.

Harley fully appreciated the potential of the situation. Queen Anne had the power of life and death over Defoe. The sureties for his good behaviour for seven years that his sentence entailed could be supplied by Harley, but by whom else? On 26 September Godolphin wrote to Harley to tell him that he had read some paragraphs of his letter to the queen. 'What you propose about Defoe may be done when you will', he assured him, 'and how you will'.[26] Defoe's release from Newgate was effected in the first days of November 1703. On the 4th the lord treasurer wrote that he had 'taken care in the matter of Defoe'.[27] 'Everyone is not a Daniel Defoe that has a party to pay his fine for him', William Pittis wrote in *Heraclitus Ridens* on 6 November, 'I hear that he is bailed out. He must have a great interest indeed that he could find sufficient bail for his behaviour for seven years'. Defoe was to have his wish of employment in the government's service, but at the price of almost absolute dependence on the good will of Robert Harley. The first round had been won in the struggle for the appointment of a ministerial apologist. The first step had been taken to form a government propaganda machine.

Defoe's release from Newgate coincided with revival of interest in an occasional conformity bill. Occasional conformity was a ruse used by Dissenters to qualify for office under the terms of the test act. By taking communion annually in the Church of England they outraged the sensibilities of High Churchmen. There were also political reasons for wishing to legislate against occasional conformity. It would reduce whig power in many corporations, as Dissenters tended to support the whig party. The first occasional bill, introduced in 1702, had been lost in the Lords, but not before it caused considerable consternation to the triumvirate. Godolphin formulated contingency plans to thwart the bill in parliament should it be reintroduced. Charles Davenant was commissioned to write *against* the proposal. On 19 October he sent the lord treasurer the draft of his *Essays on Peace at Home and War Abroad*. 'Having strenuously opposed the intended bill about occasional conformity', Davenant explained, 'I do not judge it safe to produce my thoughts upon that head unless I am let in to know how far it may consist with the present measures'. In detail he outlined the argument of his pamphlet, which was 'offered as a cure, and to heal the divisions that are among us', in other words, in the ranks of the tory party over occasional conformity and the war. It was to act as an antidote to the poison which was spreading through the tory body. Davenant was careful to remind Godolphin that, if he approved, it 'should be in the press quickly, and published before the parliament sits'.[28] Once more the idea of a 'manifesto' for the session is apparent.

Defoe immediately informed Harley that he had some papers ready for publication on his 'enlargement'. He sought ministerial sanction for their production.[29] One of these, which Defoe himself viewed as a vindication of his good intentions in writing the *Shortest Way*, was *A Challenge of Peace*. The theme was the exact corollary of the first part of Davenant's *Essays* – it sought to bring about domestic peace. The pamphlet appeared on 23 November 1703, urging both parties to reach a settlement of their differences. This, and not persecution, would, according to Defoe, be 'the shortest way with the Dissenters'.[30] Of more importance, as it transpired, was Defoe's response to the second part of Davenant's *Essays*. In discussing the war Davenant had tried to unite the nation behind the queen's administration. Harley wished to extend this theme. Although Scotland had been the bait used to lure Godolphin into accepting Defoe's services, there is no indication that Harley seriously intended using him in the north in 1704. Defoe became Harley's peculiar responsibility. Godolphin did not even know how to get in touch with him, contacting him only through Harley.[31] Defoe was destined to be the discreet writer Harley had advocated for so long, and Davenant's *Essays* gave the *Review* a cause. As Douglas Coombs has perceptively observed, 'one of the main purposes of the *Review*...was to keep before the eyes of politically conscious Englishmen the doctrines enunciated by Davenant in his *Essays*'.[32]

The *Review* was not a newspaper. It was essentially a regular political essay, eschewing the popular dialogue format, which consistently propounded the government line, however obliquely. Until its demise in 1713 the *Review* mirrored changes of emphasis within the ministry. But initially the periodical was not without its gimmicks. Until the 1705 election campaign a section called *Advice from the Scandal Club* provided diversion from 'the more weighty and serious part of the design'. In this way, it was hoped, the important points in the serious essay would be more easily assimilated 'into the heads and thoughts of those to whom it might be useful'.[33] The important task of influencing public opinion meant that the pill often had to be candied. The *Advice* consisted of answers to letters, criticisms of the errors and absurdities of Defoe's journalistic rivals, and general social comment 'upon the immediate subject then on the tongues of the town'. It took the form of spurious proceedings of a society called the Scandal Club, which purported to act as a moral watchdog. There is strong evidence that the *Advice* was successful, and that it answered the design of launching the *Review*. Soon monthly supplements to the column were being published, and finally a completely separate paper, *The Little Review*, had a run of twenty-three issues in 1705.

The Scandal Club, then, was a good idea, for the political message of the *Review* in its first year was a complex one. Defoe resolved that 'this shall not be a party paper', and he expressed a desire to free affairs 'from the false glosses of parties'.[34] This cultivation of the aura of impartiality was taken to the lengths of excluding the words whig and tory from the pages of the *Review* on policy. They are mentioned only once in the essay in the whole of the first volume, and then purely with the intention of 'stat[ing] the case between whig and tory'.[35] Defoe preached a vague concept of moderation. Through the decade of the *Review*'s existence, his use of the term was often inconsistent. It was a clever strategem, prompted initially by Harley, that allowed a considerable freedom of manoeuvre, hiding a multitude of anomalies under a cloak of impartiality. The propaganda effect of pretending to pose as a moderate patriot, uninfluenced by any party considerations, was probably quite large. Certainly if the number of attacks on the moderation advocated by the *Review* are anything to go by, the party writers were unable to tolerate such a stance.

Despite its author, and its subsequent deserved reputation as a whig paper, the *Review*, at its inception, was a tory organ. It was required to cajole the moderate tories into maintaining their support for the government's war-effort. Signs of war-weariness were evident as early as the spring of 1704.[36] Until the victory at Blenheim that summer, popularity for the war was rapidly vanishing. The tory squire did not want to pay his taxes. For these reasons it was essential for the ministry to appeal to public opinion. This, at any rate, was Harley's view. Unlike an ad hoc pamphlet, published to meet a particular contingency, a periodical allowed a gradual, almost imperceptible persuasion, and the alteration of inborn prejudice. By stating facts right, Harley hoped that ministerial propaganda would bring home to country gentlemen the necessity of a war to prevent French hegemony. Defoe, therefore, called his paper *A Review of the Affairs of France*, and after four issues it began to appear twice a week.

Defoe's task was to build up an 'official' picture of the might of France. To achieve this he extolled the virtues of absolutism in warfare, to emphasise the formidable nature of the French threat. For these reasons he was easily misunderstood, and he was soon accused of being in the French interest. On 29 June 1704 Godolphin himself wrote to

Harley, who was now, having replaced Nottingham as secretary of state, officially responsible for the press:[37]

I should not have troubled you again so soon but that the enclosed print, more scandalous in my opinion than the *Observator* itself, is fallen into my hands. I don't know what course can be taken with effect to find out the author; but I think no pains or expense could be, or be thought, too much to bring him to the punishment he deserves...this magnifying of France is a thing so odious in England, that I can't think any jury would acquit this man if discovered.

This prompted Defoe to explain the editorial policy of the *Review* in print. Writing 'à la vulgaire', but careful not to offend any 'objectors' who might be 'persons of character', Defoe pointed out that he was not an alarmist, but[38]

like the geese in the Capitol. If the Roman soldiers should have killed them, for frightening them out of their sleep, they would have soon found the Gauls at their backs, and have blamed themselves for the mistake. I leave all men to judge whether those geese gaggled for the Gauls, or for the Romans, and whether the Gauls would not have been glad to cut their throats, for telling the Romans who were a-coming.

The *Review*'s apologia appeared on 4 July; three days later Defoe wrote to Harley:[39]

I confess myself...something impatient to have it from yourself that I have explained the *Review* to your satisfaction, and that in reading it you have been pleased to note the caution I mentioned that it was to be written as if the objectors were of such quality as to whom the style should be unsuitable.

Once the *Review*'s apologia had been explained, Defoe's pro-ministerial writings brought him his pardon. Less than a month after the appearance of the apologia, Godolphin sent Harley 'the blank warrant signed by the queen for Defoe's pardon. Her majesty commands me to tell you she approves entirely of what you have promised him, and will make it good'.[40] Official sanction for the existence of the *Review* had been granted, and Robert Harley had acquired a propagandist and a paper that, in conjunction, would effectively spearhead the government's election campaign in 1705.

It had been a long fight. Until the birth of the *Review* Harley seems to have cultivated connections with the editors of two other periodicals, *Heraclitus Ridens* and *The Observator*, even though they were bitter opponents in print. William Pittis is said to have 'looked on the new Secretary as a patron and a protector'. This much is true.[41] He heaped lavish praise on Harley's parts in *The Patriots* in 1702:[42]

Just are his Thoughts, and daring is his Mind,
Boundless in Care, in Goodness unconfin'd,
Watchful to see neglected Wrongs Redress'd,
And amidst Injuries serene his Breast.

In 1701 Pittis had penned replies to Defoe's *True-Born Englishman* and to his *History of the Kentish Petition*. Unfortunately the link cannot be documented, and Theodore F. M. Newton's contention that 'Pittis was actually in Harley's employ soon after Anne came to the throne' is merely an assertion. More tentative is the view that *Heraclitus Ridens* was launched 'perhaps with Harley's encouragement'.[43] It is at any rate surprising that *Heraclitus Ridens* was prosecuted by the grand jury for libel *within a month* of the appearance of the *Review*, and the paper folded. Complete sets of *Heraclitus Ridens* were advertised in the *Review* during July 1704.

Harley's relations with John Tutchin, author of the *Observator*, are less obscure. Even Pittis wrote scathingly of Tutchin's 'three letters to Mr Speaker, the contents of which are so common'.[44] In September 1702 Harley instituted enquiries into Tutchin's whereabouts, and he was traced to Allan's Coffee-house near Charing Cross.[45] But Tutchin, after flirting with prosecution several times, was arraigned in the Commons for seditious libel in the issue of the *Observator* for 8–11 December 1703, which touched on occasional conformity. He absconded, only to give himself up on Harley's appointment as secretary of state in May 1704. On the eve of his trial, Tutchin again wrote to Harley, offering to discontinue the *Observator* 'provided the prosecution. . .might cease'.[46] He claimed to have made a similar offer to Harley often. He asked him to procure a writ of *nolle prosequi* from the attorney-general, Sir Edward Northey. Harley sent Tutchin's letter to Northey, on an unofficial basis. Northey took no notice of Tutchin's plea for clemency.[47] Nonetheless Tutchin survived due to a flaw in the proceedings. A complex technical error in the information saved him.[48] Northey, a staunch tory, was sure 'somebody done it on purpose'.[49] There was no retrial, however, and on 8 June 1705 Tutchin was discharged. In 1706 James Drake also escaped punishment on a technicality. Harley's hand is clearly suspected of intervention behind the scenes.

Harley's appointment as secretary of state went some way to levelling the scales of justice, for the ministry's proscriptive machinery was heavily weighted in favour of the tories. Defoe got away with many infringements of his bail, some, it appears, with Harley's direct connivance. Until his pardon his position as ministerial apologist was uncertain. In the face of tory prejudice Harley had his work cut out to safeguard Defoe and the *Review* in the early years of their association. In the very month that the *Review* appeared, a High Church bill for restraining the whig press was being considered in parliament. It was sponsored by Harley's High Church colleagues, Seymour, Jersey, and both secretaries of state, Nottingham and Sir Charles Hedges. Defoe published *An Essay on the Regulation of the Press* in January 1704 to argue against a return to the old system of licensing. He agreed that it should be settled 'what an author may or may not do, to bring the offences of the pen to a regulation'.[50] On 1 April an anonymous correspondent forwarded Harley an underground broadsheet on the bill for regulating the press. In mock form, *To the Honourable the Commons of England Assembled in Parliament. The Humble Petition and Representation of the True, Loyal and always Obedient Church of England, Relating to the Bill for Restraining the Press* ridiculed the pretensions of the High Churchmen, who wanted censorship merely 'because we do find that these damned whigs are a little too hard for us, when we come to downright arguments, demonstration, etc.'[51] Harley's informer wished to know whether or not Defoe's bail had been forfeited by writing and publishing this broadsheet.[52]

Needless to say, Harley did not act on information of this kind. His relations with Defoe were kept secret, and it was presumed that Defoe's fine had been paid by the whigs, and that they had bailed him out. Even Hedges, Harley's colleague as secretary of state, was totally ignorant of the facts. When Defoe was accused of writing *Legion's Humble Address to the House of Lords*, Hedges told Harley enthusiastically that he had arrested 'one Sammen...a tool of Defoe's'. He regretted that he could 'get nothing out of him against others'.[53] Even when the printer of *Legion's Humble Address*, James Rawlins, offered to make 'an ingenuous, full and free confession of the fact, and of whom [he] received the said paper',[54] Harley refused to act. No wonder one lampoon recalled the days when Defoe and Harley[55]

> ...met slyly at the *Vine*,
> To spin out Legion-Letters o'er our Wine.

Simultaneously Defoe was plagued with rumours that the messenger of the press, Robert Stephens, another staunch tory, had a warrant for his arrest in connection with a periodical called *The Master Mercury*.[56] Things were far from easy for Defoe as ministerial propagandist.

The *Master Mercury* was almost certainly Defoe's work, despite his denials. It is equally likely that he had published the mock *To the Honourable the Commons of England* without Harley's permission, and against the speaker's better judgment. Defoe lied often to Harley. He went so far as to publish *Some Remarks on the First Chapter of Dr Davenant's Essays* while extending the theme itself in the *Review* and elsewhere. Harley protected him from prosecution. He could just as easily have left him to languish in Newgate. Defoe was crucial to Harley's plans. He was to be used in the founding of an intelligence network throughout the country, and this would also facilitate the distribution of Harleyite propaganda. When Defoe was accused of writing the *Master Mercury* in September 1704, he was forced to return to London from East Anglia, where he had been touring on Harley's behalf. One important contact made was with John Fransham of Norwich, to whom Defoe sent many *Reviews* and other pamphlets in 1705.[57] Defoe embarked on a similar circuit in 1705. Although one main reason was to feel the pulse of the nation just after the elections, one of his memoranda was 'to settle a method how to write, etc.'[58] This cryptic note is best viewed in the light of the distribution of *Remarks on the Letter to the Author of the State-Memorial* in 1706.

It is clear that both Harley and Defoe were concerned with the development of a method for the effective and speedy dissemination of propaganda in the provinces. By the elections of May 1705 the *Review* was coming out three times a week. The days on which it appeared – Tuesdays, Thursdays and Saturdays – were the only days on which letters were dispatched to all the English counties by the Post Office in Lombard Street. It was no coincidence. In the propaganda campaign surrounding the General Election of 1705, one particular number of the *Review* was so important (and singular) that it might be called Defoe's election 'manifesto'. It carried no Scandal Club, and, what is more unusual, no advertisements. All four pages were taken up with the political message: 'a word in season' to the 'contending parties of this nation', advising them to 'study peace'.[59] In retrospect Defoe explained that 'some people' had given him 'public thanks' for his 'sincere endeavours'. They 'made' him print 5,000 copies of the one issue 'to be sent all over the nation to move us to peace, and paid me very frankly for them'.[60]

Harley was well aware of the influence on country gentlemen of John Dyer's manuscript newsletters. He went to great lengths to procure a complete run from one of his contacts, the *quondam* messenger of the press, John Gellibrand. As Henry Snyder observes, 'only a few issues for 1705 survive' in the Harley papers. But others were published by Defoe in 1706 in *A Collection of Dyer's Letters* on the elections. Snyder is almost certainly correct in his belief that 'Harley turned over all or part of the collection to Defoe who extracted the ones he wanted and returned the balance'.[61] What Harley's ideal entailed was a system for dispersing *printed* propaganda to counter Dyer's manuscripts. Dyer had managed to establish centres for the distribution of his propaganda. Why could Defoe not do the same for Harley? This, surely, is the 'method how to write' which Defoe hoped 'to settle' in 1705. In 1712, when the stamp act was being discussed, Defoe proposed to turn the *Review* into a manuscript newsletter in the Dyer mould. If the tax on printed paper proved prohibitive, he would 'invite all my correspondents in Britain to subscribe'. He would 'hire some large hall or great room in the City' in which scribes could copy out his essay.[62] The methods of Dyer and Harley in 1706 bear comparison.

On his circuit of England in 1705 Defoe travelled from London to the south-west, thence northwards to Liverpool, across country to Leeds, and finally south to London, via Coventry and Cambridge.[63] When the *Remarks* were 'sent into the country', batches were conveyed to all the major towns on Defoe's route. Bundles of 100 went to the large centres of Plymouth, Exeter, Bristol and Norwich, while small parcels of 12 copies were dispatched for places like Dorchester, Newbury and Leominster. But some were sent even further afield. Fifty went to Preston and Whitehaven, and 100 to Newcastle upon Tyne, not to mention 50 for Dublin. Significantly Defoe splits his list into two main sections. A total of 1,405 were sent to towns on his 1705 circuit (plus Whitehaven, Preston, and Newcastle). An additional 510 went to East Anglian towns, and these were catalogued separately, along with the south-east, Dublin and Oxford. Fifty were 'laid down in coffee-houses', and a final 100 'given about by hand'. This totals 2,065. But it is noteworthy that Defoe should distinguish so markedly between areas he had reconnoitred in 1705, and outlets that were clearly established earlier like Norwich and Dublin.

This, then, is the agency for the distribution of propaganda which Harley tried to promote through Daniel Defoe while he was secretary of state. That pamphlets could be dispatched effectively by these channels in these years is demonstrated by Defoe's list of destinations for his *Remarks on the Letter to the Author of the State-Memorial*.[64] The birth of the *Review* was not the only feature of Harley's press policy.

The production of propaganda was one thing; its distribution was another. Only when steps had been taken to establish outlets in the provinces was it worthwhile to build a propaganda machine, in other words, to assemble a circle of propagandists to produce words to order. To influence public opinion the pamphlets had to be scattered throughout the land. Otherwise Harley could only hope to persuade Londoners, or parliament men. It is evident from the extensive tours which Defoe made on Harley's behalf in 1704 and 1705 that the secretary was more interested in public opinion in the broadest sense. When Defoe was sent to Scotland during the time that the union bill was being considered in the Edinburgh parliament, it was no doubt with a similar function in mind. As Harley had no agency in Scotland for disseminating propaganda, it was necessary for Defoe to be on the spot to organise affairs in person. But the General Election of 1705 provides the first indication that Harley was using the system founded by Defoe, and Defoe was also Harley's principal propagandist.

The allied victory at Blenheim in August 1704 stimulated general approval of the war, being more 'for their 4s. in the pound than ever yet [the country gentlemen] saw'.[65] The occasional conformity issue, however, was not dead, and it was soon in the forefront of affairs in the 1704–5 parliamentary session. Plans were set on foot to ruin the Godolphin ministry. Defoe warned that 'the two ends will be reconciled to overturn the middle way'.[66] A third occasional bill was projected, to be tacked to the supply bill to ensure its success in the Lords. But Harley's credit with the tory backbenchers was not exhausted. His appointment as secretary in the room of the earl of Nottingham was not taken as a change 'from tories to whigs', but from 'violence to moderation'.[67] He was accompanied into office by Henry St John and Thomas Mansel, hardly the most lukewarm of tories. Harley's careful cultivation of support in the Commons counterbalanced the loss of the tory lords.

The allegiance of the tory backbenchers was quickly put to the test over the tack. Harley had taken upon himself the responsibility of countering the 'tackers'.[68] His good management resulted in a split in tory ranks, and this shaped electoral strategy in 1705. When it came to the question, only 134 parliament men (136 with the tellers) voted for the tack. The rest of the tory body in the Commons, numbering over a hundred, either voted outright against the motion, or abstained, slipping out of the house without entering the division lobbies. The failure of the tack demonstrated that the dichotomy between whig and tory was fluid once more. Harley sought to perpetuate this arrangement. His preparations for the general election due in 1705 had in view a non-party scheme. He mounted a campaign aimed almost exclusively at the tackers.[69]

Defoe's *Review* figured strongly in Harley's plans. It was the principal organ of ministerial propaganda throughout the election campaign. Following Harley's non-party designs, Defoe urged the moderate tories, who had not voted with the tackers, to keep in mind their country principles: 'it is our desire the government should be in the hands of Churchmen', Defoe assured them, 'it is our free choice that we should have a Church parliament, only let them be men of peace; other qualifications may be requisite, but this is absolutely necessary'.[70] This from the author of the *Shortest Way*! 'Were there but 134 Churchmen in the house of commons', Defoe demanded, 'or must none be of the Church but such as would run her upon the rocks, and force her to blood and persecution?'

Defoe's attack on the tackers was a sustained one, as he urged the moderate tories to divide from them: 'you must not choose a tacker unless you will destroy our peace, divide our strength, pull down the Church, let in the French, and depose the queen. Let all that are willing to do this vote for tackers; and all that vote for tackers must be supposed willing to do this.'[71] This appeal was directed at the moderate tories in the electorate, as well as the 'sneakers' who had failed to support the tack. It was an address to the public at large in an attempt to sway opinion on party. Defoe called for a house of commons free from the corruption of the Crown, but at liberty to work for the public good and the honour of the monarchy and the Church of England. For this to be possible, the taint of party had to be abandoned, and the beneficial effects of the tack in pulling down party barriers had to be allowed to continue to influence political alignments. As Defoe summed up:[72]

they are most truly zealous for the Church of England that with temper, moderation, and Christian charity maintain her principles without the ruin and destruction of anybody, studying to unite the Church's safety and the public interest together by promoting the peace of all parties. This is moderation, and on this the safety of the Church of England does depend.

High Churchmen did not subscribe to the Harleyite doctrine of moderation as propounded by Defoe. Mounting a counter-campaign against 'false moderation', the tackers and their supporters sought to thwart Harley's non-party schemes. The publication of the *Memorial of the Church of England* in July 1705, 'in effect a declaration of war between the "tackers" and the ministry',[73] involved a vicious assault on the very morality of the concept of political moderation. High Church writers continued to attack Defoe's *Review* until well into 1706.[74] His programme of 'moderation' offended most. *The Moderation, Justice, and Manners of the Review, Exemplified from his own Works* censured Defoe's 'sophistical way of writing', which had unfortunately 'seduced...several well-inclining people'. The author accused Mr *Review* of abusing the nation 'with pretensions of peace and moderation whilst nothing less was at his heart'.[75] Charles Leslie, meanwhile, in the *Rehearsal*, pointed out that the 'Lady Moderation' was dead:[76]

You have not heard a word of her this many a day. Every paper and pamphlet was full of her. She was the whole discourse of the town. You could hardly hear anybody speak of anything else. But now all over. Hush and dead...She died of laughing...To think how she had gulled the poor Churchmen...

At the same time the whigs themselves were not pleased with Defoe's propaganda. They regarded him as an apostate, and John Tutchin censured him severely in the *Observator*. Tutchin disliked Defoe's selectivity in attacking tories. He tarred members of the whole party with the same brush. The *Review* was assaulted on all sides. The whigs accused him of equivocation, the tories of whiggery. Leslie was greatly amused 'when even Tutchin and Defoe...those noble chiefs of the people, cannot agree, but are in open war with one another'.[77] The parties closed their ranks, and managed to ignore Defoe's efforts to divide them into moderates and extremists. Yet the efficacy of his propaganda is open to debate. The number of attacks on the *Review* in 1705 and 1706 suggest that the tories, in particular, were anxious lest Defoe should succeed in drawing off more moderate men. He was constantly being branded as a whig of Tutchin's hue. In 1705 there was a precise distinction between Harleyite propaganda and whig propaganda.

But Harley was unable to complete his experiment in non-party government. The contest over the speakership in October 1705 put an end to his plans for administering through a centre party, without the support of either whig or tory. Court tories refused to vote for the ministerial candidate, John Smith, and supported the tacker William Bromley. This confirmed Godolphin in his belief that only by relying on the whigs could he secure a regular majority in the Commons. His opinion was endorsed in the winter session of 1705–6, during which the 160 whigs 'voted always with the body of the queen's servants'.[78] Harley differed in his analysis. He retained the hope of persuading a sufficient number of tories to support ministerial policies to be able to govern without recourse to party considerations. He expressed open resentment at the encroachments of the whig Junto. In this difference of opinion lies the cause of the eventual disintegration of the triumvirate.

The gradual divergence between Harley and Godolphin serves to illustrate Defoe's role as ministerial propagandist. He continued to write with the aim of distinguishing between the tackers and the moderate tories, and he was viciously abused in print for doing so. In the spring of 1706 Joseph Browne began to 'rehearse' the *Review* in *A Dialogue between Church and No-Church*, which ran for seven issues before it was suppressed in conjunction with Browne's prosecution for *The Country Parson's Honest Advice*. (For Browne's prosecution, see below, pp. 93–5.) Defoe was accused of purchasing 'a patent to sell scandal by retail, and make a monopoly of it', with the connivance of the secretary. Mr *Review* was ridiculed as 'a friend to the queen and government' who 'gave great assistance to the people in telling them who were the fittest men to be chosen members of parliament in the last election'.[79] Ironically Defoe wrote to Harley at this juncture about a meeting 'on account of *The Review*'. He expressed himself 'impatient to mention...the subject of the three last *Reviews*'. From 30 March to 6 May 1706 (when Defoe was writing) the *Review* had been issuing anti-High Church propaganda. 'I have often endeavoured to have the like honour', Defoe concluded, 'and began to hope something might offer in which I might be useful to *you*'.[80]

The emphasis is well-placed, for Defoe had started to write to Harley's personal directions, and these were no longer at one with Godolphin's views. An additional complication arose after Marlborough's decisive victory over the French at Ramillies on 12 May 1706. Previously the dispute between Harley and Godolphin had been over strategy; now an accompanying divergence of opinion occurred over policy. While Marlborough, Godolphin and the whigs wished to carry the war into France at the expense of the country gentlemen, in order to reduce Louis XIV to his knees, Harley wanted to end the war at the earliest available opportunity now that France had visibly been defeated. After Ramillies he[81]

advised the queen to command the duke of Marlborough to march into France, when there was no army to oppose him, or else to hearken to the overtures of peace that were then made by France, telling the queen that nothing could be so fatal to her people as the carrying on a lingering war, which must destroy the trade and exhaust the strength of her kingdom.

Harley consistently expressed the country view that the war was being waged for the security of the Protestant Succession. It was undertaken 'not to augment the power of any state unreasonably, and only to keep France from hurting its neighbours'.[82] He stressed that this was 'not a worse argument now we have success, than it was when it was urged not to try for those successes'. Once more the rich vein of country theory can be seen in Harley's political thinking. The war had been won, so why not have peace?

It is profoundly important to any understanding of the relations of Harley and Defoe, and its effect on the *Review*'s propaganda, to realise that in 1706 Defoe was disseminating Harleyite views. They were not shared by his fellow ministers. 'Beyond sea affords nothing new', Harley wrote on 15 June, 'we have victories, and have improved them, and that is grown so old a story, as I wrote our general word, that I am of the opinion that he will need another victory, not to save himself, but to rescue the Modern Whigs from their own mismanagement'.[83] War-weariness had affected the very centre of power, and Harley's brother observed that 'from this time the duke and his friends made their utmost efforts for the removal of Mr Harley'.[84] In the *Review*, Defoe urged a speedy settlement. Again we should recall that he had been *in favour* of a standing army in 1697, and he had handed Harley the 'Legion-Letter' in 1701 for not declaring war on France at the instigation of the Kentish Petitioners. Like Harley, Defoe now emphasised that the war had been undertaken only to reduce 'the exorbitant power of France', not France itself. He expected the French to 'make a stand' should an allied advance be attempted. The answer was peace. 'The honest end is peace, and the best reward of victory is peace', he advised, 'an honourable, safe, and lasting peace, which I believe every honest man will join with me in a petition for'.[85] He based his opinion on the strength of the kingdom, which would be drained by prolonging the war. 'England thrives best by peace', he reiterated, 'Union at home and peace abroad is all she wants'. Now that victory had been won, one side to Davenant's *Essays* – the *raison d'être* of the early *Review* – could be forgotten.

Harley's relations with Marlborough and Godolphin rapidly deteriorated. After Ramillies the Junto pressed for the ministerial appointment of one of their number, the mooted move being to replace Hedges as secretary by the young earl of Sunderland. This would be to bring him into direct conflict with Harley over not only the press, but the whole board of government policy. An opportunity presented itself to send Defoe away from the centre of the struggle for power, and Harley took it. He was dispatched very perfunctorily to Scotland in September 1706, while Harley was fighting a dogged rearguard action to forestall Sunderland's promotion, even coaching Queen Anne herself in her resistance to the Junto.[86] Defoe was anxious about his mission. He had been ordered to set off 'without any farther conferences', and he suspected that 'something unhappy' relating to Harley was the cause.[87] It is perhaps significant that Sunderland, when appointed secretary in December 1706, appears to have made efforts to woo Defoe, and to prise him away from Harley.[88]

Defoe told Harley that he intended to discuss the impending union at length in the *Review* when in Edinburgh, adding the rider 'unless your judgment and orders differ'. He begged hints 'if you find it otherwise'.[89] But Harley did not stop Defoe from writing *ad nauseam* on the one subject upon which the ministry could present a tolerably united front. By producing propaganda in favour of union he could offend no-one, neither Godolphin nor the Junto. He published many pamphlets in Edinburgh in favour of union, and all the while he sent material back to London to be put into the *Review*, which was published and disseminated continuously for the eighteen months or so that Defoe was absent. Only once did the post fail him.[90] Nonetheless the *Review* lost much of its popularity with English audiences through its concentration on Scottish affairs. 'Union, union, nothing but union for four months together glutted [your] fancy', Defoe admitted to his readers, 'I was content to hear the readers of this paper cry it was dull, see them throw it by without reading, and hear them say, he preaches so long on the union because he has nothing else to say'.[91] One witty gentleman (possibly Joseph Browne) gave Defoe the character of 'the greatest tautologist in the world'. 'Some people are so cunning when you begin a subject', he went on, 'to buy the first paper, and that serves them a quarter of a year, for all the following papers are the same thing, only turned into other words'.[92] This was a particularly apt description of Defoe's writings on the union, of which he styled himself 'the author of every good thing'. He demanded recognition for his services on behalf of union. He did not receive it.

We have no means of assessing how much or how little Defoe's pamphlets influenced Scottish public opinion. It is dangerous to overemphasise Defoe's part in the conclusion of union between England and Scotland. It appears to have been a political job, and for this reason propaganda was merely the icing on the cake, maintaining the impression of a free and open decision by the representatives of the Scottish people in the Edinburgh parliament.[93] Defoe's sojourn in Scotland offers few clues to the actual organisation of ministerial propaganda under the Godolphin ministry. But it does suggest a number of interesting facts about the relations between Harley and Defoe. On the passing of the act of union in the Scottish parliament on 16 January 1707, Defoe expected to be recalled to London. He was to be disappointed. Harley told him to stay where he was. At the same time Defoe was contacted by 'the other, newly altered, part of [the secretary's] office'. Sunderland was approaching Defoe for information. 'I am not to be pumped or sounded', Defoe assured Harley, 'and yet would be glad to have a hint from you where I should be wary, and where not'. Defoe was uneasy, and with good cause. 'It is hard if the persons who *say they employ* [*me*] do not stand by [me]', Defoe complained, 'pray let me know if you are in anything uneasy, and the like'.[94]

Harley made no reply to Defoe, despite receiving numerous anxious letters, until 12 June 1707. 'I have set up my rest', Harley wrote obscurely, 'and therefore it is not in their power to disappoint me...and their wrath is greater against me because their weakness as well as their villainous arts happen to be detected'. He was battling hard at this point against the Junto, and he had begun to lose all faith in the probity of Marlborough and Godolphin. Now the lord treasurer was to take Defoe out of Harley's employment. 'I am sure I have taken care to represent your services in the best light from time to time where it may do you service', Harley assured Defoe, 'lord treasurer says it is not fit you should be longer at my charge, which I hope is for your good'.[95]

In February 1707 Defoe told Harley that had 'neither hands to act, mouth to speak, nor purse to receive favours but as you direct'.[96] He continued to write to Harley while in Edinburgh as Godolphin was slow to send him money. He was in dire straits. But when he finally was provided with the means and the orders to return to England, his letter to Harley of 5 January 1708 marks the change in arrangement:[97]

I have been in town five days, but have kept myself *incognito*, being willing to have my lord treasurer's commands how to dispose myself before I took any step of my own. In order to this I sent by my brother [in law] that I thought it my duty to acquaint

his lordship that I attended his lordship's pleasure, but have not yet had the honour
of his lordship's answer.

I give you this trouble to entreat your intercession with his lordship for an audience,
since I shall not be able to continue long concealed, and I have no hand to act or tongue
to speak now but by his lordship's directions, to whom I resolve to be not only a faithful,
but a punctual servant.

It looks suspiciously as though Godolphin had deprived Harley of his
personal propagandist more out of spite, than out of an urgent desire
to employ him on his own behalf. Sunderland had tried to break the ties
that bound Defoe to Harley. Finally the lord treasurer himself had
intervened. For the time being, the relationship between Harley and
Defoe was over.

In the first weeks of 1708, Harley reached a showdown with
Marlborough and Godolphin over the construction of the ministry, and
its policy of prolonging the war. The Junto were trying determinedly
to bring about Harley's removal. Harley, on the other hand, wished to
replace the government's abject dependence on the support of the Junto
by cooperation with the body of tory country gentlemen in the
Commons. The corollary to this arrangement was an early settlement
with France. For several days things were in the balance. The deciding
factor was Godolphin's ultimate belief that Harley was plotting to
replace him at the head of the ministry. He tendered his resignation.
After some hesitation, Marlborough formed a united front with
his friend. Harley could not administer without the sanction of the
captain-general. He had the support of the queen, but not of the cabinet.
He capitulated on 10 February 1708.[98]

Defoe offered to be 'the servant' of Harley's 'worst days', but he was
advised to remain in the government's service.[99] The sole vestige of the
propaganda machine Harley had tried to erect under the triumvirate was
Defoe's *Review*. It continued to act as a ministerial paper, although a
decided whig bias could be seen emerging. Nonetheless it was there in
1710 for Harley to take over once again, and so were the outlets that
had been established for the distribution of propaganda. The paper
designed to 'state facts right' survived two extensive reconstructions of
the ministry. It was a government organ, the first of its kind. The idea
had been Harley's. When he returned to office in 1710 he built on the
beginnings he had made from 1704 to 1708. Godolphin and the whigs
again neglected the opportunity to extend the means at their disposal
for organising the production and dissemination of propaganda. In the
aftermath of the Sacheverell trial they were to rue this oversight. On his

fall Harley devoted considerable energy to filling the void left when Defoe entered Godolphin's employ. The results could be recognised in the propaganda issued by the opposition during the parliamentary session of 1708–9, and the Sacheverell trial. To Harley, the capacity to appeal to public opinion in print was a *sine qua non*.

4

The Memorial of the Church of England (1705): a case study

If the employment of a ministerial propagandist on a more or less permanent footing, the establishment of an unofficial government press organ, and of a system for disseminating propaganda, were the most tangible and enduring achievements of Harley's press policy as secretary of state, his involvement with Defoe was, nonetheless, not his sole concern during these years. The events surrounding the appearance of *The Memorial of the Church of England* provide a case study of Harley in action during his time in office. In the wake of the 1705 election campaign, chiefly managed by Harley for the government, the publication of this pamphlet – a full-blown High Church attack on the Godolphin administration and its policy of 'moderation' – caused an outcry. Queen Anne was bitterly upset at accusations that she was not acting in the true interests of the Church of England. Godolphin was close to tears.[1]

In the succeeding months Harley pursued an active policy of proscription, not only in attempting to trace the author or authors of the offending tract, but also investigating the genesis of a number of other publications from both whigs and tories that tried to cash in on the controversy precipitated by the *Memorial*. As secretary, Harley was officially responsible for the prevention and suppression of outspoken criticism of the ministry, and for the prosecution of offenders if and when apprehended. From May 1705 onwards, well into 1706, he vigorously carried out these duties. At the same time he was also expected to counter the possible detrimental effects of opposition propaganda, and his efforts are an important qualification of his proscriptive activities. He arranged for the printing and distribution of counter-propaganda to defend the government from the censure of the Memorialist. This, incidentally, upheld Harley's own conduct, then simultaneously coming under fire. In this way the positive and negative aspects of his press policy can be studied in conjunction, demonstrating how little he relied on proscription as an end in itself, and how he used it as a weapon to back up his attempts to disperse Harleyite propaganda as an antidote to the invective of the party writers.

The accession of a Church of England queen was looked upon by High Church zealots as a deliverance from 'Egyptian bondage', and they anticipated a journey out of the wilderness and into the promised land. The first doubts stirred uneasily in tory minds when the occasional bill was stifled in a conflict between the two houses of parliament in February 1703, and Rochester resigned in disgrace. Behind the scenes the triumvirate began to work against the reintroduction of the bill, and they plotted the downfall of Nottingham, Jersey and Seymour, the remaining tory chieftains. The failure of the second occasional bill served merely to heighten High Church anxiety. When Nottingham engineered a confrontation with the triumvirate, refusing to administer 'with that cabinet',[2] it was a desperate gesture towards realising the thoroughgoing tory government High Churchmen had envisaged in 1702. Nottingham followed Jersey and Seymour out of office. Harley replaced him as secretary.

The attempt to tack the third occasional bill to the supply bill was a direct result of these High Church setbacks. Harley tried to exploit the fiasco during the 1705 elections, but the parties closed their ranks. In response to Defoe's call for peace and unity, High Churchmen ridiculed the concept of political moderation. The Memorialist highlighted the danger of the Church. He claimed to see 'a vast difference between that moderation which is a virtue, and a part of the moral duty of every Christian, and the moderation so fashionable, and so much recommended of late, which is nothing but lukewarmness in religion, and indifference in every thing that relates to the service of God, and the interest of his Church'. Latitudinarianism was undermining the very foundations of the Church of England. Instead, the Memorialist urged the clergy to instruct their congregations 'in the nature of *true* moderation, and exhort 'em to the practice of it'.[3]

During the elections the old tory slogan, 'the Church in Danger', was raised once more, despite Harley's attempts to strangle the cry. The attack on the 'moderation' of the ministry was pressed home after the elections, when it became clear that Harley's non-party scheme had failed. Defoe had been unable to neutralise the propaganda released by the parties during May. Party labels had not been abandoned. Godolphin, satisfied that the tories could not be safely trusted to provide suitable support for the government in the Commons, proposed to give official backing to the Junto candidate for the speakership, John Smith. Reluctantly, Harley agreed.[4] Under these conditions the publication of the *Memorial* on or around 9 July 1705[5] took on even greater significance, and High Churchmen everywhere (including placemen) began to campaign energetically in favour of the tory candidate, the tacker William Bromley. While the *Review* and the whig propagandists backed Smith, the *Rehearsal* was joined by two new High Church periodicals, William Pittis's *Whipping Post*, and James Drake's *Mercurius Politicus*, in canvassing support for Bromley. Both were launched *after* the elections. Their *raison d'être* was the contest over the speakership.

The *Memorial of the Church of England* expressed ingenuously the hopes and fears of the High Churchmen under the Godolphin ministry. It was an emotive document. The patronage of Queen Anne had promised prosperity. But the Church of England was in anything but a flourishing condition, it was argued, although the 'sudden death' of William III had 'disappointed, mortified, and humbled the Dissenters, and their abettors, the whigs'. Yet outward appearances were illusory:[6]

all attempts to settle [the Church] on a perpetual foundation have been opposed, and rendered ineffectual by ministers who owe their present grandeur to its protection, and who, with a prevarication as shameful as their ingratitude, pretend to vote and speak for it themselves, while they solicit and bribe others with pensions and places to be against it.

This transparent reference to the manoeuvres of the triumvirate against the occasional bills – the Memorialist's 'perpetual foundation' – was driven home by arguments couched in country rhetoric. The divergence between court and country was apparent even under an administration of which Harley was a prominent member. Like the Church, the house of commons was in danger from the overbearing house of lords. The Commons had had privileges 'long before the race of lords existed', but they were being wilfully ignored, while the ministers fell back on the worn-out excuses of trimmers throughout the years under the new-fangled cause of 'moderation':[7]

that the times will not bear any other measures; that they are as hearty and as firm to the interests of the Church as ever, but the enemies of it are very numerous and powerful, and must not be provoked at this juncture; that the queen must have the hearts of all her people, and in order to it give equal encouragement to all her loving subjects, without distinction of parties; that the old, seditious, rebellious race of fanatics and whigs is extinct, and their leaven worn out.

As an alternative to platitudes such as these, the Memorialist urged the promotion of measures for the preservation of the establishment in Church and State. The time was ripe for the suppression of the practice of occasional conformity. The toleration act, approved by all honest Christians, guarded against the *persecution* of the Dissenters. But if they refused to comply with the established Church, why should they be allowed civil liberties? Toleration was one thing, encouragement another. Let Dissenters live as second-class citizens, instead of permitting them to profit from their nonconformity. It was high time to think of the *true* sons of the Church, who had been neglected for so long. And together with an occasional bill to secure the sanctity of the Church, a self-denying ordinance – the old place bill of the country party – would go a long way to safeguarding the sovereignty of parliament.

Godolphin, as lord treasurer, bore the brunt of this frontal assault on government policy. His approaches to the whig lords of the Junto were openly censured. Such ill-conceived ideas had led the ministers into a situation in which they were 'courting and truckling to Wharton, Somers and Halifax, their old enemies'.[8] While Godolphin wept at the indictment of his policies, Harley could hardly have been unaffected by the rhetoric of the *Memorial*. It is ironic that in private he aired similar misgivings about the wisdom of a reconciliation with the Junto.[9] He had been branded as an apostate by the whigs in the previous reign. Now he was being called a turncoat by the tories. It was difficult to maintain non-party principles in the age of Anne. The summer of 1705 brought strange attempts at self-justification from the pen of Robert Harley in his correspondence with his High Church friends. 'I have the same principles I came into the house of commons with', he told one, 'I never have willingly, nor never will change them'.[10] The sting of being criticised on country lines was, no doubt, keenly felt.

Steps were quickly taken to apprehend the men responsible for the production of the *Memorial of the Church of England*. Thomas Hearne noted the appearance of the pamphlet on 9 July; the next day a warrant was issued to Robert Stephens and Richard Heywood to take up David Edwards, the printer.[11] Defoe immediately informed Harley that Stephens, 'too much a friend to that party', had privately sent word to all the booksellers, and had gathered in almost all of the first impression of the *Memorial*.[12] His suspicions were independently endorsed by John Gellibrand, the *quondam* messenger of the press, who assured Harley that 'the discovery of this book might...easily have been made...if you had not been tricked by Mr Stephens'.[13] Very few copies of the first edition of the *Memorial* have survived, and the probability seems to be that few were sold in the first place of the first impression of 250. David Edwards managed to make good his escape. On 31 August the *Memorial* was presented by the grand jury, and orders were issued for Edwards's arrest. His whereabouts were unknown.

In the autumn of 1705 Harley recruited Robert Clare, an out-of-work printer, as a government informer in an attempt to track down from the inside the authors and printers of pamphlets printed against the ministry. One of his tasks was to hunt out Edwards. On 17 October he was able to provide Harley with the information that Edwards was 'with his mother (or some other relation) in Flintshire, in Wales'.[14] Other sources of information had already brought contact between Harley and Edwards. On 1 October, Edwards wrote to Harley, offering his cooperation if the proceedings against him could be suspended or lightened.[15] His reluctance to come forward without previous assurances is explained when the character and standing of the men he felt to be responsible for the authorship of the *Memorial* are taken into account. He intimated that there was 'greatness and wealth in the case, tall trees, which may prove very difficult to climb to the top of'. As he told Godolphin, in the event of a mishap he trusted that the government would not stoop 'to destroy a shrub'.[16]

Conjecture upon the author or authors of the *Memorial* was rife. On 10 July Defoe named Francis Atterbury as author, with George Sawbridge and Abel Roper as the publishers. Charles Leslie was another possibility, but Defoe subsequently pointed the finger of accusation at James Drake. He emphasised, however, to both Harley and the earl of Halifax, that Drake was only the amanuensis of the duke of Buckingham. 'The duke of Bucks', he assured Halifax, 'is as plainly pictured to me with his pen in his hand correcting, dictating, and instructing, as if I had been of the club with them'.[17] Though Charles Davenant admitted that 'the town would needs believe it was written by Dr Drake, and supervised by the duke of Buckingham', he pointed out that he 'was always satisfied of the contrary from his Grace himself'.[18] Yet Hearne countenanced the rumour that Buckingham was involved,[19] and the duke of Newcastle agreed that 'the style of this scandalous libel is as imperious as King John himself, full of groundless assertions'.[20] 'I don't know particularly what Drake has written', Godolphin told Harley on 1 October, 'but I can easily imagine his great patron and his great zeal together may have encouraged him to meddle too much'.[21] The evidence appears to centre on James Drake, and indeed his authorship was asserted after his death. The 1711 edition of the *Memorial*, which contained an introductory preface giving an account of Drake's life and death, claimed that it was written by Drake in conjunction with the MP for Westlow, Henry Poley.[22]

But David Edwards ignored James Drake. He attributed the pamphlet to Sir Humphry Mackworth, in collaboration with Henry Poley and John Ward. He could not prove his case. The copy of the *Memorial* had been brought to his printing-house in the middle of June 1705 by two women, one of whom was masked. He reluctantly agreed to print 250 copies of the pamphlet within a fortnight, but when the women returned to collect the order the books had not been stitched. Several porters were then engaged to carry the books to the Mitre Tavern. The letter which called for the delivery of the order was allegedly in the handwriting of one William Shiers, and this was the basis of Edwards's case. Shiers was an employee of Sir Humphry Mackworth. The letter was in the same hand as the manuscript copy of the *Memorial*. Certainly the holograph copy of the pamphlet extant in the Harley papers is not in Drake's hand. But it is not unmistakably Shiers's, not can we say with safety whether the letter which Edwards alleged was sent for the final batch of the books was genuine.[23] The case against Mackworth depended on handwriting which was not even his. Edwards claimed to have printed a pamphlet, *Pro Aris et Focis*, from a manuscript in an identical hand, and he had seen George Strahan, a bookseller, carry the proofs to Mackworth's house on Snow Hill. *Pro Aris et Focis* has not previously been attributed to Mackworth.

But Harley acted on the testimony of David Edwards, and with the approbation of Godolphin. On 12 January 1706 a proclamation promised Edwards his pardon if he could reveal the author or authors of the *Memorial* within four days. This superseded a reward for information leading to Edwards's arrest. Three days later Edwards surrendered himself into the custody of the messenger of the press. He provided Harley with a list of persons to be seized for interrogation. On 17 January the investigation commenced in earnest, and the cabinet was informed that members of parliament were implicated. It was decided to safeguard against a breach of parliamentary privilege by telling the Commons that some of their number were under investigation. The house duly returned thanks for the queen's 'tender regard' for their privileges, but requested that the enquiry should proceed.

Nothing came of the interrogations. Harley proved unable to clinch the case against Mackworth. Edwards suspected duplicity, and complained bitterly about lax security arrangements. The suspects were rounded up inefficiently, and left together in a room where they could corroborate and rehearse their statements. Edwards's answer was a more ruthless interrogation of Shiers and Strahan, the principal witnesses.[24] They refused to be frightened into a confession. The enquiry never reached a stage at which Mackworth himself could be questioned. But David Edwards was not the only one to criticise Harley's handling of the affair. On 25 January, Shiers and Strahan were examined in the cockpit before the assembled cabinet. Afterwards William Cowper, the whig lord keeper, noted in his diary that he, like Edwards, was 'convinced, by the similitude of hands, that Shiers, Sir Humphry Mackworth's amanuensis, wrote the letter'. He was similarly dissatisfied with the manner in which the interrogations had been conducted. He felt that Harley was 'extremely bad' at the technique of questioning, managing 'neither with cunning nor gravity to imprint any awe on those examined, by which he spoiled the thing in his former examinations'. Cowper was not without suspicions that this had been with a design 'to hinder the discovery'.[25]

Cowper's reservations allowed Trevelyan to conclude that Harley was 'unwilling to employ his private agents and sources of information against a brother tory'.[26] This was not so. Harley had used Clare to locate Edwards, and he gave the latter enough rope to hang himself, Mackworth, Poley, and half the tory party. William Bromley did not share Cowper's doubts about the thoroughness of the government enquiry. 'I wish all libels were so treated', he wrote, 'and the like endeavours used to discover and punish the authors of them, as have been upon this occasion'.[27] One witness died after being interrogated about the genesis of the *Memorial*. Thomas Hearne was not slow to lay his martyrdom at the government's door.[28] Shiers and Strahan were held without being charged until they brought their writs of *habeas corpus*, and were admitted to bail. 'I have been eight days confined tomorrow', Strahan wrote on 25 January, 'my long absence will infallibly ruin my trade'.[29] This was precisely what Edwards advised Harley to do. He called Strahan 'a niggardly, covetous fellow', and suggested that if Harley should 'touch his pocket' he would presently 'squeak'.[30] William Shippen had the temerity to banter Harley's management of the case in public, and he too was interrogated and prosecuted, although he denied all knowledge of the *Memorial*.[31] Harley took his job seriously enough.

Cowper was vindictively prejudiced against Harley. 'If any man was ever born under a necessity of being a knave', he confided to his diary, '[Harley] was'.[32] An unhealthy whig bias coloured all his dealings with the secretary, whom he regarded without compunction as a tory sympathiser. But Harley was hardly prevaricating over Mackworth's involvement in the production of the *Memorial*. He had no proof, despite Edwards's accusations, with which to indict Mackworth. There was a great deal of circumstantial material, but Edwards had been unable to produce one iota of incontrovertible evidence against Mackworth. A second point of fundamental importance is the attribution to Drake. Now Trevelyan, when discussing Harley's 'slackness' in pursuing the author, presumes it was Drake whom Cowper wished to prosecute. But the whigs were after a bigger political fish. If Drake's authorship is to be accepted, then Harley would have been committing a grave injustice in succumbing to whig pressure for an immediate public indictment of Mackworth. Drake, on the other hand, was prosecuted for the views he had expressed in *Mercurius Politicus*.

Was Harley's failure to make anything of his long investigation into the authorship of the *Memorial* not simply the result of the mistaken assumption that Mackworth was involved? Room for doubt remains. Unless fresh evidence can be brought to bear on the case, James Drake will continue to have the *Memorial* attributed to his pen. But the possibility that Mackworth was Drake's patron is a tantalising one. In 1706 one poetaster offered guidance to budding scribblers: 'Mackworth and Pooley will support thy lines'.[33] Drake constantly wrote with the assistance of others: Anthony Hammond in 1701;[34] Henry Poley, it seems, in 1705. Mackworth, 'the general pamphleteer of the party',[35] also wrote pamphlets. Both men commented extensively on the privileges of the house of commons. *Pro Aris et Focis* concerned the Aylesbury case. So did the *Memorial*. On their own, of course, thematic similarities are insufficient to prove a connection between Drake and Mackworth, and it is virtually impossible to exploit stylistic evidence because the canons of both men are horribly complicated. But the simple fact that it would have been much safer and easier for Edwards to have named a lowly scribbler, such as Drake, rather than a political figure of Mackworth's standing tends to lend weight to the authenticity of his testimony. He appears to have had clear suspicions that Mackworth was implicated, and he spoke persistently of a cover-up. It is not stretching credulity too far to assume that Mackworth was involved in the production of the *Memorial*, or, at least, that he could have been, and attempts to whitewash him raise doubts, rather than allay them. Edwards proceeded to extend his efforts to produce evidence against Mackworth throughout 1706 and into 1707 when all except Harley had forgotten the affair.[36] His persistence perhaps indicates that his conjectures contained an element of truth.

If Harley's efforts to uncover the authors of the *Memorial* illustrate little more than the rudimentary machinery wielded by the government in its official dealings with the press, the other aspects of his reaction to the challenge provide a much more positive picture. Retaliation in print was swift. On 9 July 1705 Defoe informed Harley that he had already answered 'this High Church Legion'. The following day he sent 'the rough of the answer', and he asked Harley for 'any hint' he might feel appropriate, which would be 'added' to the printed pamphlet. 'If you would please to give me leave', Defoe concluded, 'I would address it to my lord treasurer or to yourself; it should be in the press today if possible'.[37] *The High Church Legion: Or, the Memorial Examined* was published on 17 July to discredit the 'satire upon moderation'. Defoe had anticipated himself in the *Review* for 12 July, which had inveighed against 'the virulent pamphlet'. The unofficial ministerial press organ continued, until well into August, to dispute the contentions of the Memorialist.

Defoe's pen proved insufficient to counter the deluge of High Church propaganda which began to roll off secret presses. 'I am concerned to see your orders betrayed and buffooned', Defoe told Harley on 16 July, 'that wretch Stephens makes the government perfectly impotent in these matters, and the booksellers and he together make sport at your orders'. The basis of Defoe's anxiety was the predicted republication of the *Memorial*, supposedly answered paragraph by paragraph. 'As this is done purely to sell the book, which the town is so eager for, and which I think the government is highly concerned to prevent', Defoe wrote, 'so the answers are always trifles, and the design, which is dispersing the original, is fully answered'.[38] Five days later copies of *The Memorial of the Church of England, Answered Paragraph by Paragraph* were seized.[39] The reply was identical in sentiment to the original pamphlet. Defoe's fears were realised, the answer serving merely as a vehicle for reprinting the *Memorial* itself.

High Church sympathisers resolved to risk further reprisals by the government for the sake of propagating the views of the Memorialist. More copies were sold, and a vindication, *The Case of the Church of*

England's Memorial Fairly Stated, was published. Several High Church writers were taken up, including Drake, for *Mercurius Politicus*, and William Pittis for his *Whipping Post*. Pittis did himself no service in admitting responsibility for the vindication of the *Memorial*. He also penned an answer to Defoe's *Dyet of Poland*, and a defiant *Fire and Faggot: Or, the City Bonfire* in response to the grand jury's decision to burn the *Memorial* at the hands of the common hangman at the sessions house, and royal exchange, and the Palace Yard in Westminster in turn in the first weeks of September 1705. Subsequently Pittis claimed to have been given 'the most solemn assurances' by Harley that a confession 'should be of no prejudice to him'.[40] 'You told me when I was under examination before you', he wrote, 'that rather than my necessities should make me comply with booksellers' requests in writing what they would put me upon, you would be assistant to me yourself'.[41] But Harley showed no signs of employing 'that pitiful creature' Pittis.[42] He was later accused of promising 'the poor scribblers' that he 'would never take any advantage of their confessions'. One writer asked:[43]

did you not use to promise you would not punish 'em, but let 'em depend on you, 'til you had completed their ruin? Did you not promise those that would plead guilty all the favours you were capable of conferring on them, which were fines, pillories, and imprisonment?

Proscription, it seems, put some pens out of action. For this Harley was affectionately styled the 'President of the Pillory'.

Simultaneously Harley made arrangements for Defoe to have support in his battle with the tory propagandists. Newcastle remarked upon the timely appearance of the *High Church Legion*, but, he continued, 'I hope by what I observed by the reading of it, that some abler pen will undertake it, for certainly they lie very open, and may be lashed to the quick'.[44] The definitive Harleyite response to the *Memorial* appeared in October 1705[45] – the month of the speakership contest. In August Harley brought about a reconciliation with John Toland, and Toland's *Memorial of the State of England, In Vindication of the Queen, the Church, and the Administration* defended the secretary to the hilt, enumerating the 'qualifications' that made Harley 'the most capable of any to encounter those who would confound all our rights, and bring us under a slavish and barbarous subjection'.[46]

Toland's favour with the court of Hanover had been short-lived. Soon he was reduced to suing Shaftesbury for subsidies, and the earl eventually declined to provide any more cash for one 'whose prophane and loose ways overbalance all the good (I think) that either he has done or can do, unless he reforms much more'.[47] In June 1705 Toland asked William Penn, the Quaker, to intercede with Harley on his behalf.[48] Penn finally sent Toland's request for an interview to Harley, accompanied by a covering letter.[49] Toland offered his services to the secretary. His pen was of more immediate use. As he later reminded Harley, his *Memorial of the State of England* was written at his 'allowance and encouragement'.[50] In 1705 he sent Shaftesbury a copy of the pamphlet, assuring him that it had given 'full satisfaction to him that encouraged the work'.[51] Toland arranged for the dispersal of copies of his *Memorial* throughout the country.[52] Whether or not he made use of the outlets founded by Defoe cannot be established. While contemporaries suggested that Harley himself had written the pamphlet ('you did but dissemble with the court when you made such a splutter to hunt out the Church-Memorialist, and afterwards turned State-Memorialist yourself'),[53] Toland made it clear that it was written 'in a very few days without any to advise me but Mr Penn, being in the country'.[54]

The *Memorial of the State of England* was designed specifically as an antidote to the *Memorial of the Church of England*, and it was a full-scale defence of the Godolphin ministry. Although it served its purpose, it did not bring the debate to a suitable conclusion. This time it was the turn of the whigs to find fault with the government, and with Toland's apology. *A Letter to the Author of the Memorial of the State of England* appeared around the turn of the year. It was a vicious assault on Marlborough and Harley. If Godolphin reaped the dubious praise of the *Memorial*, the other triumvirs were fully recompensed in the *Letter*, which took umbrage at Toland's sycophantic defence of the ministry. After vilifying the captain-general with great freedom, the *Letter* subjected the secretary to perhaps his most extensive public censure hitherto:[55]

There is a certain gentleman, whom I would have taken no more notice of than your Memorialist has done, but that you seem to be angry that he was left out...a man who has deserted and betrayed all parties...I shall not...dispute the matter with you whether this grand omission was occasioned either by hope of his assistance, or fear that he might betray their secrets, or any other inducement, so long as you agree with me that it could not be out of *love*...You say indeed that *he hated extremes in all parties*; had you said he is hated extremely in all parties you would have varied less from the mark than from the words...if his literature was as extreme and consummate as these last mentioned qualities he might well pass for the most learned man of his time.

Here the *Letter* set the precedent for the standard whig judgment on Harley's conduct and intellect which was to be repeated and amplified throughout the intervening decades to the era of Macaulay and beyond:

by establishing an opinion of his great knowledge, by inveighing much against the ill-management of the revenue, by popular harangues, and by affecting to draw all business to his own hands, by endeavouring (through his skill in the rules and methods of the house of commons) to obstruct and defeat all motions which were not of his own making, he insinuated himself into the good liking of a credulous and unwary party.

On 18 January 1706 Charles Davenant told his son about Harley's 'dexterity and diligence':[56]

There was published about three weeks ago one of the most virulent libels that was ever read, as well as the falsest, the malice of which was particularly levelled at the duke of Marlborough...and at Mr Harley. At first it was thought some red-hot tory had written the pamphlet. It was at last traced to Parson Stephens...He is is a hare-brained whig, and owned the book, though parts of it are plainly above his capacity. Trenchard, Rawlins, and his republican club are more than suspected to have had their share in the composition.

The cabinet considered information regarding Stephens and the printed *Letter* on 16 January, and Luttrell noted the following day that Stephens would soon be prosecuted.[57] In February 1706 he was up before the bar of the Queen's Bench, and despite a public apology in the *Flying Post* on 14 March, he was sentenced on 6 May to stand twice in the pillory. He was also fined 100 marks.

Although historians have accepted without demur Stephens's authorship of the *Letter to the Author of the Memorial of the State of England*,[58] Davenant's suggestion that Thomas Rawlins was responsible can be supported by documentary evidence. Stephens escaped the pillory. The reason given was that Marlborough interceded on his behalf with the queen. But Harley had information which mitigated Stephens's offence. Thomas Rawlins had written to him, unsolicited, to deny complicity in the production of the *Letter*. Harley declined to reply. Rawlins chose to pester him with a further denial. This was hardly likely to allay suspicions. Harley felt obliged to set the record straight. His reply is more than simply clarification of a confusing incident, it provides singular evidence of Harley's attitude to attacks in print upon his person:[59]

The book which was owned by Mr Stephens, had it reflected upon no-one but myself, I should have taken care to have prevented any prosecution as I was not unserviceable in preserving the unhappy man from the execution of the sentence. This was the consideration which weighed with me not to return you any answer to your first letter, because what Mr Stephens said to me could never have come to your ears but from himself, and I thought he could have best explained the manner of his doing it. I am not willing to leave town without rectifying a mistake in that letter of his, of which you are pleased to send me a copy in your second, by giving you a true state of the fact, which is this: some time after Mr Stephens's first examination he came voluntarily to me, and said that he was no more than the transcriber of that book, and that was what he meant when he said he wrote it all; that the book was brought to him in manuscript by yourself; and that he was not the author of one word of it. Then, and not till then, I showed him that letter of yours which was taken about him, and which was the occasion of his being asked at his first examination whether anyone else had any hand in it. This is all that was done in that matter relating to yourself. Neither has what he then said been publicly taken notice of by me, either to do you any prejudice, or him any service.

Yet Harley wrote to Marlborough concerning 'the *authors* of Parson Stephens's Memorial', and he told the duke that the judges had begun 'to make examples of the libellers and printers'. His idea of proscription was not repressive, but exemplary. 'Some few examples', he assured Marlborough, 'will cure, in great measure, this abominable vice'.[60]

John Toland was shocked to see his pamphlet fall under the censure of the neo-Harringtonians. He attributed the *Letter* quite categorically to Rawlins, his old acquaintance, with Stephens as merely the 'publisher'. He composed a rejoinder, apparently with Harley's approbation.[61] 'Toland is Secretary Harley's champion or penman', one of Harley's agents was told, 'to write as he desires as to the subject matter'.[62] But Toland's 'Defence of her Majesty's Administration' was never published. 'I may take it as my text that *I own myself disappointed*', Toland complained to Harley in 1707, having received no advancement as a result of the *Memorial*, 'it being none of my fault that ['The Defence'] was not published'.[63] But if Toland's vindication of the *Memorial of the State of England* was shelved, the *Letter* received its share of printed criticism nonetheless. One anonymous author answered it paragraph by paragraph, while Defoe came up with *Remarks on the Letter to the Author of the State-Memorial*. It was this pamphlet which was carefully sent to outlets throughout England (as well as Dublin), and this fact probably explains why Toland's 'Defence' was considered redundant.

Clearly Harley felt the time had come to put an end to the paper war with a decisive offering that would be given maximum promotion. The fact that over 2,000 copies were printed in the first place indicates its unusual nature, and the preservation of Defoe's list of the destinations of each bundle endorses the assumption. Harley was concerned to have the pamphlet distributed throughout the land, and this when parliament was not sitting. He wanted to influence public opinion, not parliamentary opinion, and it is doubtful if the *Remarks* were sold, rather than given away. Fifty were 'laid down in coffee-houses' in London itself, and a further 100 were 'given about by hand'.[64] Defoe was supplied with information by Harley, to clinch the collaboration on a vital piece of government propaganda. He was quick to point out that Stephens was no more than the amanuensis of more designing men. 'To usher this book into the world', he wrote, 'it was necessary to find such a thing of which *Hudibras* gives a very significant description':[65]

> ...a Tool
> Which Wise Men work with, called a Fool.

Following Harley's predilections about the evil of party, Defoe pointed out that 'these extremes of parties are the only things dangerous to this nation's prosperity', and he concluded with a eulogy on the present ministers, 'though members [of parliament] write Memorials, parsons write railing accusations, divines turn callumniators, and tools work their own ruin to gratify a party'.

By the spring of 1706 the government, under Harley's management, was beginning to get the better of the parties in print. Defoe pressed home his attack on Stephens and other anti-ministerial propagandists of both sides in the *Review*. He was the object of considerable spite in return, but the impression is that it was the opposition writers who had been reduced to the defensive. Time and time again they returned to the *Review*'s election propaganda of the previous year, as if they felt it required further confutation. A number of pamphlets chose specifically to address the *Review*, and in addition to Charles Leslie's *Rehearsal*, with which Defoe fought a running battle in 1706, Joseph Browne undertook a 'Rehearsal of the *Review*' in *A Dialogue between Church and No Church*. Harley's reaction to Browne's challenge illustrates perfectly the interaction between the twin aspects of his press policy. Proscription was used to support the positive side of things – the production and dissemination of Harleyite propaganda.

Defoe declared himself amazed at Browne's affrontery in 'rehearsing' the *Review*. 'Of all the men in the town', he wrote, 'I did not expect to be attacked by Dr Browne, for sundry reasons'.[66] One very good reason was that Browne was, at the time, languishing in Newgate, under prosecution by Harley for publishing the libellous poem commemorating Cowper's elevation to the lord keepership, *The Country Parson's Honest Advice to that Judicious Lawyer, and Worthy Minister of State, My Lord Keeper*.[67] On 1 February 1706 Browne was examined before the under-secretary, Erasmus Lewis, in Harley's office, where he confessed that the printed broadsheet was a copy of a manuscript he had given Hugh Meers to print. Browne was immediately committed to Newgate, and, on 12 February, he was indicted for libel.[68]

Despite this confession, Browne proceeded to deny that he had written *The Country Parson's Honest Advice*. In a printed letter to Harley he accused the secretary of false arrest. He alleged that Harley had 'wisely resolved, like a great man, as well as a great minister, to ruin the trade of little scribblers'. The phrase 'little scribblers' was imputed by Browne to Harley himself. Clearly there had been personal contact between the two men. Browne admitted putting the manuscript of the poem into Meers's hands, but he stressed that 'it had been handed about in manuscript, as I was well informed, some days before I saw it'. 'The printer upon oath informs you he had such a paper from my hands', Browne continued, 'but never said I was the author, or desired the publication'.[69]

Harley did not care for the freedom with which Browne had used him in print. 'I desire you will be pleased to peruse the enclosed pamphlet entitled *A Letter*, etc., by Dr Browne, and let me have your opinion whether any passages of it are penal, and how far the author of it may be prosecuted', Harley wrote to attorney-general Northey on 22 February 1706, 'it is a notorious falsehood he asserts, that no oath was made, for Mr Borrett has the original affidavit of Meers the printer'.[70] The biggest mistake made by Browne was to reflect upon the secretary's sense of fair play. In the *Letter to the Right Honourable Mr Secretary Harley* Browne had offered to 'produce vouchers' to prove his case. But, as Defoe pointed out in the *Review*, there was a definite contradiction between Browne's contention that he was 'ignorant of the author' of the *Country Parson's Honest Advice*, and his subsequent offer to 'produce' him.[71] Similarly, though Browne may not have written the poem, he almost certainly meant Meers to print it when he gave him the manuscript – he 'desired the publication'.

On 24 May Browne wrote to Harley, seeking an interview at which he would offer proof that he was 'thoroughly convinced' of his 'error'.[72] It was at this time that he laid down the *Dialogue between Church and No Church*. Five days later, on 29 May, Anne Watkins made a statement that Browne had copied the *Country Parson's Honest Advice* out of her album of manuscript lampoons. She herself had been unaware of the author of the lines, having copied them from one Patrick Roberts 'some time since Christmas'.[73] Although Browne was patently involved in the publication of the poem, doubt remains whether or not he *composed* the verses for which he was pilloried. This suggestion is supported by the existence of a large number of manuscript copies of the poem, compared to only three extant printed broadsheets.[74] Variants in the titles of the manuscripts also suggest that they had been copied from hand to hand, rather than from a single, printed version. As Browne had emphasised in the *Letter*, 'it had been handed about in manuscript, as I was well informed, some days before I saw it'.

Browne was pilloried once for his initial offence, but twice more for his impudence in the *Letter*. He had also made several very unwise assertions in his 'Rehearsal of the *Review*', in which he continued to banter Harley's press policy, and his treatment of the 'little scribblers'. On his fall from office in 1708 Harley was commemorated by several poems supposedly written by some 'favourites' of his. Browne's hand can be discerned in these. One, in particular, an 'epigram' to Harley, pointed out:[75]

> Had'st thou in Pow'r, been merciful and good,
> As Great Men ought to be, and Christians shou'd,
> The little Scriblers would have sung thy Praise,
> And soften'd thy Misfortunes with their Lays...

Since Harley's alleged policy had been one of 'large fines, and pillories', however, the anonymous poet did not hesitate to kick the fallen minister while he was down. Whenever any of Browne's works were published in 1706, it was claimed, 'the copies [were] presently seized by the then secretary of state's order, by reason there were some facts then clearing, that would be a manifest prejudice to the underhand practices of a great minister, who kept hirelings at work to do his state-drudgery'.[76] Browne, at any rate, had no doubt about the dual nature of Harley's press policy: his propaganda was backed up by the proscription of authors who got in his way. The 'Rehearsal of the *Review*' ceased in the middle of May after only seven issues, when Browne made his submissions to Harley in the vain hope of escaping the punishment awaiting him in the pillory.

In later years Harley reminded Marlborough of his proscriptive activities as secretary of state, when, 'by an impartial prosecution', he succeeded in silencing most of the 'ill-natured scribblers', 'until a party of men for their own ends supported them against the laws and my prosecution'.[77] Pittis was pilloried for *The Case of the Church of England's Memorial Fairly Stated*. Like Browne, he retaliated, publishing *A Hymn to Confinement*, convinced that Harley had double-crossed him. Drake was indicted for libel in *Mercurius Politicus*. He escaped only through an error in the indictment, and a writ lodged by Northey in the Lords was still pending on Drake's death in 1707. Ned Ward was pilloried and fined for his serial poem, *Hudibras Redividus*, and ordered to find sureties for his good behaviour for a year. Charles Leslie was under investigation for the *Rehearsal*. The most prominent High Church writers, including Sir Humphry Mackworth, received close scrutiny under Harley's supervision in 1706. He succeeded in containing the volume of propaganda generated by the *Memorial* and its sequels.

There is little evidence of a concerted tory press campaign. One scholar, writing in peculiarly Walcottian terms, speaks of 'writers retained by (or, like Sir Humphrey Mackworth, politically allied to) Nottingham, Rochester, and Seymour',[78] but I have yet to uncover any proof that connections existed between the tory leaders and the party propagandists other than of the most tenuous sort. During the 1705 elections the main tory spearhead was provided by Dyer's manuscript newsletter, which appealed in particular to the country gentlemen and the clergy, and, in print, by Charles Leslie's *Rehearsal*. Both men appear to have been independent of patrons. The most plausible case for a mastermind behind tory propaganda could be made out for Sir Humphry Mackworth, if he was collaborating with James Drake. *Mercurius Politicus* and the *Memorial* itself, however, appeared after the elections. There was a campaign in support of Bromley's candidature for the speakership, which might suggest a coordinator, but evidence for such an arrangement on the tory side is completely lacking. In reality, most publications seem to have been written and printed by independent tories on their own initiative. Even the *Memorial*, the most effective tory pamphlet of these years, was designed to run to a first edition of no more than 250 copies. Detailed arrangements for the dissemination of the *Memorial* throughout the land on the scale worked out by Harley and Defoe for the *Remarks* obviously did not exist. Two hundred and fifty copies could hardly supply the mass of country gentlemen. It was all rather hand-to-mouth.

On the whig side the evidence is not much better. Certainly their propagandists got off much more lightly when involved with the law, but none of their pamphlets created a stir of the proportions caused by the *Memorial*. Stephens was excused the pillory for his part in the *Letter to the Author of the Memorial of the State of England*, the most offensive whig offering. Marlborough and Godolphin believed that Shaftesbury had sued on the parson's behalf.[79] Rawlins, although implicated, was not prosecuted. It was alleged in print that 'Stephens's style' had been 'begun by Shaftesbury',[80] but Shaftesbury firmly censured Stephens for his freedom both in using his name, and in criticising Marlborough and Harley.[81] Stephens was, no doubt, the tool of other men, but Rawlins was not an intimate of the Junto. The whig lords appear to have been strangely inactive in print. Unlike 1701, Somers's name cannot be linked with any pamphlet with certainty in 1705. James O. Richards notes that in order 'to aid Junto policy' propaganda was produced by 'Tutchin and the other (nameless) Whig writers'.[82] The anonymity of the whig scribblers cannot be pierced, and Tutchin's connections with the Junto have yet to be established. If anything he was closer to Harley.[83] Haversham was his reputed patron, and Haversham had broken irrevocably with Somers and the Junto in 1704. By 1708 he was in the Harley camp.

The whigs did not even possess writers of known effect like Dyer and Leslie. Ridpath's *Flying Post* and Buckley's *Daily Courant* had a decided whig bias, but essentially they were newspapers. Tutchin and Defoe were periodical essayists, and they were the best critics of tory policy. Defoe was rewarded for his Harleyite election propaganda in 1705 by the duchess of Marlborough, and Halifax of the Junto wrote in favour of his ability.[84] This in itself is indicative of an absence of other writers upon whom the whigs could bestow their patronage. In attacking the tackers, it is true, Defoe was producing propaganda which could be called whiggish (and Leslie embraced the *Review* and the *Observator* as the most virulent whig periodicals), but it suggests that the Junto was either unwilling or unable to sponsor genuinely whig writings. This is the case until after the elections and the first session of the new parliament. From 1706 onwards a new determination can be discerned. As Harley remarked to Marlborough, his policy had been effective 'until a party of men for their own ends supported' the party writers. Charles Gildon was committed to Newgate in June 1706 for printing a letter from Sir Rowland Gwynne to the earl of Stamford, commenting upon the proposal to invite the heir-presumptive to reside in England. He was freed through the 'interposition' of Arthur Maynwaring, a friend of the new secretary Sunderland.[85] In May 1706 Harley had been confident that 'some few examples' would be sufficient to stem the flow of anti-government propaganda. He did not count on the connivance of the whigs within the ministry.

Sunderland's appointment as secretary of state caused a perceptible shift in official responsibility for the press. In 1705 Harley had made strenuous efforts to reform the *Gazette*, approaching Jacques de Fonvive, the efficient editor of the *Post Man*, to offer him the post of Gazetteer. Fonvive declined the intended favour, thinking it 'no way of pre-ferment'.[86] Only in 1707 did the *Gazette* retain the services of an editor of talent, Richard Steele. But although Swift believed that Steele had been recommended to Harley by Maynwaring, and that he owed his job to Harley, it is evident that, as Gazetteer, Steele looked to Sunderland for guidance. He even worked in his office. Calhoun Winton perceptively remarks that 'in all probability Addison suggested Steele's name to Sunderland, who approved and sent the nomination via Maynwaring to Harley...as a tactful gesture'.[87] Sunderland was not as tactful when it came to approaching Defoe in Scotland, as we have seen, or when it came to publishing material relating to the Greg case in January 1708. As he lost ground in the ministry, Harley relinquished power over the press. He was unable to print the proceedings, as Sunderland allowed suspicion of Harley's involvement in treasonable correspondence with France to do untold damage to his reputation.[88] Harley had to wait until 1710 before he could put into operation his full press policy. Under the triumvirate he never had enough freedom to do so.

What had Harley achieved, and, perhaps of more importance to his subsequent career, what had he learned about the press during his first spell in office? The first and most positive achievement related to the setting up of a permanent ministerial press organ to balance the official *Gazette*, with the accompanying arrangements for its distribution in the provinces. It was an enviable system for the dissemination of printed propaganda. Only John Dyer's manuscript newsletter appears to have possessed a similar network of outlets. The *Review* was subsidised, and it was a direct attempt to influence public opinion. During the elections it appealed to electoral opinion, but it extended its message long after the members had been chosen. The idea was to provide a continuous parade of ministerial (or Harleyite) propaganda. The Godolphin ministry was the first post-Revolution administration to possess such a press organ. But after Harley's fall from office the theme was not developed. From 1708 to 1710 the whigs failed to establish further ministerial papers, or to forge stronger links with existing whig journals. This was one of the principal reasons for the whig inability to respond effectively to the tory challenge over the trial of Doctor Sacheverell.

Secondly, and more difficult to assess, was Harley's victory in the paper war sparked off by the *Memorial of the Church of England*. It had been a long, hard conflict, and at the outset the government had been ill-prepared to fight a long campaign. But unlike the standing army controversy and the paper war of 1701, the fury engendered by the *Memorial* had failed to embarrass the government to the extent of altering policies or personalities. Godolphin was already committed to the whigs and the Junto candidate for the speakership when the *Memorial* appeared, and no-one lost or gained office as a direct result of the paper war. The objective of the tory writers, to redirect the swing to the whigs, was unsuccessful, much as Harley would have been in sympathy with such an outcome. All that the *Memorial* achieved, in positive terms, was a queen's speech deploring the impertinence of 'some so very malicious as even in print to suggest that the Church of England, as by law established, [is] in danger at this time', and the passing of a resolution in both houses of parliament that the Church was 'in a most safe and flourishing condition'.[89] The *Memorial* might have been instrumental in drawing attention to the issues involved, but this verdict was directly contrary to the suggestions of the Memorialist.

Writers had been recruited and commissioned to answer particularly damaging pamphlets. Toland and Defoe both countered the *Memorial*, and Defoe proceeded to defend the ministry with great effect throughout the spring of 1706. Finally, through his spirited propaganda and the efforts of Harley in silencing the more vociferous opposition pens, the battle was carried to the High Church camp, and the fight was won. That Harley was prevented from capitalising on his triumph is the fault of his ministerial colleagues, who introduced party considerations into government policies. And yet if Harley had gained this early realisation of the aims of his press policy, he might never have gone on to achieve the much more extensive control he possessed after 1710. The resources at his disposal of 1705 and 1706 were very much inferior to those he was to wield as lord treasurer. The premature existence of a system for exploiting and managing the press as a means to appeal to public opinion and to influence decisions in parliament might have stunted the growth of a government propaganda machine of real scope.

From the events surrounding the publication of the *Memorial of the Church of England*, Harley came to believe that his basic policy had been correct. It was more effective to operate a dual policy of propaganda and proscription than a single, repressive one. On his return to office in 1710 he showed no signs of contemplating a return to the licensing system, or a more strict system of censorship. He had almost succeeded in 1706 in silencing the excesses of the party writers without such repressive measures. He learned to have confidence in the essential validity of his assumptions about the press. Whigs like Cowper demanded the utmost repression of the tory writers, but Harley felt that it was unnecessarily harsh (as well as morally untenable) to censor the writings of one side while allowing the other to publish unchecked. He did not wish to see mass prosecutions and indiscriminate pilloryings. Only three men were pilloried for their writings in 1706 – Joseph Browne, William Pittis, and Ned Ward – and they had failed to act on Harley's warnings that they should write no more. Browne and Pittis specifically singled out Harley in print in retaliation. Stephens and Drake, on the other hand, remained silent, and escaped punishment. As we shall see, Harley operated a similar system of proscription in 1711, but in the intervening years he was more concerned with the production of Harleyite propaganda in opposition to the restructured Godolphin ministry.

PART TWO

1708–1714

5

The tory resurrection, 1708–1710

Harley was thrown very much back on his own resources on his fall from office in February 1708. Defoe continued to write for the reformed Godolphin ministry. Toland had proved undependable. Harley had arranged for him to be sent on a government mission to Germany.[1] Tutchin had died after a severe beating in the autumn of 1707. Davenant was too much of a courtier, and Harley had alienated other potential High Church apologists. No-one defended him from the scurrilous lampoons that proliferated on his fall, lauding him with epithets such as Harlequin le Grand and the Welsh-Monster.[2] His reaction to the situation illustrates the importance he placed on printed propaganda. His first move was to retire to his estate in the country, where he remained until November 1708. There he licked his wounds, reviewed the state of political affairs, and began to plan the overthrow of the 'family' – his collective term for the Marlboroughs and their supplicants. In the course of the summer months he initiated correspondence with leading tories in the Commons through the offices of his friend William Stratford. In particular, he forged an alliance with William Bromley, opposition candidate for the speakership. Henry St John recognised that Bromley was the linchpin of the *rapprochement* between Harley and the tackers. 'You broke the party, unite it again, their sufferings have made them wise', St John advised Harley, 'There is no hope I am fully convinced but in the Church of England party, nor in that neither on the foot it now stands, and without more confidence than is yet re-established between them and us'.[3]

The General Election of 1708 resulted in the largest whig majority since the Revolution of 1688. Harley's campaigning was sorely missed. On the tory side no-one took the direction of propaganda into his own hands. The response to the whig challenge was virtually non-existent. The danger of Jacobitism was driven home by whig pamphleteers. The theme was especially relevant after the abortive invasion attempt of the Pretender on the coast of Scotland in March 1708. But neither side campaigned with as much verve as in 1705. Defoe was in Scotland again before the elections began. The most effective piece of printed literature came from the pen of Arthur Maynwaring in conjunction with the duchess of Marlborough herself.[4] *Advice to the Electors of Great Britain: Occasioned by the intended Invasion from France* combined emotion and reason in its brief message:

if it be certain that some of the tory party were actually engaged in inviting the Pretender; and if it is not so much as suspected that one man of the whigs was in the design of the invasion, this consideration alone should be sufficient to determine the choice of all the honest freeholders in Great Britain.

The outcome was the predicted one: in this general election, where the number of contested elections actually dropped, it is no wonder that, as Professor Richards as written, in England it 'was singularly uneventful – there was less propaganda and less public interest than in any other election of the reign'.[5] The electorate expressed a preference for men who held the 'Revolution principle', and a strong whig parliament was duly elected.

It is noteworthy that the government neglected to sponsor the production and distribution of propaganda to ensure an electoral victory. Godolphin was even unimaginative enough to dispatch Defoe off to Scotland instead of making use of his pen. The *Review* continued to comment on elections both in England and Scotland, but without instructions. Nor is there evidence that any of the whig ministers arranged for the publication of propaganda. Somers once again cannot be linked with any pamphlet, nor can his Junto colleagues. The ad hoc performance of the duchess of Marlborough, effective as it might have been, hardly qualifies as evidence of a structured campaign. The whigs, in office, did little to control the press. They felt confident, with a majority in both houses, that they could stifle any tory threat. They had not remembered the lesson of 1701. But Harley had, and the whigs were to rue the failure to develop a propaganda machine when they had the power and the opportunity.

Although Harley had taken little part in the elections of May 1708, he was prepared to meet the new parliament in a determined mood of opposition to the court. His scheme involved the production of country propaganda in a vein not dissimilar to the arguments and rhetoric of the pamphleteers of the 1690s. As soon as he was out of office, he began to express doubts about the capacity of the Godolphin ministry to govern efficiently and for the public good. Gradually he came to believe that the responsibility for the state of the nation, ravaged by the expenses of a prolonged war, lay squarely on the shoulders of Marlborough and Godolphin, who, having taken over the reins of kingship in their own right, were protracting the war for their own profit. By 1708 Harley was ready to lay all the ills of the kingdom at the door of the 'mock kings'. What did the Dutch mean, he wanted to know, 'by representing this island as an ass with two men upon its back and spurring it'?[6]

The definitive anti-Marlborough thesis finally emerged in 'Plain English to all who are Honest, or would be so if they knew how'.[7] In this manuscript tract Harley anticipated in many ways the arguments that finally saw the light of day in Swift's *Conduct of the Allies*.[8] Harley employed country rhetoric to claim to see taking place in the reign of Queen Anne the evils that the country party of the 1690s had feared, 'for the mischiefs which I have seen perpetrated for at least fifty years are now united in one stream and come rolling down with fury upon us'. He recognised the corruption of parliament by the duumvirate, and the undermining of the ancient constitution of king, lords and commons. Marlborough and Godolphin had so manipulated both political parties that they themselves had near-absolute power in their hands. They conducted affairs as if the Crown was a cipher and parliament a rubber stamp. By building up an intricate system of patronage, and by interposing constantly between the queen and her subjects, they had succeeded in ensuring that all official arrangements were made through them, and by them. As a result, Britain was being governed by a family which was draining the landed men of their wealth in order to line its own pockets, rolling money into 'the long, bottomless purse'.

'It is plain', Harley wrote, 'that everything they do is calculated to support either the power or profit of one family':

Thus we see what is to be our lot. As long as these rule, victories obtained are employed for their private advantage and profit, and not to the end designed for obtaining a safe and honourable peace, but to aggrandise themselves and to prolong that war by which they get such vast wealth, and secure to themselves so much power. For you must not expect peace abroad until they have subdued all their enemies at home.

The 'family' was accused of fomenting faction in religion and party conflict in politics purely for its own ends. The divisions that had been vital at the time of the exclusion crisis were pertinent no longer. 'The nation was then divided', Harley reminded his countrymen, 'into those who were jealous for their liberty and property on the one hand, and others who were alarmed with the fear of a design to overthrow the Church and monarchy'. This dichotomy was now obsolete. Under the duumvirate both were threatened, and the safety of one went hand in hand with the preservation of the other. The duumvirs were doing their utmost to perpetuate meaningless party labels, even though 'the foundations of those parties are abolished'.

'Thus, my honest countryman, I have given you a very short view of great mischiefs', Harley concluded, 'those you feel, those which you at present groan under, and such until God be merciful and the parliament virtuous, and boldly exert itself, you and your posterity will for ever be subjected to through an insatiable avarice and boundless thirst of power'. He had the remedy. Essentially, it was that which was offered two years later in *Faults on Both Sides*. He urged a general reconciliation of the imaginary differences that divided the nation, and allowed the family to perpetrate its excesses. 'And will you still go on, blinded with mutual rage against each other', Harley asked the whigs and tories, 'while they warm themselves at your intestine fires and are secured by your wilful blindness. Unite upon common principles, against those who would rend you, and then you will quickly give the enemies to the public *their just doom*'. This, of course, was a powerful argument, and Harley proceeded to go through the supposed tenets of faith of each party in turn to demonstrate how these were being subverted under the auspices of the family. Finally, the ailment diagnosed, he exhorted both parties to rouse themselves in the new parliament. 'Be assured', he advised them, 'that as soon as they see you have purged out the opium you have taken, and begin to rouse yourselves, and act upon true principles, these heathen magicians will never stand before you'.

'Plain English' was never published in Harley's lifetime. On 26 September 1708, however, Harley wrote to Stratford. 'I have some reason to believe by hints that are sent me', he informed him, 'that you will quickly see something in writing'.[9] 'There's a dream from Harwich which sells well, and is reckoned a very cunning and insinuating paper', Peter Wentworth told Lord Raby four months later on 25 January 1709, 'it is too scurrilous and, I think, a little too big to be put in a letter. Most people I have talked with of it will have it Harley's style, by what you will see it is reckoned no foolish thing'.[10] Surprisingly, *An Account of a Dream at Harwich. In a Letter to a Member of Parliament about the Camisars*, dated 21 September 1708 (five days before Harley's letter to

Stratford), contained a scheme very similar in outline to Harley's manuscript of 'Plain English'. Dyer noted the pamphlet's appearance on 15 January.[11] That it was a Harleyite pamphlet can be proved beyond reasonable doubt. 'I hear the *Dream* was made use of as an argument for the motion of giving thanks to his Grace [the duke of Marlborough]', Harley's son Edward wrote on 30 January 1709, 'Lord William Powlet said he was sure *somebody* was the author of it, a discovery worthy of his lordship's penetration'. The *Dream* was attributed to Harley more openly than the wonted circumspection of Powlet. 'Though the taking notice of that libel was said to be contrary to the direction of the persons thought to be most concerned in it', Edward Harley continued, 'yet Mr Lechmere's zeal could not forbear it on that occasion. He, I hear, explained it all, and said that it ought to be censured, but the house burst out in a loud laugh, and nothing was determined that way'.[12] Every effort was made to afford the *Dream* the maximum publicity. For once Dyer was on Harley's side. A mention in his newsletter was a mark of recommendation to his countrywide readership.

The *Dream at Harwich* took up Harley's theme of a drugged nation, blindly allowing the family to plunder its resources. It was certainly a more sophisticated literary approach than Harley's plain speaking. Instead it sought to instruct through parable and allegory. It would seem to have been a joint effort, as Harley's letter to Stratford (always assuming it does refer to the *Dream*) would suggest. In 1709 Harley explained to him that 'our drafts and other writings seem to be near finishing, having travelled to and again between this and the north'.[13] William Bromley was almost certainly involved in the production of anti-government propaganda. He reintroduced Harley to Haversham. Thomas Mansel felt he would be glad 'to find that there are more Lord Havershams, and that they would print for the good of the public, who don't yet see their state'.[14] Mansel, at whose house Harley drafted 'Plain English', was undoubtedly another collaborator, along with Harcourt and St John, the men who had resigned in solidarity with Harley in February 1708. A final writer implicated in opposition propaganda was Francis Atterbury, Dean of Carlisle in the north, and with whom Harley was in contact in 1708. 'I had the ill luck to miss you once or twice, when I called with these papers at Lincoln's Inn', Atterbury wrote to Harley on one occasion, 'They are very handsomely drawn up...they may perhaps be touched over again in a few places without hurting them if they are designed for the press'.[15]

Harley, then, was involved in the publication of the *Dream*. Perhaps he actively assisted in its composition. But, as he hinted to Stratford, other men were busy seeing it through the press. We have no evidence to suggest the circulation of the opposition writings in 1708–9, but it is probably significant that they were short pieces. Wentworth thought the *Dream* too big to be put in a letter, but there were at least two editions of this pamphlet. One was a quarto of eight pages,[16] the other an octavo of sixteen pages.[17] Subsequent opposition offerings were broadsheets, or tracts of four pages. This devotion to detail relating to the physical bulk of the papers might indicate that they were being sent into the country, perhaps even with Dyer's newsletters. Yet the opposition was concerned not only with extra-parliamentary opinion. A concerted line in parliament was essential to achieve anything, and the propaganda released by the opposition leaders in the winter of 1708–9 was designed to facilitate this unity.

As we have seen, the *Dream* achieved notoriety within doors. It was politically subversive. The narrator was overtaken by 'a drowsiness so insupportable' that he was 'forced to submit to it'. The strategy of *The Pilgrim's Progress* is readily apparent, and the biblical imagery employed by Bunyan also formed a crucial element in the message of the *Dream*. The narrator found himself[18]

in a crowd of people holding their fingers in their ears, and most of them had their eyes fast, but all half-shut. And with them carried into, and mixed with, another crowd, where I saw nothing but disorder and confusion, treachery and violence, everyone complaining of his neighbour, but none so much as attempting to put a stop to the mischief. Some were undermining foundations, others plucking up fences, some were untiling churches, others forcing the town-house to maintain the riot.

Here, in the form of a parable, was the author's view of the state of the nation. The people, the opium-ridden country gentlemen of 'Plain English', were blind, deaf and dumb, ignorant of the undermining of the constitution, the jeopardising of the security of the Protestant Succession, the danger of the established Church, and the corruption of parliament. The image Harley had wanted to convey in 'Plain English' was 'hear no evil, see no evil, speak no evil', and this was just what the author of the *Dream* was suggesting. Harley had called for plain speech to put an end to this illusion. But in the *Dream* there were 'a sort of fellows' equipped with bags of sugar-plums, 'and if one of them did but open any eye, or lift a finger from an ear, one of these presently popped a sugar-plum in his mouth, and he sprang immediately into his old posture'.

The imagery of enchantment was paramount in the *Dream at Harwich*, and this was common in the early eighteenth century. Harley used the idea of magic in 'Plain English'. The papers of the opposition to Walpole characterised Robin as a conjurer. Swift compared Godolphin to Sid Hamet in *The Virtues of Sid Hamet the Magician's Rod* in 1710, his first Harleyite publication. One flick of an enchanted white wand, the lord treasurer's staff of office, and all opposition faded. In the *Dream* the invasion attempt was symbolised by a fire which had broken out in the northern end of the town. This false alarm 'recovered many from their blindness, and made them think of their danger…But presently I saw the old man of the hill shake his stick, and these mounted up to him by several paths in a trice, kneeled down, received his blessing, and swore they would never see or hear again while he lived.' The old man, of course, was Godolphin. The new parliament was a puppet-show organised by the conjurer. The 'town-house' was forced 'to maintain the riot', and when the chief magistrates of the town called 'for clerks and papers' it was only 'to order a collection'. This much for the new parliament, which, as one observer remarked, was meeting 'to choose Sir Richard Onslow speaker, vote supplies *pro forma*, and little else'.[19] It had declined to a mere cipher or rubber stamp.

In an 'insinuating' manner, the *Dream* pointed out the outrages which were being perpetrated by the family. The characterisation was unmistakable. Godolphin, as has already been remarked, was 'an old, swarthy man, his countenance peevish and scornful, sitting on a round ball, on the edge of a precipice'. The Junto were 'five or six jugglers' who were continually threatening to push him over the drop. Marlborough was an ill-humoured man in armour, who was sitting on a horse on a ridge which overlooked the whole town. From a distance he surveyed the scene of destruction with smug satisfaction. His wife was 'an oldish woman, of fair countenance', sitting by the right hand of 'one whose every look and every motion spoke majesty and goodness, justice and truth' – a truly idyllic portrayal of Queen Anne. The author's pent-up malice was reserved for Sarah Jennings, duchess of Marlborough. She was the queen's tormentor, as she mourned her husband Prince George's death in October 1708. The appearance of the duchess prompts comparison with Medusa herself:

her chin and nose turning up, her eyes glaring like lightning, blasted all she had power over with strange diseases. Out of her nostrils came a sulphurous smoke, and out of her mouth flames of fire. Her hair was frizzled, and adorned with spoils of ruined people…her garment was all stained with tears and blood…She cast her eyes often

with rage and fury on that bright appearance I have described, over whom having no
force, she tossed her head with disdain, and glared about on her votaries, till we saw
several possessed with her.

Not content with looting the nation, and receiving the homage of her
'votaries', this creature's insatiable thirst for power moved her to desire
absolute dominion, and the outward trappings of kingship. The parable
was transparent. As Peter Wentworth observed, 'it is agreed by all
pamphlet readers that there's nothing obscure in the *Dream*, but
everyone understands what the author means'.[20]

Despite her grief, the queen was the personification of patience. 'Sad
and dejected was her posture, yet calm and serene: none looked that way
but blessed, and every tongue praised, this appearance'. Her day of
deliverance was nigh. On the forehead of the fury, inviting comparison
with the beast in the book of Revelation, were the letters MMTU, taken
from the fifth chapter of Daniel, as Peter Wentworth noted: 'mene mene
tekel upharsin, Hebrew words'.[21] Like a practised teller of parables, the
narrator drew together the threads of his vision:

The first...is the guardian angel of the town and all the neighbouring villages, and is
designed by fate to be their preserver and deliverer. But that other figure...has
permission for a determined time to fix her seat, with audacious impudence, hard by
the angel, and with her darkness to obscure its light, intercepting every good influence,
and has power to cause all the distractions...all the villainies...are contrived and acted
by fiends under her direction. Yet her power is limited, and the angel has hitherto saved
the town from the last destruction, without whose control this pest had long before now
burnt it to ashes, and delivered the spoil to the robbers.

When the anti-queen was thrown down, however, 'all enchantment shall
cease'. The narrator explained that 'everybody will then see and hear,
and bring the miscreants and deceivers to their deserved punishment'.
This, then, was the Harleyite message, predicting the overthrow of the
family by the people.

The *Dream at Harwich* was an important country publication, popular
among 'pamphlet readers' – a clear indication that there was a regular
audience for such publications. It was damaging to the image of the
ministry. It had to be answered. 'I thought it was not proper for me
to send you the *Harwich Dream*', Wentworth told Raby, 'until I could
send you with it another sort of interpretation than the ill-natured author
would have given to it'. This despite acknowledging that the
characterisation could hardly be misconstrued! The *Interpretation of the
Harwich Dream* obscured the meaning of the pamphlet, explaining that

those with their eyes closed and their fingers in their ears were 'an unhappy set of people in England, obstinate, and ignorant of their own happiness, under the most glorious and successful reign, and the mildest government, and most careful ministry that ever was, [who] will still be deaf and blind to their own interest'.[22] 'If I thought it worth your reading I would have sent you it sooner', Harley's son was assured, 'The piece seems calculated for the mob to take them off from the obvious meaning, or else to suggest to their emissaries some colourful interpretation'.[23] Ironically, Wentworth agreed that the *Interpretation* was 'not so good as it might have been, but it will have this good effect that it will pass upon the mob'.[24]

Belatedly, the ministry realised the importance of retaining the good opinion of the electorate, even with a sizeable majority in parliament. It is uncertain who took the initiative on the government's behalf, but it would appear that 'the mob' was a term of endearment for the tory country gentlemen. A second *Dream at Harwich, Supplying all the Omissions and Defects in the First Dream* lampooned Harley, 'a little, dapper, black man' in the interest of 'one Monsieur St George',[25] with allegations of Jacobitism. Only by ousting Marlborough and Godolphin, it was argued, could a Jacobite restoration take place. But these poor essays in counter-propaganda were insufficient to silence the pens of the opposition, or their speeches in parliament. *The Speech of Caius Memmius, Tribune, to the People of Rome. Translated from Sallust* combined the rhetoric of both: 'The present circumstances of our affairs, the power of the prevailing faction, your tame submission, the loss of all justice, and the danger of speaking truth, are such discouragements that I should be silent as well as others at this time, if my concern for my country was not above all other considerations.'[26] The calls to *patria* are Roman in inspiration, but the invocation to 'friends' and 'countrymen' had found its way into 'Plain English', where Harley claimed to recognise 'the same hands who acted what was clamoured against in former reigns'. Caius Memmius reminded his audience that 'not long since we thought we had reason to complain of the squandering the public money, and of the exorbitant riches and excessive power of some particular persons, but now those very persons are so far from being contented to go off with impunity that they have again worked themselves into power'. Equally applicable to the family itself or to the Junto, its hangers-on, this was a telling point. And the ultimate message of 'Plain English', that all power was being accrued by the family, was evident in the *Speech of Caius Memmius*:[27]

In a word, whilst we lavish our treasure and husband the war, a man may venture to prophesy that unless the gods are pleased to work a miracle for us at home, as they have done many abroad, the time is not far off in which this ancient and noble frame of government will be totally abolished and we, that have so often been conquerors, shall be no longer freemen.

As late as 1709 the indelible stamp of neo-Harringtonianism is present in the writings of the opposition.

It was predictable that the government would not permit this piece of country propaganda to pass without an answering appeal to public opinion, and a speech from Livy was 'introduced to correct Sallust, and to teach his translators sober reflections and good morals'.[28] The opposition leaders were not content, however, with two editions of both the *Dream* and the *Speech of Caius Memmius*. Where arguments 'without doors' ceased, points were made in parliament itself, and genuine speeches were printed and dispersed to influence public opinion. The similarity to 1701 is readily apparent. Like the ousted whigs then, the present opposition had to appeal to the electorate directly, and to persuade them that their whig representatives were doing them wrong. Somers's own method was turned against him. In his 'annual' speech in the house of lords, Haversham exposed the sort of lack of preparation that had been obvious in Scotland at the time of the invasion attempt. He alluded pointedly to the tradition that 'even among the apostles themselves, he that bore the bag proved the traitor'.[29] Godolphin was the mark at which all opposition darts were levelled. Sir Simon Harcourt, unseated on petition at the bar of the whig-dominated house of commons, made a speech which accused the lord treasurer more or less openly of influencing election results. Whoever had convinced his defeated opponent that he should move a bogus petition against him, Harcourt observed, 'must have been a person, the most abandoned wretch in the world, who had long quitted all notions of right and wrong, all sense of truth and justice, of honour and conscience'.[30] 'As to influencing...elections', Harley had written in 'Plain English', 'speak, O! Cornwall, and answer thou, O! Scotland, and the rest of the island between will witness against them'.[31]

Harley's role as coordinator of opposition propaganda can be asserted, and, to a certain extent, documented. He adapted the methods used by the whigs in 1701 to embarrass the duumvirate and the Junto. He was frequently visited by Bromley and Haversham. A meeting was held between the three men on 8 January at which, almost certainly, Haversham's speech was concerted.[32] Oldmixon noted that Haversham's 'annual' speech 'seemed prepared for the occasion, and was not without some strokes in it levelled against the ministry'.[33] On 11 January the Lords were ordered to attend, and the house considered the state of the nation. It was then that Haversham made his mark. 'This day seven Lord Haversham made a speech', Peter Wentworth wrote on 18 January, 'and last Friday they cried it about the streets'. Harcourt's speech was 'more artfully worded than Lord Haversham's'. It, too, had been drawn up in concert. On 25 January Wentworth observed that 'Sir Simon will print his speech'. There is evidence, however, that it also circulated far afield in manuscript.[34] 'The determination of the Abingdon election has made a great noise in town', remarked Edward Harley, 'both parties are liberal of ill names to [each other]; Sir Simon Harcourt, they say, called a great man rogue and rascal, as they construe his words, which were to this effect: "A person that has long since abandoned all truth, justice, honour, honesty, gratitude, etc."; I think this is pretty plain'.[35]

A signal illustration of the importance of extra-parliamentary opinion to the opposition propaganda campaign was supplied by the debates on the question of the invasion of Scotland in March 1708. During the elections the duchess of Marlborough had prompted other whig writers to derive the maximum propaganda effect out of the affair by accusing the tories of Jacobitism. Less than a year later the *Dream* supported Haversham's speech in insinuating that, in fact, Scotland had been woefully unprepared to meet the challenge of the Pretender had he landed. This, it was suggested, was indicative of a ministerial conspiracy. In the Commons, the whig majority resolved that 'timely and effectual care was taken by those employed under her majesty at the time of the intended invasion of Scotland to disappoint the designs of her majesty's enemies both at home and abroad'.[36] Thwarted from registering an official complaint in the Commons' Journals, the leaders of the opposition published *An Account of the late Scotch Invasion, as it was opened by Lord Haversham in the House of Lords on Friday the 25th of February, 1708–9; with some Observations that were made in the House of Commons, and true Copies of Authentic Papers, in a Letter from a Gentleman in South Britain, to his Friend in North Britain*. This pamphlet openly attempted to supply those out of doors with news of proceedings in the Commons. It revealed that there had been a lack of preparation against the threat of an invasion in Scotland:[37]

the Scots gentlemen concurred with the English in blaming the conduct of the ministry, affirming it was such as gave great encouragement to the enemies of the government, while its friends look on their country to be perfectly given up...After all the observations made upon the papers, the consideration of them ended in the house of commons in the resolution above mentioned. The gentlemen that were against this resolution desired that all the papers laid before the house relating to the intended invasion of Scotland might be printed, that the world might see and judge how well-grounded it was. But those who had justified the ministry in their debates, and voted for the resolution, would not suffer the papers to be printed, so that question was carried in the negative.

In 1709 the concept of legion was used against its inventors to indict the whig house of commons of failing to act in the true interests of the electorate which had elected it: the tables had been turned, as the lesson sunk in. In lieu of influence at the centre of power, the opposition played upon public opinion.

The publication of the *Account of the late Scotch Invasion* was the climax of the opposition propaganda campaign in the winter session of 1708–9. It had caused considerable embarrassment to the ministry, which had been taken totally unawares. The stir precipitated by two brief pamphlets and two printed broadsheets was completely out of proportion to their extent. True, it was skilful propaganda, a clever blend of concrete political realism and allegorical fantasy. The symbol of the family, invented by Harley, was a powerful one (which would be used to great effect by Swift in the *Conduct of the Allies*). But it had been the absolute complacency of the government which permitted such an onslaught on its integrity. With majorities in both houses, and a parliament which still had over two years to run, the ministry neglected to take steps to preserve its public image. This was a big mistake. The electorate had expressed its opinion in the elections, but its opinion could change. Somers had forgotten 1701. Only when the opposition offensive was under way, did the government rouse itself, and try to protect its façade. In office the whigs palpably failed to do anything about the question of propaganda and counter-propaganda until forced to do so by a particular political exigency. As for Marlborough and Godolphin, their interest in the press was minute. 'I do not know who the author of the *Review* is', Marlborough had written as late as 1706, 'but I do not love to see my name in print'.[38] Attitudes like these were inimical to the development of official agencies for the production and dissemination of propaganda. It was this wilful blindness which Harley had had to combat when in office.

On the other side, preparations were being made against the opening of the 1709 parliamentary session. Harley was still cooperating with

Haversham, and the 'drafts' of the opposition leaders were doing the rounds.[39] But the amount of propaganda that these gentlemen-writers could produce was pitifully small. Help came from other quarters; unexpected help. Trevelyan observes that 'the publication that did most harm to the ministry in [1709] was a book of the lowest order, the *New Atlantis* [*sic*], wherein Mrs Manley, a woman of no character, regaled the public with brutal stories, for the most part entirely false, about public men and their wives, especially whigs and above all the Marlboroughs'.[40] Despite Trevelyan's indignant moralising, the *New Atalantis* was no worse than the verse which had greeted Harley on his fall. Arthur Maynwaring, that associate of the Marlboroughs, had accused Harley of sexual liaison with Mrs Masham, and had suggested that both of them were riddled with venereal disease.[41] But the book which did most to change the ministry was of a vastly different character, and it had nothing whatever to do with Harley. The furore which was caused by Henry Sacheverell's sermon, *The Perils of False Brethren, both in Church and State*, did infinitely more than Harley's plain speaking to bring about a ministerial revolution. At the same time, it proved once and for all that in the eighteenth century governments were subject to public opinion, and could not survive for long once electoral approval had been forfeited.

Harley's genius lay in exploiting help from whatever source it came, and any propaganda which could be turned to use was Harleyite propaganda. As Swift later observed, Harley's 'rule in politics', if it could be so called, 'was to watch incidents as they come, and then turn them to the advantage of what he pursues, rather than pretend to foresee them at a great distance'.[42] This was precisely the case with the *New Atalantis* and the *Perils of False Brethren*. Although Harley subsequently employed Dela Manley when in power, there is no firm evidence to suggest that the association stretched back to 1709. Mrs Manley's efforts did much to assist Harley's cause, and she claimed some merit in having first exposed 'the enemies of our constitution', and not without 'hazard' to herself. She wrote against the interest of the family, 'circulated their vices, and opened the eyes of the crowd, who were dazzled by the shine of power into awe and reverence of their persons'.[43] She also exposed Somers's relationship with Elizabeth Fanshawe Blount, as Harley had done in the *Letter from the Grecian Coffee-house* in 1701.[44] But though the duchess of Marlborough was convinced that Harley was involved in the *New Atalantis*,[45] Mrs Manley did not know him personally. When she sent him a copy of her *Memoirs of Europe* on 12 May 1710, she explained that only her respect had prevented her from waiting on Harley in person, 'lest I be thought to have the honour of your acquaintance, which I can only covet, never hope'.[46]

Whatever plans Harley had laid against the opening of the winter session of parliament in November 1709, whatever pamphlets he had in the press ready to be printed and published, were rendered superfluous when Sacheverell was impeached for the views expressed in the sermon he preached in St Paul's on 5 November, and subsequently published. The trial of Dr Sacheverell provided a far superior opportunity to press home the attack on the Godolphin ministry. It was said that Sacheverell had spoken out against the Revolution. His printed sermon was bought in tens of thousands. Burnet claimed that 'about 40,000 of them were printed and dispersed over the nation',[47] but this is a conservative estimate. The second octavo edition, published on 3 December by Henry Clements, consisted of 'betwixt 35,000 and 40,000'. As well as four genuine editions (two in quarto and two in octavo), there were at least six piracies, five in 1709 and one in 1710. W. A. Speck estimates that about 100,000 copies were sold in Great Britain, and there were translations into Dutch, German and French.[48]

Harley used the Sacheverell affair to woo whig dissidents. The trial itself was sufficient to unite the tory party. As Stratford noted: 'So solemn a prosecution for such a scribble will make the Doctor and his performance much more considerable than either of them could have been on any other account'.[49] The whigs intended to inflict an 'exemplary punishment' on Sacheverell, 'one that would effectively deter clergymen of his kidney from using their pulpits in future to disseminate political "poison"'.[50] Secondly, it would isolate Godolphin finally and utterly from the tories, and permit his removal. But a full-scale public trial stimulated fierce partisanship. The night before the opening of proceedings the London mob rioted in favour of Sacheverell.[51] High Church writers poured their pamphlets onto the streets. Whigs joined in battle with the High Churchmen to argue the pros and cons of the case, and to discuss the probable constitutional and ecclesiastical repercussions of the affair. The whole Revolution settlement was indeed called into question by the pamphleteers, if not by Sacheverell's sermon itself. 'Here the validity of the Revolution will be tried', wrote Defoe in the *Review*, 'Here the present constitution is to be tried, and the Lords are to give sentence upon it...Here shall be tried...the Church established by law'.[52]

Sacheverell was found guilty, but his sentence was derisory. He was banned from preaching for three years, but permitted to enjoy the benefits of preferment nonetheless, and he was soon given a rich living in North Wales. Of more importance was the decisive swing of public opinion away from the whigs. A series of addresses to the queen from counties and boroughs convinced her that the electorate which had given the whigs a majority in 1708 had changed its mind. It encouraged her to risk an extensive reconstruction of the ministry. A few weeks later, when Godolphin was at Newmarket, Queen Anne replaced the earl of Kent as lord chamberlain with the duke of Shrewsbury, a member of the alliance Harley had been trying to form. This initial foothold in the ministry was followed by the dismissal, in June 1710, of the earl of Sunderland. His replacement was a moderate tory, Lord Dartmouth, and from his appointment onwards Harley was regarded as the heir-apparent to Godolphin. Finally, prompted by Harley, Queen Anne sanctioned the removal of the lord treasurer. On 10 August Harley became chancellor of the exchequer, and second lord of the treasury, which was put in commission. The board was stacked with Harleyites, including the first lord, Earl Poulet. The tory resurrection had taken place.

The Sacheverell trial sparked off a paper war of immense proportions.[53] The display of popular feeling in favour of High Church sentiments raised the whole problem of the relationship between parliament and public opinion. As Lee Horsley puts it, 'the whigs, with their traditional respect for "the Voice of the People", found themselves the victims of *vox populi*, defeated by an enormous surge of popular support for the tories'.[54] These, of course, had been Harley's tactics in the interval since his fall. The impeachment of Sacheverell was a godsend. When the ministerial changes began to take effect pamphlets considered their scope, and whether or not a dissolution was planned. Tory propagandists argued for a new parliament. Sir Thomas Hanmer believed that 'a new ministry with an old parliament will be worse than the gospel absurdity of a piece of new cloth in an old garment, or new wine in old bottles'.[55] Bromley hoped that 'due care' would be taken to disperse 'good little pamphlets'.[56] On the other side, the whigs fought a stalling action, writing against a dissolution, against further ministerial changes, against, indeed, those changes already implemented. They manipulated the stocks to create a credit crisis which would, at the very least, embarrass the new administration, at worst, emasculate it.[57]

Harley was cheerfully pictured 'in a sculler alone, rowing against wind and tide without any person to assist him'.[58] The whigs, naturally, resented his encroachments. The tories called him, quite openly, 'a necessary ladder' which would be discarded as 'part of the scaffolding' as soon as 'the building had got its foundation'.[59] Harley's conception of the ministerial revolution was vastly different from that of the mass of High Churchmen. After the removal of Godolphin he showed a willingness to live happily with the remnant of the old government. He made determined efforts in particular to accommodate Somers, Cowper, Boyle and Halifax. He was concerned that the tory reaction should not get out of hand, resulting in a High Church ministry. This had not been the point of his opposition to the duumvirate. He wanted to *abolish* the distinction between the parties, not exchange one set of party men for another.

A clear indication of Harley's differing attitude is provided by the address of the county of Radnorshire. This stands out in the spate of such addresses presented to the queen in the aftermath of the Sacheverell trial. On 27 April it was delivered 'by Robert Harley and Thomas Harley, Esqrs., introduced by the Right Honourable the earl of Pembroke and Montgomery, lord-lieutenant of South Wales'. The sentiments were typically Harleian, and, of course, it was attributed to Harley himself.[60] Unlike the vehemence of the vast majority of High Church addresses, it spoke out against[61]

the many blasphemous, heretical, Jesuitical, atheistical, schismatical and republican books and pamphlets that have been industriously dispersed and encouraged (even in these remote parts of your majesty's dominions) *in order to foment divisions* among your majesty's dutiful subjects, disturb their peace, and alter, if not subvert, the establishment in Church and State.

Significantly the address concluded with the hope that 'all schisms, divisions and factions be laid aside, [that] we may have no contention among us'. Simply by comparing this offering with some of the more blatant High Church addresses, such as that from Westbury,[62] we can appreciate Harley's moderate anti-party feelings.

Despite the mass of writings relating to the Sacheverell trial, there is no indication that Harley instigated any of the pamphlets in favour of the Doctor. If the tory campaign had a coordinator (and it is extremely unlikely that it had), it certainly was not Robert Harley. He later was in contact with a number of High Church writers who had written on behalf of Sacheverell – men such as Joseph Trapp and William King – but there is no evidence to suggest that, in 1710, he encouraged their publications. If anything the reverse was true.[63] King published *A*

Second Letter from Tom Boggy to the Canon of Windsor, Occasioned by the Late Panegyric Given Him by the Review of Thursday, July 13, 1710 while Defoe was trying to engineer a reconciliation with Harley.[64] Trapp went even further. In *Most Faults on One Side* he actually attempted to confute the Harleyite manifesto *Faults on Both Sides*. He claimed, of course, that it had all been the fault of the whigs. This was hardly the sort of stuff to appeal to Harley at this juncture. It would be perverse to argue that Harley sponsored this attack on his own propaganda. Far from writing *in favour* of Sacheverell and High Church policies, it is more likely that Harley wanted his propagandists to damp down the heat raised by the Sacheverell trial once the change of ministry had been effected.

Faults on Both Sides: Or, An Essay upon the Original Cause, Progress, and Mischevious Consequences of the Factions in this Nation is the nearest thing we have, in print, to a full-scale exposition of Harleian ideology. It follows both Toland's *The Art of Governing by Parties* and Harley's own 'Plain English' in tracing party divisions back to the reign of Charles II. Then they were encouraged to enable the king to divide and rule. Now all true meaning had been lost. The furore over the occasional bills, of which the Sacheverell trial was merely the outcome, had given new life to outworn party labels. 'Now the factions are blown up into a flame', the Fault-Finder alleged, 'the danger of the Church cried out on one side, the danger of High Church persecution on the other'. Like the author of the Radnorshire address, in contrast to other High Church addresses, the Fault-Finder asked men 'to bury their animosities, and labour to reconcile their imaginary differences', as 'they have been all along deceived and cheated'. The healing disposition apparent in the Radnorshire address, which mentioned sorrowfully 'the great mischiefs and manifold inconveniences that have for some years past' troubled the 'faithful subjects' of the queen, is recognisable in *Faults on Both Sides*, and, although circumstances had changed, the message was the same that Harley had propounded two years earlier in 'Plain English'.[65]

Faults was published as an answer to Ben Hoadly's *The Thoughts of an Honest Tory*, which, purporting to represent the views of a true-blue tory on the Sacheverell affair, naturally enough rebounded upon both the Doctor and his party. *Faults on Both Sides* attempted to mediate between the parties, and the easiest way to bring about a reconciliation was to make the people see that both parties were partly to blame for inciting conflict in the nation. But, more important perhaps, ultimate responsibility for the state of the nation was laid at the door of neither the whigs nor the tories. Again the Marlboroughs bore the brunt of

Harleyite propaganda. *Faults* put forward as an alternative to the domination of the family, Harley's scheme for non-party government in the interests of the public good. It was, of course, fulsome in its praise of Harley and his policies. 'If his conduct shall be impartially considered', the Fault-Finder suggested, 'it will be found that his actions have shown him much more a patriot and a true whig than his adversaries'. A whig, that is, in the original 'country' meaning of the term. Harley was upheld as the shining example of a man who had tried to maintain the old values of the first whigs, while supporting the established Church and the act of toleration at the same time. Under Harley the administration would no longer seek to influence elections or parliamentary proceedings. In effect a separation of executive and legislature – that old country chestnut – would take place. 'I own to you that I have always espoused the true whig principle', the Fault-Finder explained, 'that is, to be heartily affected to the court and ministry when they act uprightly for the public good, and as heartily to oppose them when they act otherwise'.

Gradually the voice of the author of *Faults* and the voice of Harley himself merged to become one. The policy of the new regime would be to employ 'all those of the whig party who shall...concur in the promotion of the public good'. These men would be 'as freely admitted to employments and as well regarded as ever, nothing being more desired than a coalition of the honestest men of both sides'.[66] The message was loud and clear. Harley did not want a thoroughgoing High Church administration. He wished for a genuine reconciliation between whig and tory. While this was the positive side to *Faults on Both Sides*, it was also required to defend the change of ministry. The tactics of the ensconced ministers were carefully and clearly listed. The Junto had succeeded in persuading the Dutch to present a memorial to the queen through their resident envoy, Vryberg, to request her not to change her government. Then 'their next attempt was to play the bank upon her majesty' when a delegation of Bank of England officials warned the queen about the ill effects of altering her servants. When this was unable to halt the swing in public opinion and the queen's favour towards the tories, the whigs took more positive action. A run on the stock market was engineered. Lack of confidence in public credit severely handicapped Harley's chances of supplying the army in the continuing war with France. The net effect of these ruses, the whigs hoped, would be to ruin the new ministry, 'bring all things into confusion, and disable us from carrying on the war'. The Fault-Finder called these 'maxims invented by knaves to cheat fools'.[67] Yet Godolphin was certain that Harley would be unable to govern in the face of seemingly insurmountable odds.[68]

Harley himself was credited by some with the authorship of *Faults on Both Sides*, which had 'a prodigious run'. Maynwaring, in *The Medley*, was of the opinion that 'he can be nobody less than a chief minister', while one man informed Harley personally that 'divers people make thee its author'.[69] Today, however, it is generally accepted that the pamphlet was written, as Onslow remarked at the time, 'by one Clement, under the direction of Mr Harley'.[70] Whether Harley actually collaborated in the finished product is uncertain, but his influence is clear enough. Even if there are no stylistic echoes of 'Plain English', the arguments are sufficiently similar to allow the conclusion to be drawn that Clement was writing to order. The curious manner in which the tone moved from an ostensibly objective review of affairs to a more or less authoritative promulgation of the policy of the new regime indicates that this is the case. As Maynwaring put it: 'he dares assure people what her majesty's intentions are...he pretends to say what distinctions shall be kept up...he tells upon what terms they shall be admitted into the ministry, and how they shall behave themselves too, when they are admitted'.[71]

Little attempt has been made hitherto to trace the relationship between Harley and Simon Clement, nor indeed to explain why Clement should suddenly emerge as Harley's personal propagandist. The association was a prolonged one, and although many details are missing it is possible to document its development. Clement was originally a whig. Like Defoe he started life in trade. He fell into hard times when the *Regina*, a ship he subsidised jointly with fellow merchants, infringed the navigation act by being worked with less than three-quarters of her crew English seamen. This was in 1696. Clement had previously published economic tracts. In 1695 he wrote *A Short Discourse Concerning the Coin*. William III subsidised the printing of the pamphlet out of his secret service fund. Clement continued to write on financial tropics until rewarded by a recommendation as secretary to the earl of Bellomont, governor of New York and New England. Unfortunately, as Bellomont informed Somers on 7 March 1700, Clement 'disappointed [him] dirtily'.[72] It was then that Harley began to take an interest. In 1704 Clement sent him the draft of 'The Case of Prohibitions of Commerce and Correspondence with our Enemies Truly Represented. In a Letter to a Member of the Honourable House of Commons'. As far as I am aware this was never published, but the holograph is extant in the Harley papers.[73] Harley patronised Clement throughout his time as secretary of state, pushing his proposals for the import of pitch and tar for naval stores from unfrequented Baltic ports.[74] He interposed personally on Clement's behalf with George Churchill of the admiralty.[75] His persistence paid off, for there are records of payments made to Clement in 1708 for bringing tar and pitch into England.[76]

Contact between the two men continued when Harley was out of office. Clement was apparently in dire straits. It was for this reason, no doubt, that he was Harley's amanuensis in the composition of *Faults on Both Sides*. Oldmixon noted in 1711 that, among the ministry's other propagandists, they retained 'one Clement, a New England jobber, in service and pay'.[77] In 1711 Clement accompanied the earl of Peterborough to Vienna as his private secretary. He was still in Vienna on a government salary of sorts on the accession of George I.[78] Clement's son reminded Harley on one occasion of the 'friendship' he had 'expressed' for his father.[79] Simon Clement was the first of the new propagandists recruited by Harley in 1710 as the basis of his new press agency. He was quickly superseded by abler and more prolific pens, but it is his role as author of *Faults on Both Sides* which interests us here.

The publication of *Faults on Both Sides* sheds valuable light on the importance Harley placed on the press. There is a distinct proportion of propaganda in 1710 which can be classified as Harleyite, in contrast to the writings of party men. The tories were not the men to play down the High Church victory. Tory writings were useless for Harley's purposes. Bromley called for 'good little pamphlets', and Henry St John answered his prayer. He sponsored the launching of the ultra-tory *Examiner*, and he gave the paper a purpose in his *Letter to the Examiner*. It was not one which Harley appreciated. There are clear indications that St John would not have found a place in Harley's cabinet had the whigs not resigned *en masse* in September 1710.[80] St John had made no attempt to allay whig anxiety. Cowper responded with a *Letter to Isaac Bickerstaff*, while Joseph Addison's *Whig-Examiner* was followed by the *Medley* of Arthur Maynwaring and John Oldmixon when 'the old ministry saw it was absolutely necessary to set up a paper in opposition to the *Examiner*'.[81] For these reasons Harley took the precaution of stating his own policies in *Faults on Both Sides* and other pamphlets.

One of Harley's first steps on returning to office was to set about rebuilding the government propaganda machine he had outlined under the triumvirate. The recruitment of Clement was only one instance of this policy. Surveying the literature of the year, Francis Hare, Marlborough's apologist, offered the opinion that 'the most artful performance of them all' was *A Letter from a Foreign Minister in England to Monsieur Pettecum*:[82]

The rest seem to be the works of under-agents, from directions and hints marked out for them, but this I take to be the work of the chief operator himself, who, if he was not at leisure to write more largely, has in this short piece sufficiently shown what a right he has to the esteem the world has long had for him, there being in it some quick and crafty turns, and an affected appearance of fairness, with which he gilds over the blackest poison of malice and invention.

This remarkably perceptive picture of Harley's organisation of political propaganda was wrong in only one point: he did not write the *Letter from a Foreign Minister*. It, too, was the work of an underling. On 17 October Harley received a letter from Abel Boyer: 'I presumed some days ago to send you by Mr Campbell a paper of my own composing, which has been well received both at home and abroad, where I hear it has been translated'.[83] At the end of July, while the Dutch were pressing Queen Anne not to reject her whig ministers, *A Letter from Monsieur Pettecum to Monsieur Buys* was published. Purporting to be authentic comments made by the French plenipotentiaries at Gertruydenberg regarding the ministerial changes in Britain, it was in reality another whig defensive measure to prevent an entire reconstruction of the ministry. The *Examiner* devoted considerable space in its early issues to refuting the *Letter*. Clearly Boyer designed to curry favour with Harley by doing the same.

Abel Boyer had periodically tried to gain Harley's patronage since 1704. At first he offered information, and Harley, as ever, encouraged him. But after Boyer asked for permission to publish a journal of Marlborough's successful Blenheim campaign, correspondence ceased until immediately after Godolphin's dismissal in 1710.[84] On 15 August Boyer again wrote to the new chief minister. He offered advice about the credit crisis, and he trusted that Harley would 'pardon the boldness of this overture, since it results from the entire devotion I profess to your service'. He wanted to 'shelter' under Harley's 'powerful protection'.[85] Boyer made further contributions to the Harleyite cause in 1710 after the publication of his *Letter*. 'I am now printing something towards the history of the last ministry and parliament', he wrote on 17 October, 'in which, I hope, I have given such a fair account of the great things you have done for this nation, as may in some measure contribute to allaying the present ferment'. This referred to *An Essay towards the*

History of the Last Ministry and Parliament, which was avowedly Harleyite. In many ways it foreshadowed Swift's *Conduct of the Allies* when it revealed that in 1706 Harley kept the queen informed of 'many things which others endeavoured to have kept from her knowledge, particularly some advances made by France towards a general peace after the Battle of Ramillies'.[86] This implies concert between Harley and Boyer over the *Essay*, which also dealt with the credit crisis and the dissolution of parliament. Contemporaries noted that it was 'much dispersed in town and country [to] justify the change of the ministry, and promote the elections of the friends to it'.[87]

Two other writers were recruited in 1710. They were to be Harley's most effective propagandists, Daniel Defoe and Jonathan Swift. Defoe's return to the Harley fold must be explained. He had served his whig employers diligently and loyally throughout the lean years of 1708 and 1709. He backed them up to the hilt during the Sacheverell trial and its aftermath. On Sunderland's fall from office he angrily denounced the failure to make a stand in his support, which allowed the ministerial changes to proceed piecemeal. He condemned whig policy when the 'game was all in their own hands [and] it was in their power to have crushed the [tory] party, and to have kept them where they were, viz., undermost for ever'.[88] When Godolphin was ousted, the *Review* vowed that 'if tories, if Jacobites, if High-Flyers, if mad men of any kind are to stay in, or come in, I am against them, I ask no favour, I make no court to them, nor am I going about to please them'. 'I hate turning sides', Defoe assured his readers, 'never did turn in my life, nor can I ever heartily trust a man that does'.[89]

It is somewhat ironic that all the time he was publishing cant such as this, Defoe was trying to pave the way to a reunion with his former employer. He wrote to Harley on 17 July, assuring him of his support in any scheme that consisted in 'healing the breaches on both sides which have thus wounded the nation'. 'If I can be useful in so good a work without the least view of private advantage I should be very glad', he concluded, 'and for this reason I presume to renew the liberty of writing to you which was once my honour and advantage, and which I hope I have done nothing to forfeit'.[90] Harley was more than happy to accommodate a prolific pen like Defoe's regardless of the sincerity of the man who wielded it. From July 1710 onwards the *Review* gradually began to assume a Harleyite position once more, and a meeting was arranged between the two men. 'I cannot but heartily congratulate you on the happy recovery of your honours and trusts in the government'. Defoe wrote on 12 August, 'Providence, Sir, seems to cast me back upon you (I write that with joy) and lays me at your door at the very juncture when she blesses you with the means of doing for me what your bounty shall prompt'.[91]

Defoe set about the supremely difficult task of calming whig anxieties over the credit crisis. His pen was a godsend to Harley at this juncture, when only Clement could be relied upon. The tories were doing all they could to frighten the remaining whigs into resigning. In September they finally succeeded when rumours of the approaching dissolution of parliament were seen to be genuine. On the 23rd, Cowper, the last of the old ministers resigned. Only Harley's old ally, Newcastle, remained of the whigs. The game was in Harley's hands. But it was a question whether he could implement his moderate policies while under pressure from the High Churchmen for more radical measures. The fall of the stock was proving too strong a phenomenon to be checked by the *Review*. 'To cry out we are all undone', Defoe was writing, 'is to make it so; to run down public credit, to break our bank, to tear ourselves to pieces – who do we serve? – this is to ruin the whole nation, and give ourselves up to France... It is every man's interest, therefore, to support credit, establish the currency of their annuities, etc., and stand by the Bank of England'.[92]

'The people are out of humour and alarmed', Defoe told Harley, 'and to speak to them in the public paper I write would be to do no good at all, yet they should be spoken to'.[93] Once again the call was to public opinion. Defoe met the contingency as best he could with *An Essay upon Public Credit*, which argued that credit was by definition in 'no way dependent upon persons, parliaments, or any particular men, or set of men, as such, in the world, but upon their conduct, and just behaviour'. To blame the fall of the stocks on the change of ministry was absurd. 'If men of moderation and men of integrity come in', wrote Defoe, 'I see no room to fear, but our credit will revive as well under a new ministry as an old'.[94] 'High-Flying is no more consistent with the administration now than it was before', the *Review* was urging, 'it is moderation only must do the thing... the only policy of the ministry is moderation, and that's still a whig, and hated as a whig'.[95] 'I am vain of saying, Sir, the first step I took has been successful, and has done more service than I expected', Defoe wrote to Harley on 5 September, 'the town does me too much honour in supposing it well enough done to be your own'.[96]

But Harley's finest move in the paper war was the enlistment of Jonathan Swift to support his growing army of writers. As it turned out, he was to be the Oxford ministry's most able propagandist, and his pamphlets display all the essential qualities of Harleyite propaganda requirements. His *Examiner* essays, his *Conduct of the Allies* and *Remarks on the Barrier Treaty*, and his shorter publications in prose and verse are the consummation of the particular brand of propaganda in which Harley placed most value. Swift's writings for the Oxford ministry provided guidance for ministerial supporters in the Commons in the absence of party whips. They explained ministerial policy, and put forward arguments that could be expounded over again in debate. But they had a dual purpose, and a dual effect. At the same time they appealed to public opinion – to the landed gentlemen who paid taxes and elected parliament men. If Harley could control the backbenchers in the Commons he could implement his policies. But he always had to keep in mind the political nation at large. They had elected the men in parliament. The first decade of the eighteenth century had demonstrated that a minority party in parliament could organise the people 'out of doors'. Harley did not want to lose the opinion of the electorate when in office.

This issue was rendered more vital by the very fact that Harley was already in danger of finding himself virtually alone, deserted by the mass of the tory party. At the polls, the voters reflected the swing of opinion away from the whigs, registering a tory landslide in the October elections. As soon as parliament reassembled, divisions could be discerned in the ranks of those tories who had been returned. Similar divergent opinions were apparent within the ministry itself, and they burst to the surface in the power struggle which developed between Harley and St John.[97] St John, Harley's former friend and subordinate, was a hard-line tory. He did not want a coalition government. He wished 'to fill the employments of the kingdom, down to the meanest, with tories'.[98] He wanted to root out the mismanagements of the discarded whig ministers, and to punish them severely. This was the attitude prevalent in his *Letter to the Examiner*. By February 1711 a backbench society had been formed, the October Club, which expressed similar feelings to those aired by St John. It was a massive group of independent country tories which sought to revive the idea of permanent opposition to the court in whatever guise it appeared. In theory the members refused to accept places in the ministry, albeit a tory one, much as Harley had done in the 1690s. Their motto was 'we will not be harled'.[99]

It was to be Swift's job to address these dissident tories. But Swift was a whig. His friends and allies were members of the Kit-Kat Club – Addison, Steele and Somers. Yet Harley baited the trap for the pen he most wanted to write for his cause, and Swift swallowed the bait. He arrived in London in September 1710 with a mission from the Irish Church to negotiate from Harley the gift of the first-fruits – Queen Anne's bounty – which had been granted to the English clergy in 1704. But when he sought out his old associates he was greeted far from amicably by the outgoing ministers. He was soon 'talk[ing] treason' against them, comforted by the knowledge that Harley had 'formerly made some advances' in his direction. Swift resolved to ditch the sinking whig ship. He composed a biting satirical poem at Godolphin's expense, *The Virtues of Sid Hamet the Magician's Rod*, which was shot through with phallic imagery, and far above the typical political doggerel that abounded in verse. Harley recognised Swift's hand in this poem.[100] By 30 September a meeting had been arranged between the two men. 'I am already represented to Harley as a discontented person, that was used ill for not being whig enough; and I hope for good usage from him', Swift wrote, 'The tories dryly tell me I may make my fortune if I please'.[101]

Unfortunately the details of Swift's cooptation onto the editorial board of the tory *Examiner* are missing. There is some evidence that William King had been acting as general editor of the paper until Swift took over.[102] According to Swift himself, however, the previous authors, St John, Freind, Atterbury and Prior, had 'grown weary with the work, or [were] otherwise employed'. It was therefore decided that Swift should 'continue it'.[103] Yet it seems that the original authors, including St John, were not consulted. Swift did not meet St John until 11 November 1710, by which time he had already contributed two essays to the paper.[104] His dealings had been almost exclusively with Harley, who needed, firstly, to neutralise the High Church propaganda of the original issues, and secondly, to convince the tories that, at the present juncture, unity was the watchword. He felt that he had such a writer in Jonathan Swift. 'I am inclined half to believe what some friends have told me', Swift wrote on 7 October, 'that [Harley] would do everything to bring me over'. As W. A. Speck remarks, it is likely that Swift was recruited to edit the *Examiner* 'in order to moderate its tone'.[105]

It was typical of Harley to choose a *quondam* whig to address the tories. Swift was a whig who also supported the established Church. He was a clergyman, but not a Low Churchman. This was something of a paradox. By definition, whigs were almost always Low Churchmen. A whig with High Church principles was almost a contradiction in terms. Harley was a whig with a dissenting background, and yet, in essence, he too was a High Churchman. Harley and Swift were two of a rare kind. Swift, like Harley, was imbued with country ideology. He 'split tickets' on the question of the dichotomy between whig and tory.[106] His views did not fall conveniently on one side or other of the party line; they straddled it. Swift used country rhetoric to address the tories in the *Examiner*, and yet he professed a belief in contract theory, not in an 'ancient constitution'. He was not inconsistent. He did not markedly alter his political opinions on entering Harley's camp. He simply had attitudes that, for his age, appear peculiarly conflicting.

Swift did not take much convincing that the landed man was suffering through the war, or that there had been a conspiracy between the Marlboroughs, the Junto, the allies and the monied men to sap the resources of landed wealth. He provided this retrospective account of his conversion to Harley's side:[107]

Mr Harley told me he and his friends knew very well what useful things I had written against the principles of the late, discarded faction, and that my personal esteem for several among them would not make me a favourer of their cause; that there was now an entirely new scene, that the queen was resolved to employ none but those who were friends to the constitution in Church and State, that their great difficulty lay in the want of some good pen to keep up the spirit raised in the people, to assert the principles, and justify the proceedings, of the new ministers.

Swift was to influence public opinion, and to maintain the 'spirit' of moderation and unity. Harley did not want the High Church reaction to obscure the moderate principles on which he hoped to found the new ministry. The tory resurrection was in danger of becoming a rout. Swift was to try to reconcile the country gentlemen to the real nature of the regime envisaged by the prime minister, much in the same way that Defoe, through the *Review*, was at the time trying to convince the whigs and monied men that an out and out High-Flying administration was not the desire of the new ministers.

These, of course, were the sentiments of *Faults on Both Sides*, and it is significant that in his first *Examiner* essay Swift announced his resolution 'to converse in equal freedom with the deserving men of both parties'.[108] His policy was 'to let the remote and uninstructed part of the nation see that they have been misled *on both sides* by mad, ridiculous extremes, at a wide distance on each side from the truth; while the right path is so broad and plain, as to be easily kept, if they were once put into it'.[109] This is a far cry from the extremism of St John, and the tone of the previously ultra-tory *Examiner* for some considerable time after Swift's recruitment bears out the assumption that Harley had enlisted his help for that very reason. In an attempt to operate a non-party system, Harley now had two periodicals, the *Review* and the *Examiner*, preaching moderation. As Defoe assured his audience, the newly-elected members of parliament[110]

will not run the mad length that is expected of them. They will act upon the Revolution Principle, keep within the circle of the law, proceed with temper, moderation and justice to support the same interest which we all have carried on, and all wish to be well carried on. And this I call being whiggish, or acting as whigs.

Daniel Defoe and Jonathan Swift were the mainstays of the Oxford ministry's propaganda machine. Harley had succeeded in winning over the two most potent pamphleteers of his day, and the curious thing is that at the beginning of the year they were both actively involved with the whigs. Defoe had been turning out pamphlet after pamphlet against Sacheverell and the change of government. Swift, in Ireland, had been watching political developments with growing dismay, as his friends appeared on the verge of dismissal. The simple fact that Harley should *bother* to accommodate men who had no real political power, and who might just as easily have been silenced, is a signal indication of his awareness of the importance of propaganda and the need to appeal to public opinion. Explanation was more beneficial to the new ministry than silence. Godolphin, on the other hand, had the chance to retain the loyalty of each man, and he let them both go. Defoe was in his employ. Swift he treated shabbily on his arrival in London, when his pen could have been crucial to the whig cause. Under the triumvirate Harley had created an unofficial government newspaper, the *Review*; now he had two, and he had two immensely talented writers to edit them. He had, at last, the means and the authority to put his press policy into practice.

Defoe and Swift proved to be an enviably effective propaganda team. Their skills were complementary. Between them, each hardly acknowledging the existence of the other, they supplied the Oxford ministry with a continuous output of pamphlets, periodical papers and broadsheets. Defoe was a master of Billingsgate, an everyday, mud-slinging scribbler who could give and take abuse and raillery, and still publish pamphlets that display more literary accomplishment than those of his competitors. He wrote answers 'as readily as the supposed author of Swift's *Tale*.[111] His prolific output is truly staggering. With Defoe on his side, Harley never lacked a voice in print. Swift's forte was the quality of his carefully-worded pamphlets and essays. Each contribution to the *Examiner* had a specific polemical point to make, and its message was communicated by a variety of stylistic methods – irony, hyperbole, parody, satire. His polished prose made him the obvious choice for the really important work, the *Conduct of the Allies*, for instance, the culmination of the ministry's peace campaign. But the creation of the government propaganda machine, however much the individual skills of the propagandists were their own, was due to Harley. Around Swift and Defoe he assembled a host of minor writers. He made further use of periodicals. By 1713 there was a pamphleteer and a vehicle for any theme Harley wished to pursue in print. On top of all this, he had the authority of government to regulate opposition propaganda. At last the press was beginning to be controlled by government without the imposition of a strict system of censorship.

6

Swift, Defoe, and the peace campaign

John Oldmixon remarked that Daniel Defoe and Jonathan Swift were 'fellow labourers in the service of the White Staff'.[1] Under the Oxford ministry Swift gradually assumed control of the tory propaganda machine. Not only the *Examiner* fell within his sphere of influence, even after he had finished contributing to the paper on a regular basis himself, but the other principal tory press organ, Abel Roper's *Post Boy*, was evidently in Swift's pocket. 'Roper is my humble slave', he once confessed, and there can be little doubt that the *Post Boy* was, in Irvin Ehrenpreis's words, 'the ministerial paper'.[2] But Oldmixon took a jaundiced view of the relative importance of the 'fellow labourers' to the Oxford ministry. He felt that Oxford paid Defoe better than he did Swift merely because he thought him 'the shrewder head of the two for business'. Defoe, like Swift, indulged in self-delusion. He preferred to think he had retained his integrity as a writer. But it was precisely this feature of his psyche which rendered him so very useful to Oxford. He made no pretence to political power, and his conscience could be readily eased by the application of specie.

Oldmixon, then, paid no heed to Swift's careful scrupulousness to retain his independence. He regarded Swift's pomposity with cool whig cynicism. Although he refused to take money for his services to the ministry, Swift expected to be rewarded with an English bishopric, or at least an English deanery. He sent Oxford reminders when suitable positions became vacant. And though he did not receive payment for his services, he was bribed with free dinners that eased the financial burden on the impecunious clergyman. True, a genuine friendly relationship did develop between the vicar of Laracor and the men in power, but both Oxford and Bolingbroke had a happy knack of avoiding the scrounging Doctor when his wit at table did not sufficiently compensate for his willingness to dine off the family joint. In early days

Oxford's 'lying porter', Read, often refused admittance to Swift on the pretext that his master was not at home. On one occasion Swift sent Oxford a bill including an item 'for a dinner I lost by your lordship's dining abroad'.[3] Subsequently Swift believed he had political influence in his own right, pooh-poohing any suggestion that he should leave the room when confidential government matters were under discussion, as he would have to justify them in print.[4] Certainly Swift did enter Oxford's house by the front door, and not, as Defoe was forced to do, by the back, but, as W. A. Speck remarks, White Kennett's description of Swift in 1713 is not of the truly powerful counsellor to the great, but of 'the complete hanger-on at court':[5]

Dr Swift came into the coffee-house, and had a bow from everybody but me. When I came to the antechamber to wait before prayers, Dr Swift was the principal man of talk and business, and acted as a Master of Requests. He was soliciting the earl of Arran to speak to his brother, the duke of Ormonde, to get a chaplain's place established in the garrison of Hull for Mr Fiddes, a clergyman in that neighbourhood, who had lately been in gaol, and published sermons to pay fees. He was promising Mr Thorold to undertake with my lord treasurer that, according to his petition, he should obtain a salary of £200 per annum, as minister of the English church as Rotterdam. He stopped Francis Gwyn, Esq., going in with the red bag to the queen, and told him aloud he had something to say to him from my lord treasurer. He talked with the son of Dr Davenant to be sent abroad, and took out his pocket-book and wrote down several things, as memoranda, to do for him. He turned to the fire, and took out his gold watch, and telling him the time of day, complained it was very late. A gentleman said he was too fast. 'How can I help it', says the Doctor, 'if the courtiers give me a watch that won't go right?'

Swift loved to play the courtier, and to emphasise his own self-importance. It is a different matter when it comes to assessing his real influence. Defoe (if we can believe his testimony) was presented twice to Queen Anne (in 1704 and 1708). It is ironic that Jonathan Swift, confidant of the most powerful men in the government, never even met the queen. When he was given the deanery of St Patrick's in Ireland she stressed that the gift was not hers, but the lord-lieutenant's![6] This complicates any account of Swift's role in the organisation of propaganda under the Oxford ministry. The attitude taken by both Oxford and Bolingbroke to Swift's proposed history of the peace-making illustrates his ambiguous position as *chef de propagande*. A distinction should be made between those pamphlets commissioned by the ministers, and those which Swift composed and published on his own initiative. The highly unenthusiastic response to the *History of the Four Last Years of the Queen*, which was never published in Swift's lifetime, is a clear indication of the relative importance, in the eyes of the ministry, of those pamphlets written to order, and the peripheral publications which were his own idea. To the government, Swift was the man for the really important and carefully-timed pamphlet that needed to have considerable care lavished on its production. The *Conduct of the Allies* is the perfect example of the 'commissioned' work.

For the commonplace exigencies of political propaganda Swift's independent attitude was simply unacceptable. He helped to ruin his own career in the Church by publishing *The Windsor Prophecy* without consulting any of the ministers. He was advised by Mrs Masham to recall the printed copies.[7] When he was asked to counter Steele's *Crisis*, Swift allowed his prejudices to get the better of him, introducing a totally needless attack on the Scots for which, had it not been for the ministry's protection, he would have been prosecuted.[8] Swift was undependable. His political judgment was not always sound. For these reasons his pen was reserved for specific polemical tasks, like the *Conduct*. Richard Cook pertinently observes that 'the immediate *raison d'être* of Swift's tory pamphlets was the molding of public opinion for *particular* political ends, and it is in terms of these persuasive goals that the tracts can be best understood'.[9] Swift's incomparable prose had little effect on the scribbling skirmishers who were constantly tearing at the coat-tails of the government.

But public opinion was crucial to the security of the Oxford ministry, and it was not sufficient to release the occasional polished pamphlet from the pen of Swift. A constant parading of ministerial views was what Oxford required, to prevent the whigs brainwashing the nation. The ministerial press machine was two-pronged: Swift drafted the polished government propaganda release; Defoe defended and justified the conduct of the government at all times. His role as ministerial propagandist was in total contrast to that assumed by Swift. Not only was he given the supremely difficult job of addressing the dissident whigs throughout the negotiations for peace, while Swift was aiming at the landed men who needed no convincing of the desirability of a settlement, but Defoe's main recommendation was his prolific output. He could turn out pamphlet after pamphlet without overstepping the line, and without the careful supervision which had to be exercised over the manifestos of Swift. Sometimes, it is true, he deliberately wrote *against* the government, especially after the appearance of the *Conduct of the Allies*, but at least he knew exactly what he was doing. Defoe picked up the scent where Swift left off. The learned Doctor pointed to the game, and

Defoe dutifully pursued it through the mires of Grub Street. Whenever Swift descended to such depths, it was as the dilettante amusing himself by indulging in the antics of the semi-illiterate. Yet this was the abuse in which Defoe had to deal, and Oxford did not dismiss Defoe's propaganda as lightly as did Swift. Nor did Defoe's enemies. In 1713 they arranged for his arrest to silence his pen (see below, pp. 172–3). Oxford recognised the overwhelming need for a propagandist like Defoe to battle daily with the hacks who made no pretence to the erudition of a Dr Swift.

The first objective of the ministerial writers was the stability of the regime. On 1 January 1711 Swift advised Stella to 'Get the *Examiners* and read them; the last nine or ten are full of the reasons for the late change, and of the abuses of the last ministry; and the great men assure me they are all true. They are written by their encouragement and direction'.[10] Swift's conversion to the ministerial attitude on the question of war and peace was vital to the peace campaign in print as it gathered momentum in the course of 1711. The ministry had been carried into office on a wave of war-weariness, and it had quickly set about the job of making peace. Secret negotiations were set on foot through the offices of the earl of Jersey. Soon these developed to a point at which their existence could be revealed in cabinet (in May 1711). In the summer Matthew Prior was dispatched to France. He returned in August with the French diplomat, Mesnager. Agreement was reached on the preliminaries upon which official talks could begin. The revelation of the Mesnager Convention would be made when parliament met early in December 1711. The entire programme of government propaganda in 1711 was organised with this distant end in view.

The question of peace had been raised during the paper wars of 1710. As well as the Harleyite pamphlets of Clement, Defoe and Boyer, Henry St John's *Letter to the Examiner* had argued that Britain had been tricked by her allies into taking part as principals in a war that was not really in her own interests, and that it had been prolonged in order to gain a more advantageous settlement for Holland and Austria while Britain footed the bill. Blame for this state of affairs was laid at the door of the Godolphin ministry. Swift was to take up and extend this 'conspiracy thesis'. While he concurred in most of St John's thesis, Harley, in August 1710, felt that it was a little premature, with stocks plummeting, to tell home truths that could be more opportunely told once the new regime was secure. The *Examiner*, from August to November 1710, continued to adopt an unconciliatory stance. Swift was given the responsibility of editorship to take the wind out of tory sails. He submerged the issue of peace underneath the more pressing problem of gaining widespread support for the change of ministry, and for the moderate policies envisaged by Harley.

But Swift gradually fell under the influence of St John, who encouraged him to assume a more aggressive stance. He became increasingly more outspoken about the conduct of the whig ministers just as the October Club was beginning to form. Throughout January 1711 Swift was closeted with St John in 'business' conferences. 'I think our friends press a little too hard on the duke of Marlborough', he wrote on 7 January, 'The country members are violent to have past faults enquired into, and they have reason; but I do not observe the ministry to be very fond of it'. At the end of the month, however, his attitude had changed. He had been 'forwarding an impeachment against a certain great person', Marlborough, with the secretary.[11] By March he was quite open about his censure of the captain-general. 'The *Examiners...*are written very finely, as you judge', he wrote to Stella, 'I do not think they are too severe on the duke; they only tax him with avarice, and his avarice has ruined us'.[12] This change of heart was mirrored in the *Examiner* itself, as Swift moved on from the brilliant 'letter to Crassus', which indicted Marlborough for avarice, to consider the original theme of the *Letter to the Examiner* which had lain unnoticed for so long. He revealed his design to examine 'the conduct of the late ministry, the shameful mismanagements in Spain, [and] the wrong steps in the treaty of peace...in a discourse by itself, rather than take up room here, and break into the design of this paper, from whence I have resolved to banish controversy as much as possible'.[13]

If Swift was unaware of the divergence of opinion between Harley and St John at this juncture (Harley later dated his split with the secretary from February 1711 and the emergence of the October Club),[14] he was soon given no cause to doubt that the friendship was not as firm as he might have first imagined. He had previously commented disapprovingly on the backbench willingness to embark on a witch-hunt, reminiscent of the events of 1701, to indict the whig ministers of corruption. Yet this was precisely what St John was advocating. 'We are plagued here with an October Club', Swift told Stella on 18 February, 'who...meet every evening...to consult affairs, and drive things on to extremes against the whigs, to call the old ministry to account'. 'The ministry is for gentler measures', he blithely continued, despite the fact that St John was arranging as best he could to enlist the support of the October men to oust Harley from the leadership of the tory party.[15] The vicar of Laracor was out of his depth in such in-fighting. He was apparently unconscious of the sympathetic change of emphasis he had allowed in the *Examiner*. He was totally ignorant of the strained relations between Harley and St John.

He was disillusioned after Guiscard's attempt to assassinate Harley on 8 March 1711. In the *Examiner* Swift gave an account of the incident, which, he noted in retrospect, he had from St John:[16]

The murderer confessed in Newgate that his chief design was against Mr Secretary St John, who happened to change seats with Mr Harley, for more convenience of examining the criminal. And being asked what provoked him to stab the chancellor, he said that not being able to come at the secretary, as he intended, it was some satisfaction to murder the person whom he thought Mr St John loved the best.

The various strands of unconscious irony in this passage added to the fact that this representation, as Swift later admitted, gave 'Mr St John all the merit, while Mr Harley remained with nothing but the danger and the pain'. He had, however, sent the *Examiner* in question to St John for his perusal before it was printed, and, significantly, the secretary 'made no alteration in that passage'. Naturally enough, St John's callous treatment of the affair, and his affectation that Guiscard's blow was meant for himself, outraged the Harley family, and we know that the prime minister himself was unusually touchy about accounts of the incident. Boyer may have lost his interest with Harley as a result of the relevant issue of the *Political State*. Manuscript notes on the prime minister's copy of Boyer's version of the affray decry many of the details as 'groundless' or 'false'.[17] Swift was finally shrewd enough to realise that he would offend should he repeat his original account of the affair in print. He left the official pamphlet narrative of the assassination attempt to Mrs Manley. 'I was afraid of disobliging Mr Harley or St John in one critical point about it', he explained to Stella, 'and would not do it myself'.[18]

The revelation that all was not as it should be between Harley and St John was quickly endorsed by rumours that the secretary was to be dismissed. 'I am heartily sorry to find my friend the secretary stands a little ticklish with the rest of the ministry', he wrote on 27 April, 'there have been one or two disobliging things that have happened, too long to tell'.[19] Swift continued to associate with St John, risking Harley's displeasure. It was at this time that Swift sought to redefine his position as editor of the *Examiner*. On 18 May he was 'hunting' the secretary 'about some business': the following day he was alone with Harley for two hours, 'where we talked through a great deal of matters I had a mind to settle with him'.[20] Four weeks later Swift completed his series of regular contributions to the *Examiner*. The two events were not unconnected. Swift did not see Oxford from 27 May until 21 June. Clearly the decision for him to relinquish the responsibility for editing the *Examiner* was taken in the week that Harley was elevated to the peerage as earl of Oxford and Mortimer, and this might well have been the business he sought to transact with St John and Harley on 18 and 19 May.

There are reasons to suspect that Swift's laying down of the *Examiner* was not really voluntary. Ostensibly the reason was that, with the parliamentary session at an end, the regime was sufficiently secure to stand in no further need of justification in print. But this would have been totally at odds with Oxford's views about propaganda, and the *Review* did not similarly go into liquidation. The *Examiner*, moreover, was quickly revived to counter the anti-ministerial propaganda of Oldmixon and Maynwaring in the *Medley*, and George Ridpath in the *Flying Post* and *Observator*. Only on the resuscitation of the *Examiner*, it is notable that the task of editorship was given not to Swift, but to Mrs Manley. 'As for the *Examiner*', Swift wrote on 7 June:[21]

I have heard a whisper that after that of this day, which tells what this parliament has done, you will hardly find them so good. I prophesy they will be trash for the future; and methinks in this day's *Examiner* the author talks doubtfully, as if he would write no more, so that if they go on, they may probably be by some other hand, which in my opinion is a thousand pities; but who can help it?

This is not the tone of a man willingly surrendering his position as editor. Seeking a redefinition of his situation, with the object, no doubt, a reassertion of his literary independence, Swift had been told that if he intended to write without consulting the general policies of the government, then his services were no longer required.

This, at least, would explain Swift's profound depression during the summer of 1711, and his pessimistic remarks to Stella:[22]

Remember if I am used ill and ungratefully, as I have formerly been, it is what I am prepared for, and shall not wonder at it. Yet I am now envied, and thought in high favour, and have every day numbers of considerable men teasing me to solicit for them. And the ministry all use me perfectly well, and all that know them say they love me. Yet I can count upon nothing...They think me useful. They pretended they were afraid of none but me, and that they resolved to have me. They have often confessed this. Yet all makes little impression on me. Pox of these speculations! They give me the spleen, and that is a disease I was not born to.

Swift, then, had been removed from the *Examiner* after displaying opinions too much like those of St John. Oxford wanted to influence the country gentlemen to exercise a little patience over the question of peace. He did not want to make a separate peace with France, contrary to the terms of the Grand Alliance. He consistently made a nice distinction between separate treating, and a separate, concluded peace. But, as Dr MacLachlan remarks, 'St John disapproved of the carefully contrived releases and disingenuous promises [which Oxford] eked out' to the Dutch: 'He preferred shock tactics – silence followed by a *fait accompli* delivered to The Hague'.[23]

This was, in essence, more than simply a disagreement over policy; it was a misunderstanding of Oxford's whole attitude to propaganda. The audience of the *Examiner*, it has been convincingly demonstrated, was made up principally of landed gentry and provincial clergymen.[24] As an organ of propaganda it was unrivalled in its capacity to influence these sections of the electorate. St John wanted to pervert Harley's message. He failed to comprehend that propaganda could play a vital role in the peace campaign. Oxford, on the other hand, fully appreciated the part that the press had to fulfil in the run-up to the meeting of parliament, when the question of peace would be in the forefront of affairs. Swift seemed to be in agreement with St John. He was relieved of responsibility for government propaganda until Prior arrived back in England with Mesnager.

At the end of July 1711 Oxford sent Swift a letter, 'with an offer of £50, to be paid to [him] in what manner [he] pleased; because, he said, he desired to be well with [him]'. Although he affected to be in a rage at the impertinence of the offer, Swift was soon writing on behalf of the ministry once again. 'The *Examiner* has been down this month, and was very silly the five or six last papers', he told Stella on 24 August, 'but there is a pamphlet come out in answer to the seven lords who examined Greg. The *Answer* is by the real author of the *Examiner*, as I believe, for it is very well written'. 'There is now but one business the ministry wants me for', he wrote on 25 August, 'and when that is done I will take my leave of them'.[25] This, apparently, is the first direct reference to the *Conduct of the Allies*. Oxford had engineered a reconciliation with Swift for a specific purpose – the mounting of the ministerial peace campaign. 'Do you know', Swift wrote to Stella, 'I have ventured all my credit with those great ministers to clear some misunderstandings betwixt them, and if there be no breach I ought to have the merit of it? 'Tis a plaguy ticklish piece of work, and a man hazards losing both sides. 'Tis a pity the world does not know my virtue.'[26]

Defoe, like Swift, was carefully coaxed back into line after a period of strained relations subsequent to a trip to Scotland in the government's service around the turn of the year 1710–11. While in Edinburgh he published a pamphlet called *Atalantis Major*. He was reluctant to own his authorship, equivocating shamelessly in a letter to Harley in which he asked the prime minister for his 'favourable construction' upon his conduct 'in an age so nice as this'. He pretended to be making an attempt to track down the author. 'I have some guess at the man', he claimed, 'but dare not be positive'.[27] After the assassination attempt Defoe was isolated from his benefactor for some weeks, and his conscience got the better of him. 'I am very unhappy not in my private affairs only, which are melancholy and ruinous from the discontinuance of your favour', he wrote on 19 June 1911, 'but in not having the occasion and honour of laying before your lordship several matters of importance relating to the public'. 'I had once, my lord, the honour of your promise that if I did anything offensive you would be my first reprover', he continued, 'if I knew anything in which I should displease your lordship, I should avoid it diligently'.[28]

The character of Oxford's relations with both Swift and Defoe is clarified by his conduct towards them in June and July 1711. Both men had overstepped the line. Oxford required subordination. But they were essential components of the propaganda machine. On 28 June the *Review* began a series of papers dealing with the south sea trade on the inauguration of the South Sea Company. 'I can no way express my humble thankfulness to your lordship for the relief which the return of your goodness and bounty has been to me', Defoe wrote to Oxford two weeks later, 'I extremely wish for an occasion to render myself useful, as the best method to show myself grateful'.[29] The peace campaign provided the opportunity to put Defoe's sincerity to the test. There was more to Oxford's programme in print than merely Swift's *Conduct*. Defoe paved the way for the reception of Swift's pamphlet. The 'peace crisis' best illustrates the two writers working in conjunction, and yet neither knew what the other was writing, nor indeed realised that the whole offensive was being coordinated by Oxford.

Douglas Coombs points out that Defoe had been 'commissioned to prepare the way for the simultaneous revelation of the second Mesnager Convention and of the expected Dutch acceptance of it'.[30] Whether or not St John approved of Oxford's 'carefully contrived releases', these were the tactics adopted by the ministry in the autumn of 1711. From Prior's return to England onwards the *Review* carried occasional papers on the state of war and peace, defending the intentions of the ministry:[31]

To give up Spain to the House of Bourbon is a thing so absurd, so ridiculous, you ought as soon to think of giving up Ireland to them. The reasons may hold on both sides alike, and the ruin of the English commerce may be argued equally from both...if we must make peace with the giving up of Spain, I hope, gentlemen, you will not do it sword in hand. It is time enough for that when you are beaten...that Spain should be abandoned...never entered any men's heads.

And yet this was exactly what Oxford was proposing to do, albeit with safeguards to ensure that the thrones of France and Spain would never be united. The time was not yet ripe for the telling of truths. The problem of revealing that there was to be peace without Spain had to be handled subtly. To the last, Oxford retained the hope that the Dutch would agree to the preliminaries that had been hammered out between France and Britain. His optimism was to prove to be well-founded.

The way in which Defoe's stance gradually altered *before* the publication of the *Conduct of the Allies* is striking. On 6 October he brought out *Reasons why this Nation Ought to put a Speedy End to this Expensive War: With a Brief Essay, at the Probable Conditions On Which the Peace Now Negotiating, may be Founded. Also An Enquiry into the Obligations Britain lies under to the Allies; and how far she is obliged not to make peace without them.* The very title of this pamphlet reveals its complementary nature with Swift's *Conduct of the Allies.* Still conciliatory, it nonetheless makes the point that peace must be made, and the insinuation that this might not necessarily embrace the allies is present. The idea was to be planted in the minds of the people, before the full-blooded peace manifesto was supplied by Swift. Defoe observed that the cost of the war had increased drastically since 1709, when, in negotiating with France, 'we treated them as if the King of Spain had been a prisoner of war, and the King of France fled from Versailles'. He emphasised that allied war aims had evolved since the signing of the Grand Alliance: 'The first pretence...the reducing the exorbitant power of France, by degrees this title to the war was dropped...and then we had it changed for these words: for the obtaining a lasting, safe, and honourable peace.'[32] Now, Defoe alleged, the whigs were trying to change the title 'a second time, and call[ing] it a war for the recovering the whole monarchy of Spain'. The original objective of the war, the reduction of the exorbitant power of France, had been achieved. Now the cry was for 'No Peace without Spain'.

Defoe stressed that peace was the solution, and peace could not be made without negotiation. Not content with expressing his views through the *Review*, Defoe adopted a variety of personae to drive home the same argument in a large number of tracts treating the same theme. He even denied the exact points put forward by the *Review* on occasion, to give the illusion of a number of propagandists urging essentially similar policies. Defoe was a team of government writers on his own; a team controlled exclusively by Oxford. Britain had borne the burden of the war, Defoe wrote (anticipating Swift), why could she not be trusted with making the peace? It was ridiculous to suggest that the allies were unaware of the British peace overtures, or that they would be excluded from a treaty. Again pre-empting Swift, he observed that it was not as if 'Britain was under the tutelage of the Dutch...or that their politics were the standard by which every step we took was to be tried...This is making such an idol of the Dutch as the Dutch themselves do not desire, *or can have reason to expect*'.[33] Leaving the possibilities open, Defoe energetically put forward the government line throughout October and November 1711 in battle with the skirmishers of Grub Street. Oxford was the influence behind Defoe's pen. 'I believe, my lord, I need not give your lordship an account how I am treated in print by the *Observator*', he wrote soon after the publication of the *Conduct of the Allies*, 'for espousing the just article of peace'.[34]

All the while Swift was painstakingly drafting the crucial pamphlet. 'I dined today in the city concerting some things with a printer, and am tomorrow all day busy with Mr Secretary about the same', Swift wrote on 30 October:[35]

I won't tell you now, but the ministers reckon it will do an abundance of good, and open the eyes of the nation, who are half bewitched against a Peace. Few of this generation can remember anything but war and taxes, and they think it is as it should be, whereas it is certain we are the most undone people in Europe, as I am afraid I shall make appear beyond all contradiction.

The manuscript of the *Conduct of the Allies* was circulated among the senior ministers for their comments and suggestions. St John was particularly active in supplying facts and information for inclusion in the pamphlet. But Oxford was the man behind the propaganda campaign, and he was consulted extensively about the content.[36] St John's *Letter to the Examiner* spelled out the attack on the allies, but the 'conspiracy thesis' in all its ramifications owed much to the bitterness of 'Plain English'. Swift intended to 'open the eyes of the nation, who are half bewitched against a Peace': the enchantment imagery of the *Dream at Harwich* and of 'Plain English' itself is once more in evidence. The drugged electorate was to be made aware of the scope of the designs of the family against the landed man. 'I cannot sufficiently admire the industry of a sort of men', Swift wrote:[37]

wholly out of favour with the prince and people, and openly professing a separate interest from the bulk of the landed men, who are yet able to raise, at this juncture, so great a clamour against a peace, without offering one single reason, but what we find in their ballads. I lay it down for a maxim that no reasonable person, whether whig or tory (since it is necessary to use those foolish terms) can be of opinion for continuing the war upon the foot it now is unless he be a gainer by it, or hopes it may occasion some new turn of affairs at home to the advantage of his party, or, lastly, unless he be very ignorant of the kingdom's condition, and by what means we have been reduced to it.

The *Conduct of the Allies*, at any rate, intended to remove any ignorance about the state of the nation. The polemical approach was essentially factual, with little trace of irony. It was an historical treatise presenting the treaty obligations of Britain and her allies, and the way in which the war had developed to the extent that they were now being wilfully ignored. Swift's evidence was supposedly objective. Of course it was far from being an unbiased account. But it informed the public without appearing to lead them by the nose, and this was the point. The trick was to provide the impression that they were drawing their own conclusions from the evidence supplied by Swift. The *Conduct* had a precise public relations job to perform. At the same time it had a specific political objective. This, in simple terms, was to provide a government line on the question of the conduct of the allies when the issue was debated in parliament. Oxford, as we have seen, was always keen to prepare the ground for the opening of a parliamentary session in the days before party whips. The climax of his propaganda programme was to create an atmosphere in parliament which would prove congenial to the revelation of the peace preliminaries. There was no doubt that the peace issue would be the main focus of discussion. The *Conduct of the Allies* was meant to counter whig cries of 'No Peace without Spain'.

Swift's thesis was straightforward: he claimed[38]

that no nation was ever so long or so scandalously abused by the folly, the temerity, the corruption, the ambition of its domestic enemies; or treated with so much insolence, injustice, and ingratitude by its foreign friends.

Through 'plain matters of fact' he intended to prove three points:

First, that against all manner of prudence or common reason we engaged in this war as principals, when we ought to have acted only as auxiliaries.

Secondly, that we spent all our vigour in pursuing that part of the war which could least answer the end we proposed by beginning of it, and made no efforts at all where we could have most weakened the common enemy, and at the same time enriched ourselves.

Lastly, that we suffered each of our allies to break every article in those treaties and agreements by which they were bound, and to lay the burden upon us.

In this way, Swift sought to pre-empt the expected complaint that the Grand Alliance had been transgressed by separate British negotiations with France. And by the exposition of the conspiracy thesis, aimed at the family and the monied men, he insinuated that the late ministers had been involved in a scheme to accrue to themselves all political and economic power in the state. This pricked the latent paranoia of the landed man:[39]

It is the folly of too many [Swift pointed out], to mistake the echo of a London coffee-house for the voice of the kingdom. The city coffee-houses have been for some years filled with people whose fortunes depend upon the Bank, East-India, or some other stock. Every new fund to these is like a new mortgage to a usurer, whose compassion for a young heir is exactly the same as that of a stockjobber to the landed gentry. At the court end of the town the like places of resort are frequented either by men out of place, and consequently enemies to the present ministry, or by officers of the army. No wonder, then, if the general cry in all such meetings be against any peace either *with* Spain, or *without*, which, in other words, is no more than this: that discontented men desire another change of ministry; that soldiers would be glad to keep their commissions; and that the creditors have money still, and would have the debtors borrow on at the old extorting rates while they have any security to give.

It might be thought that the sale of 11,000 copies of the *Conduct of the Allies* before the end of January 1712, the preparation of the seventh edition, and the fact that they were evidently 'sent in numbers into the country by great men, etc., who subscribe for hundreds',[40] are sufficient indications of its successful appeal to public opinion. Once again the importance of the physical size of a pamphlet is apparent. The fifth edition was printed 'in small', specifically for the purpose of distributing the copies across the nation.[41] Similarly the vote of the house of commons against the motion of 'No Peace without Spain' – the ostensible aim of the pamphlet – and its usefulness to the ministry in the debate on the conduct of the allies, when, as Swift jubilantly informed Stella, 'those who spoke drew all their arguments from my book, and their votes confirm all I write', would seem to point to the success of the peace campaign as handled by Oxford. Swift mentioned the court majority of 150, and explained that 'all agree it was my book that spirited them to these resolutions'. Ultimate justification, in Swift's eyes, was provided by the votes of the house. They were 'almost quotations' from the *Conduct*, 'and never would have passed if that book had not been written'.[42] The publication of the pamphlet, on 27 November, had been carefully timed to have the maximum beneficial propaganda effect. Parliament was due to debate the peace issue on 7 December, and the *Conduct* was confidently expected to stifle the 'No Peace without Spain' lobby. In the Commons the events had all gone according to plan.

It was not as simple as that. There was a large government majority in the Commons, but not in the Lords. In the upper house Oxford had to marshall his strength with caution. And in December 1711, at the height of the peace crisis, he was guilty of his most glaring failure in parliamentary management in the Lords. It was known that the earl of Nottingham would make a speech against peace without Spain. He had reached an agreement with the whigs on the issue in return for the safe passage of a diluted occasional conformity bill. Swift observed that Oxford spoke 'as if he wished a ballad was made on him'. In an incident that amounts to a considerable comment on the organisation of ministerial propaganda under Oxford, Swift resolved to 'get one up against tomorrow'.[43] The ballad, 'two degrees above Grub Street', was *An Excellent New Song, Being The Intended Speech of a Famous Orator against Peace*. It appeared on 6 December, the day before Nottingham's anticipated speech. Swift supplied Dismal with an alternative message, the gist of which was that no-one was to make peace, no matter how favourable or necessary, while Nottingham was '*Not in game*'. Despite a strong mutual antipathy between Nottingham and Oxford, the earl had expected a position in the tory ministry. One was never found for him. Clearly Swift got most of his information for the poem from Oxford and Dartmouth:[44]

> An Orator *dismal* of *Nottinghamshire*,
> Who has forty Years let out his Conscience to hire,
> Out of Zeal for his Country, and want of a *Place*,
> Is come up, *vi & armis*, to *break the Queen's Peace*.

Ironically Nottingham very nearly succeeded in doing precisely what Swift predicted, despite Oxford's preparations for the revelation of the Mesnager Convention. The prime minister failed to ensure that all the court supporters in the Lords had arrived in London by 7 December.

He might have adjourned the debate. Instead he allowed Nottingham and the whigs to pass a motion of 'No Peace without Spain'. His propaganda campaign did not prevent this check to the initiative for peace. Oxford saved the day by the unprecedented step of creating at a stroke twelve new court peers to reverse the decision of the house of lords. Now the peace programme was able to proceed according to plan. Swift did not defend the arguments he had propounded in the *Conduct of the Allies*. He worked on a sequel, *Some Remarks on the Barrier Treaty*, which appeared on 21 February 1712. It was Swift's final word on the question of peace. It dealt savagely with the pretensions of the allies, censuring Dutch high-handedness in the peace negotiations, and their overbearing demands for a secure barrier against French encroachments in the Netherlands. He suggested that 'a reasonable person in China... would conceive their High-Mightinesses the States-General to be some vast, powerful commonwealth, like that of Rome, and her majesty to be a petty prince', whom they could 'depose at pleasure'.[45] It had been left to Defoe to defend the points made in the *Conduct of the Allies*.

Some Remarks on the Barrier Treaty was a sequel in another sense, for it was published after the resolutions of parliament had made it quite clear that the ministry had triumphed on the question of peace. Defoe, with all his sympathy for the Dutch alliance, wrote in the *Review* on 23 February:[46]

1. The state of our late parliament resolutions can be understood to mean no more than to tell you all that the true reason why this war had not been long ago ended has been the deficiency of the confederates in their quotas and proportions, and tells you in particular where they are, and whose fault it has been.
2. That if these quotas and proportions had been paid duly, and the forces furnished, there would have been no more need to debate about carrying on the war, or making a peace, but it would have been over long ago.
3. That a treaty of peace is more reasonable for us now, if it were only to let our allies see that if they will not do their part we must be fools no longer.
4. And that if they will have us make no peace, but the war must go on, they must be more just and more punctual for the future.

Although this was a slightly more equivocal statement of the government attitude to war and peace, it illustrates the way in which Defoe was called upon to support Swift in print, and it provides a fine example of the chief ministerial propagandists working in tandem. *Some Remarks* came out on 21 February: Defoe chipped in with the *Review* two days later. 'It must be owned they have been very industrious to find advocates suitable to their cause', one opposition pamphleteer commented on the government's peace campaign, 'they have furnished the *Review* with arguments, and the *Post Boy* with history: but the one being never read, and the other only laughed at, it was necessary, at the opening of a new session, to have a master genius take the work in hand'.[47]

In *A Further Search into the Conduct of the Allies, And the Late Ministry, as to Peace and War*, Defoe noted 'the reception a former work of this kind has met with in the world, and the little which has been said against it as to matters of fact'. He imputed this 'to the truth, coming in with an irresistible force upon the minds of men, and which always carries its own evidence along with it'. This remarkably perceptive assessment of the polemical strategy of the *Conduct of the Allies* owed much to Defoe's own partial conversion to the government line. He admitted that 'few imagined' that the failure of the allies to meet their quotas would 'be so surprising, the account so large, and the particulars so many as they appear to be'.[48] Defoe's own incredulity must not be overlooked. He was a firm supporter of the Dutch alliance, yet he pointed to the votes of the Commons as proof of a fact 'which the credit of a single author was by no means sufficient for, viz., that the Dutch had any share in the deficiency, and in the injuries which this nation has suffered under the weight of this confederacy'.[49] On the appearance of the *Conduct of the Allies*, he had published *in defence* of the Dutch. *A Defence of the Allies and the Late Ministry*, although it praised the steps taken by the Oxford ministry towards a general peace, was, as its subtitle would suggest, 'A Detection of the Minifest Frauds and Falsities in a late Pamphlet, Entitled, *The Conduct of the Allies and of the late Ministry, in the Beginning and Carrying on the War*'.

Defoe's changing attitude to the conduct of the allies can be documented by his pamphlets and letters. *A Justification of the Dutch From several late Scandalous Reflections*, like the *Defence of the Allies*, actually went on the offensive to assert that 'the Dutch insist upon and require no more than what they ought to have'.[50] He was quickly disillusioned by Oxford about the stance he was to assume, and the official attitude to Swift's propaganda. Gradually he modified his views on the allies. The Emperor bore the brunt of his anger. In the *Review*, he 'could not but reflect, and that with regret, how many years ago this war had been finished in a happy, safe and honourable peace had the former Emperors but exerted themselves, as by their own interest, and their firm engagement to the allies, they were bound to do'. 'But the case is plain', he observed, 'the true German principle is to hold what they have, and make us fight for the rest'.[51] He pursued this line not only in the *Review*, but in pamphlets. *Imperial Gratitude, Drawn from a Modest View Of the Conduct Of the Emperor Charles VI...Being a farther View of the Deficiencies of our Confederates* alleged that 'the sum of the case is this: the Emperor will part with nothing, and we must fight on till we get him all'. Defoe asked all men to judge 'whether it is reasonable that we should carry on the war to oblige, and in dependence upon, the promises of *such* an ally?'[52]

Defoe turned out paper after paper on the question of war and peace. From October 1711 until July 1712, in addition to the thrice-weekly *Review*, he wrote no less than 13 pamphlets dealing with the issue. He argued for and he argued, in part, against the ministerial line, using an armoury of rhetorical devices and adopting a number of personae. In the end he toed the government line without flinching. 'It seems necessary, and I believe it is your lordship's aim, to have the Dutch friends and not masters, confederates not governors', he wrote to Oxford, 'and to keep us from a Dutch, as well as a French, management'. To this end he proposed the publication of pamphlets 'written without doors, and for the use of those chiefly who know nothing but without doors'. This was after the publication of the *Conduct of the Allies*, and the resolutions of parliament concerning the allies, and the object was to retain public opinion on the question of peace. *A Further Search into the Conduct of the Allies* and *Reasons against Fighting* were written 'to undeceive an abused people, and let them see how the whole nation was imposed upon'.[53] Finally Defoe was prepared to consider the possibility of going to war *against* the Dutch in *The Justice and Necessity of a War with Holland, In Case the Dutch Do not come into Her Majesty's Measures, Stated and Examined*. His conversion to Oxford's point of view was complete.

Swift's *Conduct of the Allies*, then, stimulated a lengthy controversy in print which was carried on for the government chiefly by Defoe. Swift contributed two major pamphlets to the peace campaign; one of them after the issue had, to all intents and purposes, been settled. Yet for the sake of the reputation of the ministry in the eyes of the electorate, Defoe defended it against all-comers. He prepared the way for the publication of the *Conduct*, and he cleared up the mess afterwards. Printed propaganda was used to the full in an attempt to channel the energies of the tory backbenchers into a position of solidarity over the peace question. They were spoon-fed with points to make in debate, and with ready-formulated resolutions on the conduct of the allies. At the same time Swift's manifesto was distributed widely to influence public opinion, and Defoe's back-up pamphlets were similarly published to keep those 'without doors' informed of the decisions of parliament, and the facts on which these had been based. The nation was saturated with the views and opinions of the ministers on the question of war and peace.

The peace campaign, therefore, is the finest example of the organisation of propaganda under the Oxford ministry. This account has been simplified to highlight the respective roles of Swift and Defoe. The government made use of many other writers, and their contributions will be noted in a later chapter, in contrast to the efforts of the opposition propagandists. But the basis of the propaganda offensive was supplied by Swift and Defoe. Swift was the gentleman-writer, adopting an attitude of ill-concealed exasperation that it was necessary to explain such self-evident matters at all. He presented a full-blown conspiracy thesis in which the tory country gentlemen wished to believe. After all the October Club had been formed with the intention of enquiring into the mismanagements of the late ministry. Now Swift was supplying evidence of the corruption they had implicitly but vaguely suspected all along. Defoe was the ministerial whipping-boy, shielding Swift from the party hacks who were after the blood of the man who had written the *Conduct of the Allies*. He reiterated the themes propounded by Swift. Oxford's organisation of political propaganda was well thought out, and admirably thorough. Suitable editions of the *Conduct* were printed to be 'sent in numbers into the country by great men'. Here we can recognise Oxford's concern for the effective distribution of his propaganda. The pre-publication copies of the *Conduct* had been similarly sent to 'the great men', and Oxford had had it 'by him on the table' when Swift called on 27 November.[54] Swift's reference, then, would appear to have been euphemistic. The suggestion is that bundles of his pamphlet were dispatched through a system comparable to that which obtained during Oxford's time as secretary of state. Perhaps it was the one established by Defoe. Some of his pamphlets were specifically designed to meet the demands of public opinion. By the end of the parliamentary session in 1712 the ministry was secure, peace had been won, and public approval of the government was assured. Oxford could turn to the problems raised by the freedom of the press and ponder the alternatives. The result was the stamp act of 1712.

7

The stamp act of 1712

The institution in 1712 of a stamp duty on pamphlets and newspapers by the Oxford ministry marks a crucial change in government thinking about the press. A return to press regulations did not take place. The stamp act – an entirely new piece of legislation – continued in operation until 1885. Walpole retained his predecessor's measure, increasing the levy, and he was imitated by successive governments throughout the eighteenth and nineteenth centuries until it reached a maximum of fourpence on all newspapers. Advertisements, taxed in Oxford's original duty, were subject to particularly heavy tolls. This was a far cry from the halfpenny tax imposed by the Oxford ministry in 1712, but the solution to the problem of maintaining some sort of control over the press which was worked out under Oxford, if not by him, was the foundation of the new system. The licensing system, as it turned out, had finally been superseded by a different attitude towards literature, which attempted not to suppress it, but to exploit its popularity.

The break with the past is more striking than merely this, however, for the Oxford ministry deliberately and determinedly blocked more repressive steps to reintroduce press regulations. When the house of commons, in April 1695, refused to concur with the demands of the Lords for a renewal of the licensing system, the reasons given were based on the assumption that the act was 'a law which in no wise answered the end for which it was made'.[1] Many attempts were made between 1695 and 1702 to restore official control over the press, some involving modifications of the licensing system. When, in January 1702, Harley, as speaker, advised Archbishop Tenison to introduce a bill in the Lords if he considered it necessary, it seems his Grace did just that (see above, p. 55). Although it was rejected on a third reading on 22 January it proved sufficient for the Commons to order the appointment of a committee to look into the problem of seditious libel. Fifty-seven members were named, including those future champions of the stamp act, Harley and Walpole.[2] The resolutions of this committee were not recorded, but the accession of Queen Anne witnessed a High Church motion, in 1704, for restraining the predominantly whiggish press (see above, p. 68). The measures proposed envisaged a return to the old licensing system. Defoe agreed that 'the offences of the pen' ought to be brought 'to a regulation', and he called for the registration of all printing presses, and the acknowledgement of authorship on the title-page of pamphlets. Nonetheless he damned the old system of censorship *per se*.[3]

The situation was largely unaltered on Harley's return to office in 1710. No new regulations had been imposed, though many had been suggested. Instead successive queen's speeches, and a royal proclamation, had decried the licentiousness of the press. Similarly, on 19 January 1712, Queen Anne sent a message to the Commons regarding the proliferation of libellous and scandalous publications. 'This evil seems to be grown too strong for the laws now in force', the message ran, 'it is therefore recommended to you to find a remedy equal to the mischief'.[4] This was the first official statement about the press under the Oxford ministry. The tory majority in the Commons resolved to 'effectually cure the problem'. Once more a parliamentary committee was set up to look into the question of press regulations. For some little time afterwards nothing happened. Finally the resolution to deal with the press was stiffened when a complaint was made about a 'pretended Memorial', printed by the whig *Daily Courant* on 7 April 1712, which reflected upon the proceedings of the house. On 12 April a committee of the whole house met to consider the import of the queen's message in the light of this 'false, scandalous, and malicious libel'.

The report was due to be read on 15 April 1712; it was finally considered on 3 June. It had been put off no less than seven times.[5] It called for the registration of all printing presses, and advised the house that 'to every book, pamphlet, and paper, which shall be printed, there be set the name, and the place of abode of the author, printer, and publisher thereof'.[6] But the bill was lost after its second reading when parliament was prorogued on 8 July 1712. In the meantime a duty on printed paper had been introduced, and it had proceeded onto the statute-books. This tax had not even been considered in parliament when the committee of the whole house debated the queen's message on 12 April. The report of the committee was due to be read, after its initial postponement, on 22 April. It was again put off. Instead, on the same day, the committee of ways and means reported several resolutions concerning stamp duties on paper. It was proposed that a tax be levied on 'all pamphlets and newspapers, printed or written'. This passed the house of commons, and received the royal assent on 22 May 1712 (10 Anne c. 19). It effectively prevented the institution of a more rigorous system of censorship based on compulsory imprints bearing the names of the author, printer and publisher of each individual book, pamphlet or paper. By the time the resolutions of the committee on the queen's message were reported to the house, the stamp act was in being, and the implementation of a tax on newspapers and pamphlets, starting on 1 August 1712, was imminent.

This, then, was the genesis of an act which was to remain on the statute-books for over a century and a half. Clearly some problems of interpretation are raised. Was the introduction of a system of compulsory imprints intentionally prevented, and, if so, why? What was a stamp duty expected to achieve? What of the queen's message to the Commons relating to the licentiousness of the press? Did this envisage taxing the press, or, as seems more likely, its repression? 'The parliament, by the queen's recommendation, is to take some method for preventing libels', Swift wrote on 26 February, 'I don't know what method they will take'.[7] But Swift was premature in his news, and the stamp act hardly fulfils the description of 'a method for preventing libels'. The question of the effect of the stamp duty on the circulation of pamphlets and newspapers will have to be considered in due course, but more immediate issues are raised by the very institution of the tax.

Although the Radnorshire address had spoken out against the books and pamphlets 'that have been industriously dispersed and encouraged ...in order to foment divisions',[8] Harley displayed no urgency to deal with the press on his return to office. He appreciated, none better, the rudimentary nature of the proscriptive machinery of government, but he appears to have gone to the opposite extreme to eschew the prosecution of his opponents in print. This was part of his twin policy of propaganda and proscription. The peace campaign illustrates the interaction between the two: at the same time that Defoe was preparing the way for Swift's *Conduct of the Allies*, Secretary St John began to flex his official muscles. The contrast between the lenity of the first year of the new ministry and the burst of activity which occurred in the autumn of 1711 was brought home by Oldmixon, who complained that 'on the first day of the term fourteen booksellers, printers or publishers, who had been seized and confined by warrants from Secretary St John, a great painstaker in such dirty work, appeared at the Queen's Bench bar, for printing and publishing some pamphlets and ballads on the managers of the peace'.⁹ 'We are fain to send messengers among your printers and booksellers', another contemporary observed, 'to stop a little this madness and folly of the press'.¹⁰

The impression given is not that the Oxford ministry from the outset chose ruthlessly to proscribe its opponents. Rather it indicates that until the lead-up to the peace crisis the government had been unduly lax in dealing with the opposition propagandists. Further evidence of this comes from an unexpected quarter. Marlborough had already complained about the treatment he was receiving in print to St John, who assured the duke that he had given a 'proper hint' to the editor of the *Examiner*.¹¹ In the autumn of 1711 Marlborough again contacted the ministry about the press. This time Oxford himself dealt with the captain-general's complaints. Marlborough had been besieging Bouchain in the *Ne Plus Ultra* line of French fortifications in Flanders. It fell on 3 September – it was the duke's final military victory. On 19 October he wrote to Oxford about several printed libels. 'The title of one is *Bouchain*', he noted, 'and the other an answer to it'. 'The authors of these papers... are not only my enemies', he continued, 'they are yours, too, my lord, they are enemies to the queen, and poison to her subjects'.¹²

Interpretation of the sincerity of Marlborough's motives is complicated by the probability that his own apologist, Francis Hare, was responsible for *Bouchain: Or, A Dialogue between the Medley and the Examiner*. Mrs Manley forwarded 'Dr Hare's pamphlet of *Bouchain*' to Oxford, with the assurance that she had penned the ministerial reply, *A New Vindication of the Duke of Marlborough*.¹³ Presumably it was, in fact, Mrs Manley's pamphlet to which Marlborough took exception. A rejoinder, *The Duke of Marlborough's Vindication, In Answer to a Pamphlet falsely so called*, quickly made its appearance. Nonetheless Oxford's swingeing reply to Marlborough is worth considering for the light it brings to bear on his thinking about the press:¹⁴

When I had the honour to be secretary of state, I did, by an impartial prosecution, silence most of [the party writers] until a party of men for their own ends supported them against the laws and my prosecution... I have made it so familiar to myself by some years experience that, as I know I am every week, if not every day, in some libel or other, so I would willingly compound that all the ill-natured scribblers should have licence to write ten times more against me on condition that they would write against nobody else. I do assure your Grace I neither know nor desire to know any of the authors, and

I heartily wish this barbarous war was at an end. I shall be very ready to take my part in suppressing them.

Although Oxford, like Marlborough, was equivocating when he pretended entire ignorance of the authors of the pamphlets in question, it should not be allowed to obscure the fact that he promised to look into the problem. 'The queen ordered last Sunday night in cabinet', he continued, 'that the authors of all libels shall be impartially sought out and punished'. This, surely, is the crucial step along the road to legislation. Swift observed that it was St John 'who advised the queen in that part of her message' to the house of commons on 17 January 1712 relating to the press. According to Swift, St John 'had only then in his thoughts the repressing of the political and factious libels'. Significantly, he continued: 'I think he ought to have taken care, by his great credit in the house, to have proposed some ways by which that evil might be removed, the law for taxing papers having produced a quite contrary effect, as was then foreseen by many persons and hath since been found true by experience.'[15] The stamp act did not result in the suppression of political literature. But was it meant to? Rather, I think, St John envisaged a more repressive system of controls. Irvin Ehrenpreis suggests plausibly that St John was the man behind the move for the reinstitution of press regulations, concluding that he 'invented' the stamp act 'as a new repressive measure'.[16] David Stevens also refers to the new tax as the climax of 'Bolingbroke's repressive campaign'.[17] They are correct in assuming that the secretary wished for a strict system of censorship, but this was not the stamp act. He desired the registration of printing-presses, and the implementation of a system of compulsory imprints, in order to maintain close control over the press. This, surely, is what he envisaged when he composed the section of the queen's message relating to the press. As his bill was headed off in the Commons, so his policy was superseded by Oxford's new thinking about the press.

Ehrenpreis observes that 'Bolingbroke's attitude towards the Fourth Estate was much more like Swift's than like Oxford's'.[18] 'A rogue that writes a newspaper called *The Protestant Post Boy* has reflected on me in one of his papers', Swift told Stella on 10 October 1711, 'but the secretary has taken him up, and he shall have a squeeze extraordinary'. He promised to 'Tantivy' Boyer 'with a vengeance'.[19] This humanitarian attitude to his brethren of the quill was censured most strongly by Boyer in later years:[20]

what man in power ever used it with more wantonness, insolence, and severity than Henry St John, while secretary of state? His barbarities in such prosecutions are notorious. Among the rest, a harmless woman that kept a pamphlet-shop without Temple-Bar, for selling the Hanover Ballad, and publishing the *Protestant Post Boy*, (written by Mr Philip Horneck and Mr A. Boyer, the editor of this *Political State*) was by him committed to Newgate, where she died with hard usage...Mr Boyer himself was by this hare-brained Titan's orders twice taken into custody, and prosecuted upon very slight pretences.

Although, as Phyllis Guskin remarks, Sarah Popping, who published the *Protestant Post Boy*, in conjunction with Benjamin Harris, was alive if not well in 1716,[21] Boyer's accusations were echoed by others. St John's 'repressive campaign', launched with Oxford's approbation at the height of the peace crisis in the autumn of 1711, was endorsed by Swift. 'The pamphleteers begin to be very busy against the ministry', Swift wrote on 21 September, 'I have begged Mr Secretary to make examples of one or two of them, and he assured me he will, they are very bold and abusive'.[22] Oldmixon viewed the stamp act as merely 'another instance of the ingratitude of these men, in offering to lay the least restraint upon printing'. He awarded St John pride of place as 'the greatest libeller and state ballad-maker in Britain'.[23] Clearly the secretary was regarded as the champion of censorship. The corollary to such a policy is surely not a stamp duty, but wide-ranging controls like those listed in the report to the Commons on the problem of regulating the press on 3 June 1712.

While St John's press policy appears to have consisted of the widespread adoption of censorship controls, Oxford still retained a belief in the use of selective proscription as a weapon to be wielded side by side with the dissemination of government propaganda. When, in January 1711, the committee of ways and means considered a proposal to stamp printed papers, Harley was still managing the supply.[24] Swift's recorded attitude is interesting. 'They are intending to tax all little printed penny papers a halfpenny every half-sheet, which will utterly ruin Grub Street', Stella was informed, 'and I am endeavouring to prevent it'.[25] He expressed his misgivings about the scheme to St John. Unfortunately the secretary's response was not reported. Whether or not Swift's efforts played a part in the rejection of the motion, it was delayed, not permanently blocked. And by 1712 Swift was more concerned at the failure of the stamp act to control the press. There is no evidence to suggest St John's interest in the levying of revenue on newspapers and pamphlets – his attitude throughout was repressive. The idea for a stamp duty was Oxford's.

The proposal to raise revenue by a stamp on printed paper was current soon after the lapse of the licensing act, as soon as it was realised that the tremendous growth in political literature would permit it. In 1704 an estimate of the circulation of the periodicals then in existence was sent to the treasury, along with a scheme to tax them.[26] Soon after the motion in parliament in 1711 to raise supply through a levy on paper, a schedule of proposals was sent to the treasury which included newspapers, under the heading 'things upon which money is like to be raised'.[27] By October, plans were on foot for the installation of four new presses for printing stamps. James Lightbody sent Oxford numerous suggestions for stamps of better quality that would not be as easy to forge as those then in regular use.[28] Although ostensibly these stamps were to be used for almanacs, by 1712 it was being said that they were 'for newspapers, almanacs, etc.' Preparations had already been made for raising revenue on printed paper when the queen's message regarding the licentiousness of the press was sent to the Commons. When the committee of the whole house, presumably under the leadership of St John, decided to adopt proposals leading to the institution of a system of compulsory imprints, the consideration of the committee's report was postponed for almost two months while the committee of ways and means rushed the stamp tax into law.

It would be misleading to suggest that Oxford was diametrically opposed to compulsory imprints. In theory imprints were already compulsory by the stationers' regulations, and it may well have been this to which Harley was referring when he reminded Tenison in 1702 of 'sufficient authorities given by the laws in being'. Defoe's *Essay on the Regulation of the Press* also argued for compulsory imprints in 1704. One of Oxford's memoranda reads: 'About regulating the press, see Scobell's *Collection*, folios 44 and 45'.[29] Scobell, in the pages to which Oxford was drawing attention, chronicled a commonwealth act 'against unlicensed and scandalous books and pamphlets, and for the better regulating of printing'. Again compulsory imprints are in evidence. Interestingly enough, though, this was also a revenue-raising device. Fines, levied by the stationers' company, were to be divided between the poor of the company and the commonwealth itself, 'to be yearly by them answered, and paid into the receipt of the public exchequer'.[30] Two schemes, with two very different ends, were being weighed in Oxford's mind in 1712.

Contemporaries debated the intent and consequences of the stamp act. Several petitions were submitted to the house of commons while the measure was under consideration. All were against the proposals.[31] *Reasons humbly offered to the Parliament, in behalf of several Persons concerned in Paper-making, Printing and Publishing the Halfpenny News-papers, against the Bill now depending* took the debate into print. Defoe was suspicious of the tax. He ridiculed those who predicted that 'the people will easily come up to the price, the papers will sell as before, and a great sum of money will be levied by it'. 'Little taxes raise great sums of money, great taxes none at all', he warned, 'little taxes give spirit to trade, great ones smother it'.[32] It is noteworthy that in committee the proposed duty was cut from a penny to a halfpenny, apparently for reasons similar to those aired by Defoe. As I have remarked, Swift was against the tax. His misgivings were twofold. Firstly he did not think it would effectively prevent the publication of libels (despite his dire prediction on the implementation of the tax that 'Grub Street is dead and gone').[33] Secondly, the imposition of a system of compulsory imprints would have suited him much better on a personal level, as well as being more likely to discourage the opposition writers. As a government-backed pamphleteer, he had little to fear from press regulations on the purely practical level. But taxes on pamphlets affected his activities too.

Swift's feelings can be documented. His reaction to the failure of the bill for registering printing presses was bitter disappointment. It is true, as Irvin Ehrenpreis remarks, that Swift was against one clause in the bill. He did not want the author's name to be included in an imprint. Again this was for mainly personal reasons.[34] But he was in favour of the rest of the proposed press regulations, as his account in the *History of the Four Last Years of the Queen* makes clear:[35]

a bill for a much more effectual regulation of [the press] was brought into the house of commons, but so late in the session that there was no time to pass it...However it came about this affair was put off from one week to another, and the bill not brought into the house till the 8th of June. It was committed three days later, and then heard of no more.

Swift was clearly a sponsor of this bill. It was for 'a much more effectual regulation' of the press; it did not seek to raise money by it. The almost off-hand 'however it came about this affair was put off from one week to another' indicates profound dissatisfaction with the outcome. Swift criticised St John's handling. He felt 'he ought to have taken care' to secure the enactment of press regulations, not a tax.[36] The implication is that the secretary failed to manage the Commons on this occasion, as he had failed in the past over other matters.[37]

But someone sponsored the stamp act. It appears that ministerial thinking altered in the course of the session. A system of compulsory imprints was replaced by a scheme to raise revenue by the press. The tax was, no doubt, intended to fulfil two functions. It would act as a restraint on the publication of opposition propaganda without ruining the book trade. We have Swift's sentiments on the inefficacy of the stamp act in silencing the whig press, but this was retrospective. One contemporary explanation of the measure was simply that 'some members' in the committee of ways and means 'suggested a more effectual way for suppressing libels, viz., the laying a great duty on all newspapers and pamphlets'.[38] It was genuinely feared that the book trade would suffer severely as a result of the tax. Representatives of the trade offered to implement more far-reaching controls voluntarily if the levy were to be lifted. Significantly, this was refused, although the tax was reduced to a halfpenny on broadsheets, and a penny on pamphlets up to and including a folio sheet in size.

It is evident that there was some little debate as to the relationship of the stamp act and the proposed bill for the registration of printing presses, and whether resolutions reached in the committee of ways and means would interfere with those of the committee on the press. 'So many difficulties arose in this affair that it was thought fit to leave it as they found it', one writer explained, 'only a good tax was laid upon all paper, pamphlets and newspapers, to punish the licence of the proprietors'.[39] In the pro-ministerial *Plain Dealer*, William Wagstaffe discussed the motion for registering printing presses. He concluded that 'it is impossible for the invention of man to contrive a law as shall put an effectual stop as we could desire, *without a total suppression of the press*'.[40] In essence, this was Oxford's attitude, and he did not intend to silence the press altogether. 'We have a ministry, the readiest to patronize, and the best qualified to judge', Wagstaffe explained, 'who will refine our wit, and cultivate our knowledge, as they improve our trade, and revive the genius of the nation, as they restore her credit'.[41]

Oxford did not expect the stamp duty to raise large amounts of revenue. Yet supply was on his mind nonetheless. David Stevens writes that the act 'was not made chiefly for revenue purposes, but with the hope that the charges might prove prohibitive for the whig journals'.[42] There is truth in this, as we shall see. The stamp act was meant to exercise some degree of control over the press. But the avidity of Oxford to have regular, accurate statements of the number of stamped sheets purchased by the printer of each newspaper on the inauguration of the duty on 1 August 1712 indicates that, at any rate, the prime minister was not indifferent to the revenue factor. Over £1,000 was levied during the first seven weeks of the tax on newspapers alone. True, this amount was tiny, in a total budget of around £7 million p.a. The yield for advertisements and pamphlets was even smaller. In the whole of the first year of the tax adverts raised £911 16s. 0d., and pamphlets £133 5s. 0d.[43] These figures were gross. The running costs of the scheme were, no doubt, extremely high. As one contemporary observed, 'whatever may be represented to the contrary by private persons, for their own ends, experience shows that the greatest part of the duty will be spent in the salaries of commissioners and other officers to levy it'.[44] It would be reasonable to assume that the net revenue of the stamp act in the first year of its existence should be calculated in thousands, not tens of thousands, of pounds.

But it was not as simple as that. The stamp act has been dismissed as a revenue-raising device because its yield was so small. Such an interpretation is grounded on a fundamental misunderstanding of the scheme. Narcissus Luttrell provides an important clue to Oxford's real purpose. On 20 January 1711 he reported a motion in the committee of ways and means 'for laying 1d. per pound on English hops, and 2d. upon Flemish; and a stamp upon printed papers'. The revenue raised in itself by these measures would be limited, but they were accompanied by 'a proposal for raising a million and a half by way of lottery'. The money which came from the stamp act in 1712–13 was similarly intended for a lottery. Lotteries were big time. In a budget of £7 million per annum the odd thousand pounds raised by a stamp act might be neither here nor there. But £1,500,000 raised by a lottery which in its turn had been funded by the returns of the stamp duty is a different matter. As Luttrell noted on 23 January: 'Yesterday...the Commons... were in a committee upon ways and means for a fund for the new lottery'.[45]

Oxford, then, did not want to destroy the press through the stamp act. It was primarily a revenue-raising device. Swift's reaction was based on a misinformed opinion of what the prime minister was up to. The stamp act did not destroy Grub Street, though the first shock of the duty was severe enough. 'The *Observator* is fallen, the *Medleys* are jumbled together with the *Flying Post*, the *Examiner* is deadly sick', Swift informed Stella, 'the *Spectator* keeps up, and doubles its price'.[46] The act was one more nail in the coffin of the ailing *Review*. Defoe reduced the number of issues to two per week, selling at 1½d., including the halfpenny tax. By this strategem he hoped to encourage subscribers to pay the same amount each week for less printed matter, and he published on paper of better quality. But by now the *Review*'s circulation was no more than 400 to 500 per edition.

The weekly sales of newspapers have been calculated as falling *in toto* from a figure of 67,000 to around 44,000 – a circulation figure passed as early as 1705.[47] At least five periodicals appear to have published their last on the institution of the stamp duty: the *Observator*, the *Medley* (which Swift said was 'jumbled together' with the *Flying Post*), the *Plain Dealer* of William Wagstaffe, Boyer's *Protestant Post Boy*, and the *Supplement*.[48] But there was no absolute decline in the circulation of newspapers. Swift's early pessimism was quickly belied in a way of which he did not approve. 'These devils of Grub Street rogues that write the *Flying Post* and the *Medley* in one paper will not be quiet', he wrote on 28 October 1712: 'They are always mauling lord treasurer, Lord Bolingbroke and me. We have the dog under prosecution, but Bolingbroke is not active enough. But I hope to swinge him. He is a Scotch rogue, one Ridpath. They get out upon bail, and write on. We take them again, and get fresh bail, and so it goes round.'[49] It was for reasons such as these, no doubt, that Swift was so antipathetic to the stamp act after it had been introduced.

Surprisingly, the stamp tax had very little effect on the number of pamphlets and poems that were published once the initial shock wore off. Only when we compare figures for 1713 with those of the peak years of 1710 and 1714 can be discern a decline. Morgan's *Bibliography* lists 720 items for 1713, compared with 493 in 1709.[50] His collection is, of course, by no means complete, but it might be used as a crude guideline. By 1714 the book trade had recovered completely from the imposition of the stamp duty. Maxted's figure for 1714 is the highest in the whole of the eighteenth century. He calculates that 1,006 items were published that year.[51] Admittedly figures for 1710 to 1713 are missing, and it is likely that the exceptional events of 1710 resulted in more publications than in 1714. But even these tentative records permit the conclusion that the stamp act did not have any significant long-term effect on the growth of the book trade. Foxon's *Catalogue of English Verse* endorses this interpretation. One hundred and forty-two poems are listed from 1711, 171 from 1713, and 188 from 1712 itself.[52] But the poem on affairs of state seems to have suffered an absolute decline. Only 25 have survived from 1713, compared with 82 from 1711 and around 65 from 1712. Perhaps, as W. A. Speck surmises, 'the genre was becoming less fashionable'.[53] The *annus mirabilis* of the poem on affairs of state was 1710.

The political pamphlet, then, continued to harass the Oxford ministry. This must represent a partial failure of its press policy. While the stamp act was designed to fund a lottery, it was also intended to reduce the amount of opposition propaganda that found its way onto the streets. This much can be assumed from Oxford's words to Marlborough in the autumn of 1711. But the government was forced to make further official statements about the press after the introduction of the stamp act. When Queen Anne opened parliament on 9 April 1713, her speech included a paragraph relating to the press. Swift had a hand in this carefully-worded address, which ran:[54]

I cannot, however, but expressly mention my displeasure at the unparallelled licentiousness in publishing seditious and scandalous libels. The impunity such practices have met with has encouraged the blaspheming everything sacred, and the propagating opinions tending to the overthrow of all religion and government. Prosecutions have been ordered, but it will require some new law to put a stop to this growing evil, and your best endeavours in your respective stations to discourage it.

In the last year and a half of its existence, the Oxford ministry had to turn to proscription to combat the propaganda campaign launched by the whigs. Their writings were subsidised quite heavily after the implementation of the stamp act, and this partly accounts for the failure of the tax to stem the flow of publications. Ridpath, editor of the *Flying Post*, decided to flee the country, while Richard Steele was expelled from the house of commons for writing seditious libel. The old, ambiguous laws governing libellous and treasonous publications were still the only means of prosecuting printers, publishers and authors. The licensing system was not revived. To point to the stamp act, therefore, as an instance of the Oxford ministry's repression of the press seems specious. The government had allowed opportunities for introducing more stringent regulations to pass. After the creation of the twelve peers, there was no practical reason why the government could not impose press legislation had it wished to do so. We must assume that Oxford did not desire to operate a system of rigorous censorship.

This is not meant to imply that Oxford was entirely happy with the situation, especially in 1714, or that he failed to appreciate the shortcomings of the ministry's press policy after the initiative had been seized by the whigs. His positive answer to propaganda threatened to rebound on him dangerously as the whigs finally learned to recognise the benefits of a concerted press programme. Godolphin had never imagined that printed propaganda could be anything other than, at best, a necessary evil. Walpole developed the policies ultimately adopted by the whigs in 1713–14 relating to the press, but they owed everything to Oxford. Even if he did not come up with satisfactory solutions to all the problems posed by the increase in the production and circulation of political literature after the expiry of the licensing act, it was nonetheless the stimulus provided by Oxford to find answers that did not involve censorship as such, which led to the imposition of a stamp duty instead of an extensive system of controls. Perhaps, had the ministry survived for any considerable time after the experience of Steele's trial and Swift's impending prosecution for the *Public Spirit of the Whigs*, Oxford would have reconsidered the question of censorship. He had chosen, in 1712, to use the stamp duty to attain a twofold aim: the raising of revenue, apparently to fund a lottery; and to maintain some sort of curb on the licence of the opposition propagandists. In so doing, he had shelved the question of the registration of printing presses, and the imposition of compulsory imprints. But it was only shelved. The threat, aired in the queen's speech on 9 April 1713, that 'some new law' would have to be found to discourage the licence of the press indicates that this was the case. Oxford had experimented with a stamp duty, and in some ways it had been found wanting. The 'new law' was almost certainly envisaged as a system of compulsory imprints. As it stands, however, the stamp act must be assessed in terms of the Oxford ministry's reluctance or inability to introduce regulations. In the long run it might have benefited more by operating a strict system of controls. Walpole, however, retained the stamp duty. The growth of government tolerance of the press owes a great deal to Oxford's determination to organise political propaganda on an effective scale, and not a little to the institution of the stamp act.

8

The organisation of propaganda, 1710–1714

Although Defoe and Swift were the biggest wheels in the government's propaganda machine, there were other cogs to ensure its smooth functioning. Defoe, again in contrast to Swift, was a loner, and he was probably the only propagandist with whom Swift had no contact, and over whom he exercised no control. Oxford retained Defoe's services as a personal propagandist. Not even Bolingbroke was aware of the prime minister's connections with Defoe. But a team of writers surrounded Swift on the tory side, and in this sense he can be said to have organised government propaganda for the Oxford ministry. He was the middle man between the ministers and both the party hacks and the printers. His opinion was sounded on the quality of tory propaganda, and on the need for pamphlets on certain questions. Although this was evident as early as the spring of 1711,[1] it was really only after the resolution of the peace crisis a year later that he began to act as *chef de propagande*. He was free from the responsibility of regular editorship of the *Examiner*, and he had no major writings to prepare. 'I have nothing to do now, boys', he wrote on 29 February 1712, 'and yet I was dictating some trifles this morning to a printer'.[2] After the anxieties of December 1711 and Oxford's creation of twelve court peers, the government propaganda machine was able to tick over under its own steam, with the minimum of ministerial supervision. Swift came into his own. St John continued to consult him, especially concerning the imminent institution of press regulations, but the press was beginning to take care of itself. The machine assembled by, and through, Oxford was at its best in 1712 and 1713.

Who were the writers upon whom Swift could depend? First and foremost was Abel Roper, editor of the *Post Boy*. Roper did well under the new regime. His tory paper was the staple printed diet of party sympathisers throughout the kingdom. Geoffrey Holmes writes that 'it would not be surprising if many numbers of the *Post Boy* passed through the hands of upward of 50,000 readers'.[3] The newspaper was dispatched from London in a similar, though more rudimentary, manner to the way in which modern newspapers are distributed. It was a most important government organ for the regular dissemination of the ministerial slant on events. In the summer of 1710 Roper was recommended for the post of Gazetteer.[4] Although the suit was unsuccessful, he was rewarded for his services (past and future) by a 'place in the secretary's office'. Oldmixon noted that this was arranged by Harley with a view 'to print libels on the duke and duchess of Marlborough, the earl of Godolphin, the earl of Wharton, the lord Somers, and all the illustrious patriots who were removed' from office in 1710.[5] Roper's involvement with the new ministers was well-known, if slightly exaggerated by some opposition writers. He was supposed to be 'far into the secret' of the negotiations with France in 1711.[6] It is less far-fetched to assume, as another whig did, that Roper was 'furnished... with history' by the ministry for his writings.[7] Ridpath was similarly convinced that 'this fellow writes by the lord Bolingbroke's order'.[8] His situation in the secretary's office was sufficient proof. We can be certain that Swift inserted passages in Roper's *Post Boy*. He himself acknowledged, in no uncertain terms, that Roper was his 'humble slave'.[9]

Abel Boyer had also sued for the position of Gazetteer when it was still in the possession of Richard Steele. He recalled 'some services performed to a great minister... while he was secretary of state'.[10] 'I am informed that great exceptions are taken to the *Gazette*, which is at present perfunctorily written by a young clerk to the original author, who, it is supposed, bestows his best thoughts and pains upon the *Tatler*', Boyer informed Harley on 15 August 1710, 'If, therefore, it was thought fit to take the *Gazette* from him, I leave it, Sir, to your consideration whether I may be a proper person to write it'.[11] On Richard Steele's dismissal in October 1710, Boyer renewed his suit. 'Mr Steele having resigned his place of Gazetteer, several of my friends would persuade me that few men are better qualified than myself to succeed him', he wrote, 'But though I am not so vain as to believe them, yet I will not be so far wanting to myself as to neglect this opportunity of putting your honour in mind of the most humble and most devoted of all your servants'.[12] Boyer's sincerity was not proof to the ministerial stance on the question of peace. Although his *Political State* counted as almost a fifth ministerial paper in the first months of 1711 (the others were the *Examiner*, the *Review*, the *Post Boy*, and the *Gazette*), he was prosecuted in the autumn of 1711 for his views in the *Protestant Post Boy*, written in direct competition with Roper's paper, and for a pamphlet, *An Account of the State and Progress of the Present Negotiations for Peace* (see above, p. 154). 'One Boyer, a French dog, has abused me in a pamphlet, and I have got him up in a messenger's hands', Swift wrote on 16 October, 'the secretary promises me to swinge him'.[13] 'However I may have been represented to you', Boyer had the impertinence to write to Oxford, 'I hope I have given both your lordship and the world sufficient and repeated proofs how heartily I am devoted to your lordship'. He claimed that his *Account* was 'mainly designed to serve your lordship in case, which seemed not impossible, the negotiations should break off'.[14] Boyer's interest with the prime minister, it seems, was good enough to allow him to escape serious punishment, but he forfeited his chance of reward in the process.

The Gazetteership was finally filled, after a vacancy of over a year, at the beginning of 1712. It was Swift's doing. He saw to it that it went to one of his nominees, William King. 'I have settled Dr King in the *Gazette*', he told Stella on 31 December 1711, 'it will be worth £200 a year to him'.[15] Despite King's early editing of the *Examiner*, he had not impressed Oxford. Swift was required to undertake that King would be 'diligent and sober'. He was not. The post proved uncongenial to King, for it necessitated regular writing. He displayed little enthusiasm to write for the Oxford ministry. Oxford displayed a similar lack of enthusiasm about employing someone who had supported Sacheverell so wholeheartedly. By 1 July 1712, King had been replaced by another Swift nominee, Charles Ford. The appointment was singular in that Ford was not an experienced journalist by any means. But he was trusted by Swift. He performed the office faithfully, if not brilliantly, and he was still Gazetteer on the accession of George I. Swift made sure he had interest with the editors of the official newspaper.

The successive editors of the *Examiner* were also directly or implicitly associated with Swift. He gave Mrs Manley the task of composing the 'official' account of the assassination attempt. She took over as editor of the *Examiner* when Swift relinquished the position in June 1711. Mrs Manley attempted to sue for Oxford's protection as editor. 'My friends have told me that I had some little pretence to be considered for what I had done as well as suffered', she wrote on 19 July 1711, and in October she explained that she had been responsible for 'Monsieur De Guiscard's *Narrative*, and that *Examiner* of Anthony and Fulvia, where by Agrippa's character your lordship's was designed'. 'Had I either instructions or encouragement', she continued, 'I might succeed better'.[16]

In the course of the winter, however, she became seriously ill. 'I am heartily sorry for her', Swift told Stella, 'she has very generous principles for one of her sort, and a great deal of good sense and invention'.[17] The *Examiner* went into temporary liquidation. But when Mrs Manley recovered she began to receive payment from Oxford for her services to the ministry. She was still under his patronage when he was dismissed in July 1714. As an ex-mistress of Richard Steele, she bore severe ill-usage from the whig propagandists. 'It is nothing to me', Steele wrote on one occasion in the *Guardian*, 'whether the *Examiner* writes against me in the character of an estranged friend, or an exasperated mistress'.[18]

In fact Steele was wide of the mark, and he knew it. Neither Swift nor Mrs Manley edited the *Examiner* by 1713. 'I have got an under-spur-leather to write an *Examiner* again', Swift told Stella on 5 December 1711, 'and the secretary and I will now and then send hints; but we would have it a little upon the Grub Street, to be a match for their writers'. William Oldisworth, the new editor, was, according to Swift, 'an ingenious fellow, but the most confounded, vain coxcomb in the world, so that I dare not let him see me, nor am acquainted with him'.[19] Nonetheless Swift was in contact with Oldisworth. 'The *Examiners* are good for little', Swift wrote in January 1712, 'I would fain have hindered the severity of the two or three last, but could not'. 'I am of your opinion that Lord Marlborough is used too hardly', he assured Stella, 'I have often scratched out passages from papers and pamphlets sent me before they were printed because I thought them too severe'.[20] Oldisworth risked prosecution for his extreme remarks, but it is clear that Swift could include material in the *Examiner* whenever it suited him, as Steele insinuated when commenting on the authorship of the ministerial paper. He left no doubt that he regarded Swift as ultimately responsible for the overall content of the *Examiner* as overseer, and that he was a 'miscreant' – an unbeliever. Oldisworth might laugh at Steele's suggestions that he had 'lain' with the author of the *Examiner*, and deny Swift's complicity in the paper's production, but Swift had contributed two essays in January 1713. His connections were real enough, if only spasmodically exercised. Steele's allegations were hardly unfounded, even if Swift had not personally been to blame for Oldisworth's habitual abuse of Marlborough.

We can be certain of Swift's relationship with John Arbuthnot, author of the 'John Bull' pamphlets, without raising the old chestnut of their authorship. Swift collaborated with Arbuthnot on *A Fable of the Widow and her Cat*, 'a ballad made by several hands, I know not whom. I believe lord treasurer had a finger in it; I added three stanzas; I suppose Dr Arbuthnot had the greatest share'.[21] Swift saw the poem through the press. He also appears to have been instrumental in seeing the first of Arbuthnot's pamphlets, *Law is a Bottomless Pit*, into print. It was published on 4 March 1712, with *John Bull in his Senses*, the second part, appearing on the 17th. It is coincidental that Swift was dictating 'some trifles' to a printer on 29 February, and again on 10 March he 'dined with a friend in the city about a little business of printing, but not my own'. In the same breath he advised Stella to 'buy the small twopenny pamphlet called *Law is a Bottomless Pit*, 'tis very prettily written, and there will be a second part'.[22] He seems to have been carrying out his new role as organiser of ministerial propaganda. Arbuthnot's clever 'John Bull' pamphlets,[23] in an allegorical style similar to that used in the *Dream at Harwich*, were fine essays with which to influence public opinion upon the peace question now that the peace crisis had been resolved. They were, at any rate, widely read, if the high sales figures are any guide.

Along with Swift and Oxford, of course, Arbuthnot was one of the founder members of the Scriblerus Club. His allegory in the 'John Bull' pamphlets appears to owe not a little to the Harleyite view of the war in Europe. It is the story of a law suit ensuing on the death of Lord Strutt (Charles II of Spain). The demise occasions 'great quarrels' in the neighbourhood. Prior to his death, Lord Strutt was persuaded to settle his estate 'upon his cousin Philip Baboon' (Louis XIV's grandson, Philip of Anjou). John Bull (personifying the English nation) decides to act as counsel for the whole neighbourhood, before he realises that he has got in beyond his depth. He is forced to extricate himself as best he can, leaving the lawyers (the Emperor and the Dutch) to enjoy the benefits they have accrued from the case. Despite the connection of Mrs Manley's name with the pamphlets, no doubt on account of her political allegories in the *New Atalantis* and *Memoirs of Europe*, Arbuthnot's hand is beyond dispute.

There are, however, close similarities between passages in the 'John Bull' pamphlets and the essays of William Wagstaffe in the *Plain Dealer*. John Bull, we recall, was an honest 'plain dealing' merchant. It has been suggested that Wagstaffe and Arbuthnot collaborated on another tremendously popular pro-ministerial offering in the first months of 1712, *The Story of the St Albans Ghost*.[24] 'I went to Lord Masham's tonight, and Lady Masham made me read to her a pretty pamphlet called the *St Albans Ghost*', Swift wrote on 22 February, 'I thought I had written it myself; so did they, but I did not'.[25] It was yet another attack on the Marlboroughs in a style very similar to Swift's, but Wagstaffe is now generally regarded as the author of this best-selling tract which went through five editions by July 1712. Wagstaffe's relations with Swift and the Oxford ministry are obscure, but his *Plain Dealer* was possibly a ministerial periodical in 1712 although there is no firm evidence to support the assumption.[26] True, Wagstaffe referred to the ministry as 'the readiest to patronize', but this was more likely to have been a hint rather than an acknowledgement. Certainly the *Plain Dealer* toed the government line, and provided support for the *Post Boy*.[27]

In the *Plain Dealer* Wagstaffe linked 'John Bull, and the late Apparition'. The *Story of the St Albans Ghost* was also mentioned in the same breath as Arbuthnot's writings in *A Complete Key* to the allegory of the satire. In the third and fourth 'editions' of the *Key* notes were included on the *Story*.[28] Wagstaffe is suspected of authorship of the *Key*. His writings were once again connected by association with Swift's *Conduct*, the 'John Bull' pamphlets, and Davenant's 'Tom Double' tracts in an *Elegy on the Death of Pamphlets*:[29]

> What, shall whole Reams of Breathless Pamphlets die
> And no one Living sing their Elegy?
> O *Barber*, deal the dismal News around,
> No *Conduct* now must rise from *Fairy Ground*;
> No dull *Tom Double*, or *John Bull* appear,
> To make us what in Truth we never were;
> No Mother *Haggy*, nor St *Alban*'s Ghost,
> To recommend an *Atheist* to a Post.

Charles Davenant had indeed attempted to secure Harley's patronage once again in 1710. He wrote to the new prime minister on 27 August about 'Sir Thomas Double (for he is now a knight) with whom I still correspond', who felt that recent events would 'prove as fatal a blow to the Modern Whigs, as to the king of France'.[30] Davenant published *Sir Thomas Double at Court and in High Preferments*, so Swift explained, 'to make his court to the tories who he had left'. Davenant 'teased' Swift to 'look over some of his writings that he is going to publish; but the rogue is so fond of his own productions that I hear he will not part with a syllable'.[31] Davenant was suspected of a hand in the *Letter to the Examiner* and the *Essay upon Public Credit*.[32] He had, however, adhered to the Marlboroughs after Harley's fall in 1708, and only his possible collaboration in the early issues of the *Mercator* indicates any ministerial sanction for his later writings.

John Toland suffered a similar fate. He, too, had always pursued his own advantage regardless of Harley's predilections. In Germany he made free with Harley's name and exaggerated his authority and his credentials.[33] When he subsequently tried to make peace with Harley in the summer of 1710 these factors weighed against him.[34] In 1711 he renewed his suit, thinking it 'strange if a person of my liberal education and experience in foreign courts (to mention no other qualifications) should not be found useful... to so learned as well as so politic a minister, to whom I have been gaining all the credit abroad that was possible'.[35] He objected to Oxford's 'tools', Swift and Prior, attacking the *Conduct of the Allies*, 'the *Examiner*, and such open opposers of the Protestant line'.[36] 'Instead... of your Priors and your Swifts', he told the prime minister, 'you ought to dispatch me privately this minute to Hanover'.[37] He complained bitterly about being denied access to Oxford, who, if he needed further warning, had been advised that 'Toland betrays what he knows to the whig lords'.[38] He never again penetrated Oxford's councils, and the prime minister was able to assure Cowper on 15 March 1712, with all likelihood of sincerity, that 'he had not seen Toland in 2 years'.[39] Toland, like the hardened turncoat he was, repaid his former benefactor's kindness with the malicious *Art of Restoring* in 1714 which drew unkind parallels between Oxford and Monck.

Oxford had no shortage of available propagandists in 1712. It was an embarrassment of riches. He turned down the services of men who, in leaner years, he might have been glad to employ. Toland was one. Simon Clement was allowed to accompany Peterborough to Vienna. His pen was no longer required. Another 'reject' was Francis Hoffman, author of a pamphlet on the Greg affair in July 1711 in the controversy in which Swift participated with *Some Remarks upon a Pamphlet called A Letter to the Seven Lords of the Committee appointed to Examine Greg*. In September 1711 Hoffman sent Oxford a scheme for a pamphlet called 'An Account of Church-ills and State-ills, and the History of an Irish Duchess, and of the Killycranky Fleet, together with several letters from Dunkirk, Paris, Toulon, Dublin and Almanza, with a frightful apparition of Guiscard's Ghost to a Duchess'.[40] Needless to say, this far-reaching pamphlet was never published, but Hoffman did print *An Impartial Character of the Noble Family of the Most Honourable the Earl of Oxford* in 1712, in which he eulogised the whole Harley family, and there is evidence of contact between Hoffman and Oxford after the earl's fall from office.[41]

Even collectors of customs were moved to compose verses on Oxford's behalf. Henry Crispe published *On the Honourable Board of Commissioners of Her Majesty's Custom-House, London; in the Year of Peace, 1713* in 'the hope of its doing some small service in the world'.[42] As prime minister, Oxford had no need to recruit propagandists; they flocked to him in search of patronage. The production of pamphlets and broadsheets almost took care of itself, and Swift was on hand to organise things. 'I have been over-seeing some other little prints', Swift wrote early in 1712, 'and a pamphlet made by one of my under-strappers'.[43] This might well refer to the anonymous *Representation of the Loyal Subjects of Albinia*, which has been claimed for William Wagstaffe,[44] but the identification of many of Swift's understrappers is mere guesswork. Some were men like Joseph Trapp, useful in a pinch, whom Swift accommodated as chaplain to Bolingbroke on his elevation to the peerage. Trapp was championed by Henry Sacheverell, and although Swift thought him 'a coxcomb, and the other...not very deep', evidence of contact extending into 1714 exists.[45] Swift was often supervising the work of other writers in 1712. In the fortnight before the implementation of the stamp duty on 1 August he 'published at least seven penny papers of [his] own, besides some of other people's'.[46] There is no way of assessing how much peripheral propaganda of this sort passed through Swift's hands as unofficial ministerial *chef de propagande* – pot-boiling broadsheets designed to act as a constant counter to opposition writings in the never-ending appeal to public opinion. But if, for some particular contingency, propaganda had to be released, Swift was able to coordinate its publication.

Without depreciating the value of Swift's own propaganda for the Oxford ministry, this was quite probably his most important function. Swift supplied a crucial link in the chain of production. Defoe made his own arrangements with printers; he did not arrange for the mass printing of ministerial propaganda: Swift did. His relationship with John Barber, in particular, was intimate. The two men often dined together to discuss business. This paid dividends. Barber was one of Swift's team. On 30 October 1711, when the *Conduct of the Allies* was being concocted, Swift was 'in the city concerting some things with a printer'.[47] The aptness of the phrase is striking. Barber contributed to the government's programme. In return Swift sent large amounts of government business his way. He was, of course, the printer of the *Examiner*, and it appears that Swift's contact with Mrs Manley and with William Oldisworth was through Barber. Mrs Manley was actually living with the printer.[48] All this would account for the considerable time Swift spent with Barber. When Jacob Tonson surrendered the printing of the *Gazette*, Swift arranged for Barber and his partner, Benjamin Tooke, to take over.[49] Of more interest, perhaps, is the fact that Defoe's *Mercator* was also printed by Tooke and Barber. This concentration on one set of printers and publishers was Swift's most original contribution to Oxford's press policy. It effectively imitated (and neutralised) the way in which the whigs used their printers, the Tonsons.

Once printed, the pamphlets which Swift had seen through the press were usually disseminated widely. As we have noted, an edition of the *Conduct* was printed 'in small' by Barber, to be sent into the country 'by friends'. Defoe had supplied the prototype for a system of outlets, even if we cannot be certain that it was the same one which he himself had established in 1705. With this arrangement, the ministers dispersed their propaganda. Although details are missing, this seems to have been what happened. Where government arrangements ceased, unofficial distribution took place. 'I am a country member', one letter to the *Examiner* began, 'and constantly send a dozen of your papers down to my electors'.[50] This may have been written by Swift himself, of course, but this does not mean that the practice did not take place. One Scarborough clergyman certainly had his regular *Examiner* sent up from London, 'and all the week after carries it about with him to read to such of his parishioners as are weak in the faith'![51]

The principal aim of ministerial propaganda after the conclusion of peace at Utrecht in 1713 was to counter opposition claims that the Protestant Succession was in danger under the Oxford regime. And, by the publication of suitable propaganda, a positive purpose was provided by the design of ensuring the peaceful accession of the Hanoverians whenever it should occur. The signing of the Treaty of Utrecht, however, also intensified the conflict between Oxford and Bolingbroke, which had been kept below the surface until the end of the war. Oxford noticed an opposition clique emerging in April 1713, comprising Bolingbroke, Harcourt, Atterbury and Lady Masham. The secretary pushed his scheme for a treaty of commerce with France and Spain. The Commons were not so sure. Hanoverian tories joined with the whigs to throw the bill out – the ministry's first major setback in the lower house since St John's mishandling of the leather duty in April 1711. With a general election in the offing, the ministerial propagandists turned to repair the damage done to the ministry's reputation.

In May 1713 a new government paper made its appearance. Defoe had been considering the question of trade with France in the *Review*, and in *An Essay on the Treaty of Commerce with France: With necessary Expositions*. He planned to start a long discourse on the subject 'when, on a sudden, I found my province invaded, and that work taken out of my hands by an unexpected paper without an author'. *The Mercator: Or, Commerce Retrieved, Being Considerations on the State of the British Trade* had government backing; Defoe refused to write on trade in the *Review* 'when an account vouched by such authorities shall come out three times a week'.[52] In June 1713 the *Review* stated its last facts right. Defoe did not mourn its demise. He was already writing the *Mercator*. He explained that he was 'set...upon that work' by Arthur Moore, the chief manager of the negotiations over the treaty of commerce. Moore 'undertook the support of it', but failed to reimburse any of Defoe's expenses. Defoe wrote to Oxford about the affair.[53] If, as has been suggested, Defoe was assisted at the birth of the *Mercator* by Moore and by Charles Davenant, he quickly seems to have taken the responsibility of editorship into his own hands. 'I hope I have not been an unprofitable servant in the new undertaking which I am embarked upon', Defoe asked Oxford on 1 August, and as late as May 1714 he was trying to persuade the prime minister to adopt measures 'to have that paper made more useful, I mean as to more purposes than its single, original design'.

The *raison d'être* of the *Mercator* was to defend the government over criticism about the abortive bill of commerce. Oxford's attitude to the proposed treaty was equivocal. He did not push it in parliament, and Bolingbroke pleaded with him to exert himself to retrieve 'a bad game'.[54] How much the issue was complicated by the crisis within the ministry which was resolved 'in the corridors of Kensington and Whitehall' in July and August 1713 is difficult to say. Oxford routed the Bolingbroke faction, forcing his opponents within the government, as Professor Holmes remarks, to bow 'not just to his continued premiership, but to a remodelling of ministerial offices which directly curtailed their own departmental authority and placed "Treasurer's men" at almost every strategic point available'.[55] Oxford calmly replied to criticism of his inactivity concerning the treaty of commerce by asserting that it would be passed in the new parliament if it failed in the old.[56] His inscrutability over the content of the treaty itself is virtually impenetrable. Almost certainly, however, it was he who arranged for Defoe to write about the issue in the *Mercator*. Although Moore was a friend of Bolingbroke, the secretary was still ignorant of Defoe's connections with Oxford; at least he was slow to extricate the author of the *Mercator*, which was defending his own pet project, from impending prosecution in 1713 for three pamphlets with misleading titles. If Defoe received remuneration for the *Mercator* it was not from Bolingbroke, either directly or through the offices of Arthur Moore.

The whigs had learned many lessons about the manipulation of public opinion through propaganda from Oxford over the years. In the final eighteen months of the Oxford ministry they moved onto the offensive. In the process they again succeeded in coming up with a few variations of their own. Paradoxically, they attempted to silence the ministry's own propagandists through prosecution. On 23 March 1713 Defoe was arrested for an old debt. His apprehension had been arranged by the whigs, who pressed his creditors to prefer charges. According to Defoe, although he owed £1,500, he persuaded his antagonists to accept no more than £150, 'and of that but £25 in money'.[57] He remained in confinement for eleven days before securing his discharge. On 11 April he was once again arrested for publishing three pamphlets, *Reasons against the Succession of the House of Hanover; And what if the Pretender should come?*; and *An Answer to a Question that Nobody Thinks of, viz., But what if the Queen should die?* His enemies had made sure that he was taken up on a Friday, so that he would have to spend the weekend in gaol before he could arrange bail. It was a ruse to silence his pen.

Despite the unfortunate titles of the three pamphlets, two of them were thoroughly ironic, while the last was simply a sober reminder that the queen was mortal, and that firm precautions should be taken to secure the safety of the Protestant Succession. As Defoe remarked, he was 'the first man that ever was obliged to seek a pardon for writing *for* the Hanoverian Succession, and the first man that [the whigs] ever sought to ruin for writing *against* the Pretender'.[58] But Defoe had angered the whigs by his ministerial writings. While they had been subjected to occasional government harassment, he had escaped scot-free. Three whigs in particular were smarting under the rigours of prosecution at this moment. George Ridpath, editor of the *Flying Post*, was tried in February 1713, and found guilty of writing seditious libel. He was out on bail. Thomas Burnet had been prosecuted for defending Marlborough too vehemently in *A Certain Information of a Certain Discourse, that happened at a Certain Gentleman's House*. He, too, was out on bail. In 1711 William Benson had libelled the queen in *A Letter to Sir Jacob Banks, by Birth a Swede, but Naturalised, and a Member of the Present Parliament*. All three, then, had grievances to nurse. They seized the manuscripts of Defoe's pamphlets from the printer's, taking them to lord chief justice Parker, a noted whig sympathiser. Parker committed Defoe to Newgate.

On 12 April 1713 Defoe wrote to Oxford of his predicament, explaining the circumstances surrounding his arrest. 'The pretences are several, some too simple to name', he informed the prime minister, 'but they were heard to say that they had all been prosecuted, and the *Review* had a full liberty, but they would bring me in whether the ministry would or no'.[59] Oxford secured Defoe's release on bail the next day. Two days later Parker wrote to him, 'believing that probably your lordship will think it for the honour of her majesty and the ministry that directions be given to the attorney-general to prosecute at her majesty's charge, and that the reason why it has not been done already is that such scribbles have not fallen within your lordship's notice'.[60] Oxford, of course, wanted no such thing, but it proved amazingly difficult to extricate Defoe. 'Mr Benson will bring an information on purpose to try if I can obtain a stop to be put to their proceedings by *nolle prosequi*', Defoe pointed out, 'which will give them an occasion of railing, which is what they desire'. 'I'll petition (I mean in print) to be brought to trial', he suggested as an alternative, 'and shall have abundant room to expose them for attacking me in a thing they cannot make out, and thus the pretence of being protected by your lordship or the ministry will be quite taken away'.[61]

Defoe was nearly hoist with his own petard. The pages of the *Review* echoed to his cries of injustice. On 22 April he was arrested a third time, and he was held in the Queen's Bench from then until 3 May, when he was released after issuing a public apology to lord chief justice Parker.[62] Even then his prosecution was not dropped. 'I am surprised, my lord, with notice given me...that notwithstanding all that has been said, and your lordship's orders...they are proceeding formally against me on account of the old affair of the three pamphlets', Defoe wrote on 9 October, 'and that if your lordship is not pleased to interpose, I shall be made a sacrifice to a party who would sacrifice your lordship and the queen also, if it lay in their power'. Northey told Defoe to petition the queen, there being 'no other way to be effectively safe but to obtain her majesty's pardon'. Even when this was arranged Defoe discovered to his horror that Northey had ordered him to plead on the charges brought against him, 'and that if the pardon be not obtained before I am obliged to plead, I shall still be brought upon the stage'. Finally his pardon came through just in time.[63]

Defoe's embarrassment was only one manifestation of a new whig resolution over the press. In 1710, with the reaction to the Sacheverell trial, the whig propagandists were reduced very much to the defensive. According to one contemporary observer, things got so bad for them that 'the hawkers would not cry' the whig pamphlets 'at last'.[64] Somers did nothing. On the appearance of St John's *Letter to the Examiner*, Cowper penned an answering *Letter to Isaac Bickerstaff*, but the *Tatler* remained strangely non-political. The *Flying Post* and Buckley's *Daily Courant* continued to report the news with a whig bias, but, after Defoe's defection, there was no whig equivalent of the *Examiner* until Joseph Addison took up the gauntlet in the *Whig-Examiner*. Assisted by Arthur Maynwaring, Addison intended to give 'all persons a rehearing, who have suffered under any unjust sentence of the *Examiner*'.[65] Junto backing is apparent, but very much in the background. Maynwaring was the key figure. Addison quickly backed out of the whig campaign, leaving Maynwaring to launch *The Medley* to succeed the *Whig-Examiner*. Hitherto Maynwaring's approach had been somewhat lackadaisical, but from 1710 to 1712 – the final two years of his life as it turned out – he shrugged off his languor and ill-health to direct whig propaganda. As Henry Snyder remarks, 'the full range and extent of his political writings is virtually impossible to establish with perfect confidence',[66] but his leadership is clear.

Maynwaring was responsible for two of the most effective whig pamphlets in 1710 itself, the *Letter from Monsieur Pettecum to Monsieur Buys*, and *Four Letters to a Friend in North Britain*, but they were insufficient to forestall the change of ministry. The efforts which he put into the *Medley* were a different matter. Confidant of the Marlboroughs, Maynwaring also appears to have provided hints and editorial advice for Francis Hare, the family's apologist. Of perhaps more significance is the recruitment of John Oldmixon, a willing hack who repaid Maynwaring's attention with a eulogistic biography which included a collection of his posthumous works. Oldmixon was the drudge behind the *Medley*, but Maynwaring's talent for organisation is readily apparent, as Richard Steele and Anthony Henley also contributed to the paper. The folding of the *Examiner* in June 1711 after Swift's series of essays was accounted a victory by Maynwaring. His friends and collaborators assured him that 'it is possible to scribble these men down', and it was to be attempted in the forthcoming winter session of parliament – the session which turned out to be the peace crisis.[67]

When St John took up the fourteen booksellers, printers and

publishers in the autumn of 1711, it is interesting to note, as Henry Synder points out, that Maynwaring 'was responsible for virtually all the libels named in the indictments'.[68] He did not write them all himself, but he had seen them through the press. Some, like *Bouchain*, had been by Hare, but Maynwaring can be discerned in the background, coordinating the whig attack on the government's peace campaign. It was Maynwaring, most probably, who first replied to Swift's *Conduct of the Allies* in *Remarks on a False, Scandalous, and Seditious Libel*, and he was, no doubt, behind Hare's quartet of tracts, *The Allies and the Late Ministry Defended*. When Swift and St John arranged for the resuscitation of the *Examiner* under William Oldisworth, the *Medley* also reappeared. From 3 March 1712 until the introduction of the stamp duty, 45 issues of the *Medley* were published, the last on 14 July. It is probable that it was Maynwaring's own ill-health, as much as the imminent imposition of a tax on newspapers, that was responsible for the *Medley*'s lapse. On his death, the initiative passed to other whigs.

A propaganda machine, then, however rudimentary, began to be assembled by the whigs under Maynwaring's guidance. It would be unwise to overestimate the success with which he motivated the opposition. The ministry was never threatened by the whig offensive in print, merely embarrassed. Nottingham's motion of 'No Peace without Spain' did much more to endanger Oxford's government than reams of Maynwaring's writings. But it demonstrates an awareness of the importance of public opinion. Like Somers in 1701 and Harley in 1708–9, Maynwaring was trying to write the ministry down. He did not, however, have the assistance of a Sacheverell. But the whigs did not surrender the initiative on Maynwaring's death; rather, they sought to extend his policies. On 7 October 1712 Oxford's son observed that they had 'resolved that they would one and all do what in them lay to prevent a peace, and made a collection for printing all the virulent pamphlets that have been written against the queen and this ministry'.[69] A year later, as the whig propaganda campaign neared its climax, Defoe commented bitterly upon whig tactics. He revealed that they had taken[70]

such measures to stifle everything that is not for their turn by clamouring at it in their *Flying Post*...that nothing can be spread into the country but by force of management, and indeed no printer will now print at his own charge, which is the reason that the world is over-run with their pamphlets, which they disperse privately two or three editions at a time, and no man stirs a hand to oppose them because they must do it at their own hazard and expense.

In only three years the wheel had come full circle. In 1710 the whigs had had difficulty in getting their pamphlets cried by the hawkers; in 1713 it was the independent tory writer who, according to Defoe, was able to publish only at his 'own hazard and expense'. The ministry, 'by force of management', could arrange for the publication and distribution of pro-government pamphlets, but it was an expensive business. The day of the independent pamphleteer was dying. The stamp act did not kill off Grub Street, it merely altered the strategy adopted by the opposition in disseminating its propaganda. To get round the problem of the halfpenny tax, the whigs imitated the ministry in arranging for the publication of pamphlets, commissioning them, subsidising their printing, and often dispersing them free of charge.

The resemblance between the propaganda machines and propaganda agencies of government and opposition at this time is striking, as the gap in organisation and technique between them narrowed after 1710. The *Conduct of the Allies* had been sent into the country, one 'edition' in particular, the fifth, as Swift remarked, being, in terms of numbers, 'as many as three editions', precisely because it was designed for that very purpose. Four thousand were produced, instead of the usual 1,400. Clearly it is this type of arrangement to which Defoe was referring in his correspondence with Oxford. 'Two or three editions at a time' were being run off, and they were being dispersed throughout the kingdom 'privately'. We can safely assume that Defoe was talking in figures of around 4,000, perhaps more, for he reported that 6,000 copies of *Neck or Nothing* had been printed for distribution in the provinces in 1714. By then the whig campaign had come a long way since the days of 1710.

After Maynwaring's death on 13 November 1712, George Ridpath, editor of the *Flying Post*, appears to have donned the mantle of coordinator. If Swift was right in his hunch that Ridpath had taken the *Medley* under his wing on the introduction of the stamp act, then it would serve to endorse this assumption. One very good example of organised whig propaganda is the publication, in March 1713, of a particularly nasty poem, *The British Embassaddress's Speech to the French King*. Swift called it 'the cursedest libel in verse...that ever was seen'. It was printed by William Hurt, who also printed the *Flying Post*. The connection did not go unnoticed. Ridpath had recently been convicted of seditious libel in his newspaper, but when the *British Embassaddress's Speech* was published he was out on bail. The small scraps of paper on which the poem appeared were 'handed about, but not sold'.[71] It was the publication of this libel, apparently, which was principally responsible for the paragraph in the queen's speech to parliament on 9 April 1713 relating to the press. It is interesting that Steele was launching his offensive upon the *Examiner* at this time in the *Guardian*. The arrest of Defoe on account of the 'three pamphlets' also occurred in April 1713, and Ridpath had a hand in that affair. The suggestion is that a concerted attack on the ministerial propagandists, and Swift and Defoe in particular, was being put into operation, with Ridpath as a key figure. In May 1713 he fled the country. He had delved too deep too quickly for safety. Even Queen Anne had been accused of entering into a conspiracy to prevent the succession of the Hanoverians. The *British Embassaddress's Speech* 'exposed' the way that, 'to baffle all the *Hanoverian* line':[72]

> A Set of Ministers she lately chose,
> To Honour and their Country equal Foes:
> Wretches, whose Indigence has made 'em bold,
> And will betray their Native Land for Gold.
> *Oxford*'s the Chief of this abandon'd Clan;
> Him you must court, for he's your only Man.
> Give him but Gold enough, your Work is done,
> He'll bribe the Senate, and then all's your own.

It is hardly surprising that care was taken to mention, in the queen's speech, that 'some new law' would be necessary to prevent the publication of this sort of malicious libel. Oxford's careful drafting of the speech can be documented.[73]

The whigs were not slow to take up the challenge thrown down by the *Mercator*. A rival whig paper on trade, *The British Merchant*, edited, as Oldmixon noted, by Henry Martin, bailiff of Southwark, 'an ingenious, judicious man', proved more than a handful for Defoe.[74] 'Nothing is more plain', Defoe told Oxford during the election in October 1713,[75]

than that the disputes upon the subject of the commerce with France are carried on not merely as a dispute about trade, which most of the people now so hot about it understand little of, but as an arrow shot at the present administration, a handle taken hold of, and an opportunity which they think is given them to raise a tumult against the ministry, and enflame the people.

The interaction between propaganda and public opinion was becoming apparent to all, and the whigs were making giant strides in 1713 and 1714 to compete with the propaganda machine at the government's disposal, arranging for the distribution of pamphlets in the provinces, and embarrassing the administration with a barrage of outspoken criticism. They learned from Oxford's example.

The key figures in this development were Richard Steele and Samuel Buckley. Steele was behind the propaganda campaign which culminated in the publication of *The Crisis*. He argued against the proposed treaty of commerce with France, and exposed the danger that the nation was in until the defences of Dunkirk were demolished. His whole theme was the security of the Protestant Succession, and he played variations on it up to, and after, his expulsion from the house of commons. Samuel Buckley, editor of the *Daily Courant*, became increasingly important after Ridpath's flight to Holland. His organising skills, accumulated over the years in the running of the first daily newspaper, were of great benefit to the whigs. Apparently the channels used to distribute the *Daily Courant* were taken over by the whig pamphleteers. In 1714 Defoe noted that 6,000 copies of John Dunton's *Neck or Nothing* had been dispersed, some as far afield as Scotland.[76] Dunton was included by Swift, along with Ridpath and Steele, in a list of whig propagandists considered worthy of attention.[77] The whigs were making determined efforts to break in on the ministry's near-monopoly of public opinion.

It was through the pages of *The Guardian* that Steele attacked the treaty of commerce and the failure to demolish Dunkirk. He made a number of sorties against the *Examiner*, a feature of the whig campaign. After resigning his place in the stamp office, Steele revealed his intention to stand for parliament. He was elected for Stockbridge. It was as MP that he began to display an awareness of the role of public opinion. Defoe told Oxford that 'the new champion of the party', would 'try an experiment upon the ministry, and shall set up to make speeches in the house and print them, that the malice of the party may be gratified, and the ministry be bullied in as public a manner as possible'.[78] We should recall that Harley had used similar tactics in 1709, when Harcourt and Haversham printed speeches in the country cause. But Steele was demonstrating a resolution and a perception which had been apparent when Somers fought the last, great, whig propaganda campaign in 1701. For over a year he was to harass Oxford and the ministry. As Calhoun Winton notes, 'the question of whether Steele originated the policy or merely implemented it cannot be resolved in the light of present evidence',[79] but the new whig initiative is not in doubt.

The facility with which the ministerial propagandists responded to Steele's challenge is a measure of the efficiency of Oxford's machine. Oldisworth answered Steele's *Guardian* essays over the failure to guarantee the demolition of the Dunkirk fortifications, in accordance with the terms of Utrecht. The *Examiner* was given sterling support by

Defoe in *The Honour and Prerogative of the Queen's Majesty Vindicated and Defended Against the Unexampled Insolence of the Author of the Guardian*. Steele's *The Importance of Dunkirk Considered* was deflated by Swift's *The Importance of the Guardian Considered*, while Wagstaffe's scurrilous *Character of Richard Steele* went through several editions. Abandoning the *Guardian*, Steele launched *The Englishman*, maintaining his offensive. The publication in January 1714 of his *The Crisis* was the climax of his campaign to discredit the ministry over the question of the security of the Protestant Succession, and Queen Anne's near-fatal illness served merely to underline the crisis within the nation. For several days at the end of December 1713 her life lay in the balance.

Parliament was due to meet on 16 February 1714. As Irvin Ehrenpreis notes, 'Swift's friends badly wanted an authoritative reply to the whigs' masterstroke'. On 23 February Swift published his response to Steele's challenge, *The Public Spirit of the Whigs: Set Forth in Their Generous Encouragement of the Author of the Crisis*. This, the last of Swift's pamphlets on behalf of the Oxford ministry, 'deserves on several grounds to be described as one of his finest works'.[80] It was a cutting attack on not only the fatuousness of Steele's exercise in verbosity, but the whig propaganda machine *per se*, and its propaganda campaign. Denying that there was in any sense a *crisis*, or that the ministry had done anything 'tending towards bringing in the Pretender, or to weaken the Succession in the House of Hanover', Swift made a liberal use of invective to undermine Steele's position, ridiculing the clamour made by the pamphlet in question, and its absurd dedication to the clergy. The second half of the *Public Spirit of the Whigs* defended the ministry's conduct in the negotiations leading to peace. Steele's prosecution for seditious libel gilded the government's victory over the opposition press.[81]

But Swift did not escape without a scare either. When Steele was indicted for the issue of the *Englishman* for 16–19 January 1714; the *Crisis*; and the *Englishman: Being the Close of the Paper so called*, Wharton retaliated in the Lords by censuring the *Public Spirit of the Whigs*. With Steele's pamphlets in mind, Queen Anne had spoken out against 'some who have arrived to that height of malice as to insinuate that the Protestant Succession in the House of Hanover is in danger under my government', in her opening speech to parliament on 2 March 1714. This was taken as a pointed reference to Steele's writings, and the Commons stressed that they would on all occasions show their 'just abhorrence...of the licentious practices in publishing seditious papers and spreading factious rumours'.[82] But Wharton turned the queen's speech against those who had drafted it. He called the *Public Spirit of the Whigs* 'a false, malicious and factious libel'; exactly the sort of thing the queen must have had in mind when making her speech. John Barber, Swift's printer, and the publisher John Morphew were taken into custody. Wharton thought this step insufficient. He said it was imperative for the 'honour' of the house of lords that they should discover the 'villain' responsible for the *Public Spirit of the Whigs*.[83]

In a completely unnecessary digression, Swift had described the Scots as 'a poor, fierce, Northern people', little better than parasites on the body of the English, who were prepared to revoke the act of union and jeopardise the safety of the Protestant Succession.[84] The *Public Spirit of the Whigs* was voted 'highly dishonourable and scandalous to the Scottish nation, tending to the destruction of the constitution'. A reward of £300 was offered for information leading to the apprehension of the author of the libellous tract. Patently it was a set-up. Even the earl of Nottingham was involved in trying to ensnare Dr Swift.[85] He was one of the men named to draw up an address to the queen concerning the *Public Spirit*, and notes extant in his own hand show that he was trying to prove either that the author was writing falsehoods, or that he had been trusted with state secrets – either libel or treason. But Swift never claimed authorship of the *Public Spirit* publicly, and when Wharton called for the rigorous examination of Barber, his journeymen and his servants, he was pre-empted by the Harleyite earl of Mar, secretary of state for Scotland, who informed the Lords on 6 March 'that he had already ordered John Barber to be prosecuted, which put a sudden stop to all further enquiries about that matter in a parliamentary way'.[86] As Abel Boyer put it, 'Jonathan...being under the wings of some great men, escaped discovery and punishment'.[87] A screen was lowered on the findings of the secretaries of state, but, like Defoe before him, Swift had experienced at first hand the inadequacies of the protection afforded 'those who scribble for the government'.[88]

It had taken, then, the expulsion of Richard Steele from the house of commons to head off the whig programme of anti-ministerial propaganda. Significantly it was Auditor Harley who made the formal complaint. On 18 March 1714 Steele made his defence, assisted by the ablest of the whigs in the lower house, Walpole and Stanhope. Despite memorable speeches in favour of the defendent and against the conduct of the ministry, the court supporters insisted on the question. Steele was found guilty of writing seditious libel by 245 votes to 152, and he was duly expelled the house. The publication of *The Crisis* was the culmination of the whig propaganda campaign against the Oxford ministry. Oxford had won. But by 1714 *both* parties had fairly sophisticated means of producing and disseminating propaganda at their disposal for the first time. In office the whigs notoriously neglected propaganda, and disregarded public opinion; out of office they developed propaganda techniques, and attempted to influence profoundly public opinion, and to organise extra-parliamentary forces to counter-balance tory majorities at the centre of power. Oxford did not fail to pursue a propaganda machine and a propaganda agency *in office*. After 1710 he developed extensive government control of the press, not through strict censorship, but through propaganda and counter-propaganda, and a limited system of press regulations involving the old laws regarding seditious libel and treason, and the new stamp duty. In 1714 his arrangements amounted to a tory propaganda machine with which the new whig machine could be combatted.

Oxford had met the exigency even though, at the time, his personal political power was being severely eroded by Bolingbroke, and he was thinking seriously about resigning. Oxford did not retain the lord treasurer's staff of office for long after Swift moved to Upper Letcomb in Berkshire in May 1714 'upon finding it impossible after above two years endeavour to reconcile my lord treasurer, and my lord Bolingbroke; from the quarrel between which two great men all our misfortunes proceeded'.[89] Arbuthnot informed Swift soon afterwards that 'the dragon dies hard, he is now kicking and cuffing about him like the devil'.[90] Oxford, in the event, did not relinquish power easily, more especially as Bolingbroke was, to all intents and purposes, the heir-apparent. On 27 July 1714, however, a weary monarch took his staff and placed it, on 31 July, not in the hands of Bolingbroke, but of the trusty duke of Shrewsbury. The next day she died. It was the end of the Stuart monarchy – the end of an era; the whigs were triumphant.

With Oxford's dismissal the government propaganda machine ran down. It had, of course, been in low gear for the last few months since the victory over Richard Steele, the acknowledged 'champion of the party'. And with Swift in the country, full responsibility for the organisation of propaganda rested with Oxford once more. He had retained overall authority to the end, in any case, as the setting up of the *Mercator* demonstrates. Despite his close association with Swift, and with Roper and the *Post Boy*, Bolingbroke's role in relation to the press was a minor one. All financial backing for government propaganda came, officially, out of the prime minister's tiny intelligence fund. Oxford made up for this deficiency by digging deep into his own pocket. His own affairs were in a sad state by the end of his treasurership, but he had taken care to reward his family of writers. Swift had finally accepted a bill for £100 to cover the expenses of his attempt to avoid discovery as author of the *Public Spirit of the Whigs*.[91] The *Examiner* ended for good on 27 July 1714, the day prior to Oxford's dismissal. As Oldisworth was receiving payment from the prime minister, a connection between the two events can be discerned.[92] Mrs Manley also received remuneration for her services to the ministry during these weeks.[93] Oxford sent Defoe his final payment of Queen Anne's reign, his quarterly £100, on the day the *Examiner* folded.[94]. The *Review* had ceased to exist long before. The *Mercator* published its last issue on 20 July 1714. All these happenings were unlikely to have been coincidental. Oxford appears to have been making a final effort to reward his propagandists while it remained in his power to do so. Charles Ford was allowed to continue as Gazetteer for only three weeks after the death of Queen Anne before he was replaced by the editor of the *Daily Courant*, and manager of the whig propaganda campaign, Samuel Buckley. The last vestiges of Oxford's propaganda machine were quickly removed.

It had, then, been Oxford's creation. Bolingbroke, even had he had the inclination, had no means to keep this team of writers together. He did not hold the treasurer's purse, and his private income was much smaller than Oxford's. Through four long years of the Oxford ministry, the prime minister's propagandists had served him well. The government had weathered the peace crisis, and had signed the Treaty of Utrecht. It had withstood whig criticism concerning the security of the Protestant Succession, and even if it proved unable to prevent the launching of the propaganda campaign spearheaded by Richard Steele, it had responded magnificently to the challenge. At one time, in May 1713, five regular government periodicals were in existence, and there were others like the *Plain Dealer* and Boyer's *Political State* that displayed sympathy with the ministry, if not actual connections. Pamphlets defending Oxford and justifying the conduct of his ministry proliferated from all sides.

Oldmixon claimed that the Oxford ministry had succeeded not only in controlling the press, but in utilising it to its distinct advantage. He felt that the government, from 1710 to 1714, was 'chiefly indebted' to the press for its 'strength, by the greatest abuses of it that ever was known'.[95] A cynical view from a bitter opponent of the regime, and yet unwitting praise indeed. Earlier administrations had been at the mercy of the licentiousness of the press. Oxford had turned a problem into a weapon to be wielded more efficiently when in power than in opposition. Previously it had been the preserve of the critic of government, who sought to mould public opinion to his own ends. Adapting the tactics of opposition, Oxford used propaganda positively to explain government policy to MPs and to the political nation. The aim was to achieve policy objectives. He altered the role of ministerial apologist from one which was essentially defensive, to a twin one in which there were practical applications in the process of administration. He had come up with a solution to the problem of what to do about the press, and Walpole imitated his methods of producing and distributing propaganda. As J. H. Plumb observes, Oxford 'tried to achieve the impossible: the system of Walpole with tory materials'.[96] In the purely practical aspects of government this is true. But in the areas of intelligence, propaganda and counter-propaganda, Oxford was at least the equal of Walpole. The Robinocracy of Walpole owed a tremendous amount to the efforts of 'Robin the Trickster'.

Epilogue: impeachment and after

On 6 August 1714 Oxford wrote to George I, offering his congratulations on the new king's accession to the throne. 'I had the honour in the two preceding reigns to express my love to my country by promoting what is now come to pass', he pointed out, 'your majesty's succession to the crowns of these kingdoms'.[1] This was no mere cant. Of the three men who had assisted William III in the drafting of the bill of settlement, only Oxford was still living. Rochester died in 1711; Godolphin in 1712. In many ways it would have been true to say that of living Englishmen, the former lord treasurer, despite whig fears, had done most to secure the peaceful succession of the Hanoverians. He regarded it as his life's work.[2]

But his day was over. Oxford was greeted silently and coldly by the new king. Inactivity gave way to illness soon after George I's landing in England.

> What gave great Villiers to th' assassin's knife,
> And fixed disease on Harley's closing life?...
> What but their wish indulg'd in courts to shine,
> And pow'r too great to keep, or to resign?[3]

Johnson's cynicism overlooks Oxford's two-year confinement in the Tower of London. It was this that finally broke his health. Bolingbroke fled to the court of the Pretender at St Germain to forestall impeachment. Whig malice lighted on Oxford. On 11 April 1715 a secret committee was appointed to look into the suspected mismanagements of his ministry. He was impeached on 10 June; the articles of impeachment were brought against him on 7 July; and on 9 July 1715 he was committed to the Tower, where his health rapidly deteriorated. He survived narrowly a further severe illness.

In print Oxford was subjected to a barrage of invective from the whig scribblers. Ridpath returned from his self-imposed exile to spearhead the campaign. Mrs Manley generously offered to undertake 'a true account of the changes made just before the death of the queen', but Oxford did not take her up on it.[4] Swift waited until Oxford had been impeached before beginning his *Enquiry into the Behaviour of the Queen's Last Ministry* and even then he thought better of printing it. Despite his arrest in August 1714 for reflecting on one of the regents, the Hanoverian tory Anglesey, Defoe defended Oxford single-handedly. He was already preparing to vindicate him in print before Queen Anne's death.[5] He proceeded to send the disgraced minister materials for his approbation.[6] But in encouraging Hurt, the former printer of the *Flying Post*, to publish a rival paper of the same name in direct competition with Ridpath's, Defoe had gone too far. 'It is long that I have been endeavouring to take off the virulence and rage of the *Flying Post*', Defoe explained to Oxford, 'the use they make of this is that I have insulted my lord Anglesey, and that your lordship has employed me to do so'.[7] Henceforth Oxford severed his connections with Defoe. In his *Appeal to Honour and Justice*, Defoe claimed to have corresponded with Oxford 'but once' since the landing of George I in England on 8 September 1714.[8] The final link with the Oxford ministry's propaganda machine had snapped.

Defoe nonetheless defended Oxford in several pamphlets, from the three parts of *The Secret History of the White Staff*, through *An Account of the Conduct of Robert, Earl of Oxford*, to, as late as 1717, *Minutes of the Negotiations of Monsieur Mesnager*. The *Secret History* sought to explain Oxford's conduct in office:[9]

The Staff proceeded with a steady resolution to maintain the authority and power he possessed, and had, as before, successfully frustrated and disappointed all the measures of those who would have overthrown and pulled him down. But it was apparent that, victory being obtained, he had no further schemes of opposition to pursue; that it was not in his design to crush and ruin the persons he struggled with, or to erect any dominion over them, as Britons; that he had no state-tyranny to erect, no secret designs to betray the constitution, and this negative produced a war between him and those who, to outward appearance, were in the same interest with him, which at last broke out into a flame, which produced unlooked-for events.

The whole tone of the pamphlet is conciliatory; its theme moderation; and it was intended to remind the whigs of the leniency with which they had been treated by the *quondam* lord treasurer. The *Secret History* is remarkable for its lucid and accurate picture of the power struggle between Oxford and Bolingbroke. It contrasts starkly with Bolingbroke's retrospective admission that in office he wanted to 'fill the employments of the kingdom, down to the meanest, with tories'. The whole of the second part of the *Secret History* was devoted to proving that far from condoning Jacobitism, Oxford had been the sworn enemy of all Jacobites. The final part dealt with the reasons why both sides became 'haters of the Staff', and it gives the lie to subsequent whig interpretations of Oxford's political career:[10]

either side was impatient of having any control upon their measures, and, being bent upon the perfecting their own designs, any middle between those extremes must, of necessity, differ with both. Moderate councils were those the Staff purposed to establish, that he might have kept a balance between two furious parties.

But, of course, no vindication of Oxford's conduct could do any good. The *Secret History* was attacked by whigs and tories, Hanoverians and Jacobites. There was a general refusal to accept that Oxford had not collaborated in its publication. Oldmixon, who wrote the whig rejoinders, was emphatic:[11]

One cannot doubt but the *Secret History of the White Staff*, a pamphlet which Defoe wrote soon after King George's accession to the throne, was by the earl of Oxford's direction, and that the most natural hints for it came from him, because the whole treatise is calculated for his vindication, and Defoe depended upon him too much to dare to publish any such thing without his participation and consent.

Certainly Oxford was aware, in August 1714, that Defoe was planning a justification of his policies. But in his private correspondence he persistently and vehemently denied having anything to do with the *Secret History*. He wrote to William Stratford on 22 March 1715:[12]

Their part towards me is barbarous. Formerly I was blamed for things I did not do, and now they pretend to father libels upon me, which I was so far from knowing of them, that I never to this day read them, and I can make it appear that they owned they knew so much but only took that handle to vent their malice and spite, for it is most certain that they who do the injury never forgave.

'The report about the author of the *White Staff*, though industriously propagated, begins like others that have such a foundation to die of itself', Stratford wrote, 'But though your old enemies contrived it, I am afraid your lordship's old friends had the greatest share in spreading it'.[13] In less partial times the *Secret History* might have served the turn of defending Oxford in print. But Defoe misjudged the response, much as he had done over a decade before when he published the *Shortest Way with the Dissenters*.

Ultimately Oxford was forced to deny publicly that he had had any hand in the pamphlets that attempted to vindicate him. In the *Gazette* for 5–9 July 1715, just before he was sent to the Tower, he inserted an advertisement:[14]

Whereas some months since a pamphlet entitled *The Secret History of the White Staff*, and lately another pamphlet entitled *An Account of the Conduct of Robert, Earl of Oxford*, have been printed and published, these are to inform the public that neither of the said pamphlets have been written by the said earl, or with his knowledge, or by his direction or encouragement, but on the contrary he has reason to believe from several passages therein contained, that it was the intention of the author or authors to do him a prejudice, and that the last of the said pamphlets is published at this juncture to that end.

Unless one is to be thoroughly cynical, and to accept that Defoe was prepared to go to any lengths to make his peace with the whigs (Defoe came to trial on 15 July 1715 on account of his reflections on Anglesey in the *Flying Post*), then it must be conceded that Oxford was being unduly critical of Defoe's unbidden efforts on his behalf. They may not have had the desired effect, but they display at the very least a willingness to help an old patron.

Oxford's advertisement in the *Gazette* was his last direct contact with the press. (We can discount the theory that he was the real author of *Robinson Crusoe*.)[15] In the Tower he developed an antipathy towards the whig propagandists which was all the more bitter for being futile. He censured Ridpath as 'a fellow that run his country rather than abide its justice'. Steele, he believed, was 'not capable of writing or acting any more than nature designed'. He was an incendiary: a 'blower of bellows...to gunpowder'. Boyer, who had tried so hard to gain Oxford's patronage, was finely drawn as 'the greatest scoundrel in the world that understands neither French nor English'. Oxford even had strong words for 'a little toothdrawer', Fonvive, who 'has got above £15,000 by news, viz., by cheating the postage and having the common prints come franked'.[16] In the twilight of his political career Oxford finally began to be ruffled by the libels and lampoons showered upon him. He was not well, and his sojourn in the Tower had done nothing for his peace of mind.

On 26 June 1716 the proceedings of the house of commons against him finally petered out, and he eventually had the temerity, a year later, to petition parliament to be brought to trial. A dispute between the two houses over whether he should be tried first for high treason, or for high crimes and misdemeanours, finally resulted in Oxford's discharge by the

Lords, upon the failure of the lower house to prosecute the articles submitted against him. His conduct in office was tacitly vindicated by his release from the Tower on 1 July 1717, but he never again took an active part in politics. He was forbidden the court at the express order of George I, and he lived an almost uninterrupted life of retirement at Brampton Bryan until his death in May 1724 on a rare visit to London.

On the death of Thomas Parnell, one of the members of the Scriblerus Club, Pope dedicated an epistle to Oxford:[17]

> In vain to Desarts thy Retreat is made;
> The Muse attends thee to the silent Shade:
> 'Tis hers, the brave Man's latest Steps to trace,
> Re-judge his Acts, and dignify Disgrace.
> When Int'rest calls off all her sneaking Train,
> And all th'Oblig'd desert, and all the Vain;
> She waits, or to the Scaffold, or the Cell,
> When the last ling'ring Friend has bid farewel.
> Ev'n now she shades thy Evening Walk with Bays,
> (No Hireling she, no Prostitute to Praise)
> Ev'n now, observant of the parting Ray,
> Eyes the calm Sun-set of thy Various Day,
> Thro' Fortune's Cloud One truly Great can see,
> Nor fears to tell, that MORTIMER is He.

Oxford's reputation with the circle surrounding Pope and Swift was assured. The Scriblerians retained a fondness for the man who had sat with them when he was lord treasurer, discussing letters, not matters of state. Swift finally came to his friend's rescue in *Gulliver's Travels*, in which Gulliver's conduct in Lilliput has been recognised as an allegory of Oxford's conduct in office.[18] When, in 1742, the duchess of Marlborough besmirched Oxford's name in an account of her own conduct during the reign of Queen Anne, the disciples of the late lord treasurer sprang to the defence of one 'grieviously misrepresented by all parties for the great crime of being of none'. A review of the duchess's book aimed to do justice to 'this nobleman's character': 'Perhaps some better hand may be tempted to finish the piece, which we have only sketched, and whenever this shall be done, the earl of Oxford will be known to posterity for a perfect statesman'.[19]

Posterity has not been kind to Robert Harley. He has received a bad press. Macaulay was ruthless in his indictment of Harley as a man whose intellect 'was both small and slow', and who 'was unable to take a large view of any subject'.[20] From Macaulay's time onwards this view has generally been accepted, rather than Pope's, or the Reviewer's. It has taken a long time for Harley to be rehabilitated. To Churchill he was 'a base and hardy hypocrite', while W. A. Shaw delighted in derogating 'the sinister, unpractical brain which ... was responsible for sponsoring if not for originating the South Sea Company'.[21] Really only Keith Feiling, of an earlier generation of historians, seems to have appreciated that there was more to Harley as a politician than the cant of Macaulay might suggest. The examination of Harley's voluminous papers proves that Feiling's judgment was sound, and in the last decade or so opinions on Harley's statesmanship have been widely reconsidered.[22]

Harley's contribution to the development of the political press serves merely to endorse this reassessment of his merit. His handling of the press exorcizes once and for all Macaulay's spectre of a man of average ability, for he was a true pioneer in the techniques of government propaganda and counter-propaganda. In its place we have Shaftesbury's view that Harley had 'a head, indeed, but too able', so that the whigs did not have 'a genius equal to oppose to him'.[23] This opinion, as we have noted, embraced even Somers. Like Harley, Somers published propaganda on his own initiative. He went to great lengths, when out of office, to appeal to public opinion 'without doors'. The formative whig propaganda campaign of 1701 appears to have been managed chiefly by Somers, and the Kentish Petition and the 'Legion-Letter' were innovations. During the December elections addresses were arranged from electors, and several were printed in the seminal pamphlet, *The Elector's Right Asserted*. Throughout the reign of Queen Anne it was impossible for the representatives of the people in parliament to ignore public opinion. Knights of the Shire, and MPs for large boroughs, were sensitive to the reactions of their constituents. This was especially so in election years.

The tories in general, and Harley in particular, did not lose sight of the mobilisation of opinion in the country by the whigs in 1701. *A Word of Advice to the Citizens of London, Concerning the Choice of Members of Parliament at the Ensuing Election* recalled, in 1705, the character of the men 'listed under the banner of *moderation*': 'their name is Legion, 'tis a name they delight in, and 'tis their own upon more accounts than one'.[24] The tactics of one party were adopted by the other, and the Sacheverell trial led to a deluge of addresses to the queen urging her to dispense with the services of the whigs.[25] Opinion in the country mattered. The defeat of Walpole in 1733 was, like the whig embarrassment in 1710, 'one of the most spectacular triumphs of extra-parliamentary forces'. The Excise Crisis bears testimony to the crucial importance of printed propaganda, and the pressure which could be brought to bear by public opinion. Although, as Paul Langford remarks, 'there were other factors at work even in this', the voice of the people made itself heard loud and long, just as it had done in the seven general elections between 1701 and 1715.[26]

The lesson had not been wasted on Robert Harley. He gained knowledge of the press and the value of propaganda during William's reign, and as secretary he was able to implement his press policies. Defoe's *Review* answered the crying need for an unofficial government paper to balance the unpopular *Gazette*: it was the first paper of its type. It aimed to explain affairs to the electorate at large. At the same time it sought to cajole uncommitted members of the house of commons. There were no party whips in the early eighteenth century. The press was one of the ways developed by Harley to rally party adherents. He realised the usefulness of printed reminders about the ministerial line, and he backed this up by organising meetings of government supporters in the Commons. He was given *carte-blanche* by Godolphin to do this; even Sir Charles Hedges followed Harley's instructions. These were techniques Harley had acquired during the 1690s, and he had had opportunities for experiment during the standing army controversy and the paper war of 1701, where the interaction between propaganda and proceedings in parliament and in the country was apparent to all. The full extent of the policies Harley wished to implement can only be appreciated when he himself was at the head of the administration, and the ministerial propaganda machine embraced five press organs in 1713.

Harley was not in favour of censorship, although he felt that some sort of restraint was necessary to prevent too great a licence being taken with the servants of Church and State. He practised proscription, but he refused to victimise individuals unless there were good grounds for doing so. He did not advocate a return to the licensing system, nor the imposition of a strict set of press regulations. Throughout his career he was impervious to attacks on his own person in print. 'I thought I had been famous for being against vindications myself, by prints', he wrote in 1715, 'or giving any answer to libels but contempt'.[27] In fact Harley enjoyed the piquancy of the well-written lampoon. Swift recalled the occasion, Harley's fiftieth birthday, on which the lord treasurer had handed him 'a scurrilous printed paper of bad verses on himself, under the name of the *English Catiline*, and made me read them to the company'.[28] Unlike Godolphin, he greeted the worst malice of the party hacks with laughter, not tears. The unkind comparison with Catiline failed totally to move him to anger:[29]

> Hail Mighty Hero of the *British* Race,
> Famous for Cunning now, as once for Grace;
> Whate'er the Arts of former Times could do,
> Is, to your Glory, far out-done by you.
> *Nero* rejoyc'd to see his Flaming *Rome*,
> But you at once whole Kingdoms can consume;
> And owing 'tis to your Great Arts alone,
> That they are better pleas'd to be undone.

Instead of a repressive and negative press policy, Harley set out to organise a coterie of writers who would work according to his directions, and he produced and distributed propaganda that had a definite objective: the separation of moderate tories from extreme tories in 1705; the justification of the change of ministry in 1710; the success of the government's peace programme in 1711. It is clear that Harley appreciated the power of the press, and that he accepted the new phenomenon. He sought to come to terms with it, not to strangle it. But what did he expect his propaganda to achieve? There were two broad categories. One was totally positive. It was directed towards a specific goal, and although the fight against a standing army was the best early example, the supreme illustration was provided by Swift's peace pamphlets. Completely divorced from any consideration of whig propaganda, they appealed directly to both parliamentary and public opinion, stating simply, in terms of black and white, the case for a settlement. The second category possessed more negative characteristics. These pamphlets were concerned primarily with countering the arguments (and the raillery) of the opposition writers. Harley himself had penned efforts of this type in 1701, and throughout the Oxford ministry Defoe dealt in counter-propaganda. The appeal to public opinion was often indirect, the objective being to counteract whig writings to safeguard the reputation of the ministry, and to retain its credibility as an administration working for the national good. Such tracts were to serve as 'antidotes' to the 'poison' of the party scribblers.

But no piece of political propaganda in the whole of the post-Revolution period altered anything *on its own*. Sacheverell's sermon led to the change of government in 1710. Had he not been impeached, there might never have been a ministerial revolution in that year. But *In Perils of False Brethren* did not *cause* Harley's return to power, any more than the

Conduct of the Allies, to use the most plausible example, defeated Marlborough and secured the making of peace at Utrecht.[30] The dialectic is, of course, more complex than that, as Paul Langford remarks in relation to the Excise Crisis. The *Conduct* exploited rampant war-weariness. It provided a slogan and a platform upon which those who desired a settlement might be united. It did not *cause* the war-weariness, or even make its audience aware that it was heartily sick of the war. These things were self-evident. The *Conduct of the Allies* supplied a focal point for the uneasiness of the country gentlemen in the symbol of the 'family', and the 'conspiracy thesis' transformed the discontent of the landed men into a formulated programme of political action, presenting facts and arguments to be used in debate. Swift rallied the converted, and the attitude of the men in parliament ensured the success of Oxford's peace campaign.

Symbolism is crucial to successful propaganda. The age of Swift and Defoe had its share of bogeys and scapegoats, its national or group phobias. Popery, Jacobitism, standing armies, placemen, pensioners, the corruption of parliament, the subjugation of the landed by the monied interests. These were the fears on which Swift wove symphonies in his pamphlets. We can recognise various parallels with the symbols of our own day: immigration on one hand, reds-under-the-bed on the other. Ultimately, in the *Conduct of the Allies*, Swift elaborated a conspiracy thesis of almost the same national magnitude as that which Goebbels nourished in Nazi Germany regarding the Jews. The landed squire believed implicitly in his social superiority over not only the unpropertied, but also the merchant and the tradesman. The suggestion that his natural rights were being undermined by stockjobbers was exploited mercilessly by Swift. The landed man, like any other, feared what he did not understand. He was baffled by the mumbo-jumbo of the City, and his anxieties were played upon by Swift, who supplied an object for his hatred, with the Marlboroughs, and above all the figurehead of the duke of Marlborough himself, as his whipping-boys.

Harley recognised, then, the value of positive propaganda, and he appreciated the crude psychology upon which it depended. His contribution to the rise of a free press, not often remarked, is crucial. The eighteenth century saw a gradual decline in restrictions, and, what is more, an altered attitude towards the press. Commenting on Johnson's anonymous reports of parliamentary debates in *The Gentleman's Magazine* during the era of Walpole, Boswell remarked, almost incredulously:[31]

Parliament then kept the press in a kind of mysterious awe, which made it necessary to have recourse to such devices [pseudonyms]. In our time it has acquired an unrestrained freedom, so that the people in all parts of the kingdom have a fair, open, and exact report of the actual proceedings of their representatives and legislators, which in our constitution is highly to be valued...

Harley would have concurred with Boswell's sentiments. By imposing a set of rigid restrictions Harley could have shackled the press, reversing the trend set in motion by the expiry of the licensing act. Instead of merely repressing troublesome opposition writings, Harley tried to understand the problems posed by the new situation of a relatively free press. It is to his credit that to some of the problems he came up with first class answers. Walpole had the example of Harley's press policy as a yardstick against which he could measure his own. Walpole, like Harley, practised proscription, and the young Dr Johnson was forced to remain anonymous as a parliamentary reporter, but Walpole preferred to follow Harley's lead in raising revenue through the stamp tax than operating a rigorous system of censorship. Of perhaps more importance is the fact that Walpole also built a propaganda machine. He was hard pressed by opposition writers – by the circle which sponsored *The Craftsman* and other anti-ministerial publications – and by a literary opposition embracing Pope, Gay, Swift, and Fielding.[32] The only prototype for the counter-propaganda agency which kept the opposition writers at bay was provided by the Oxford ministry.

Most of the innovations in government propaganda techniques from the expiry of the licensing act to the death of Queen Anne occurred when Harley was in office from 1704 to 1708, and again from 1710 to 1714. And in the main he was their originator. Had it not been for Harley, the Godolphin ministry would not have had the *Review*. From 1708 to 1710 the whigs, in office, failed to build on Harley's beginnings, and government control of propaganda was not extended to the whig periodicals already in existence. No concerted programme was put forward to influence public opinion; the whig majority in parliament was deemed to be sufficient. The Sacheverell trial proved the point. It was left to Harley, on his return to office, to complete the work. He did not make the same mistake. Public opinion was carefully and intensively cultivated, despite large tory majorities in two parliaments, and ministerial propaganda releases were constantly being arranged. Only when they had proof of their error did the whigs begin to challenge the quality of the output of the ministerial team led by Swift and Defoe. The whig propaganda campaign reached its climax with Steele's *Crisis* in 1714, and new thoughts upon the press were starting to emerge from the largely anonymous managers of the whig programme. Walpole, like Harley twenty years before, was given a firm grounding in propaganda in opposition. The Oxford ministry was embarrassed, but not defeated. It always managed to retain the edge over its opponents through the dual weapons of proscription and counter-propaganda, with which it fended off the attack.

Oxford's ministry was the first to employ the techniques of opposition in office. For the first time since the Revolution of 1688 a government was not only able to match the printed propaganda of its adversaries, but to surpass it in output and efficacy. The overwhelming need for control through restrictions was replaced by the realisation of control through the well-timed release of official propaganda and counter-propaganda. Boswell may have been critical of an age in which it was imprudent to report events in parliament, but he would have been even more shocked to have lived under the conditions imposed by the system which obtained prior to 1695. The stamp act did not destroy Grub Street; it provided an alternative to censorship. The growth of the press in the reign of Queen Anne was consolidated under the regime of Walpole. The wheels of change had been turned by Robert Harley. True, after 1715 the age of Swift and Defoe gave way to a period in which journalists of less talent were responsible for political propaganda, but readership endured and increased after the glorious years of the first decade of the eighteenth century. Censorship did not return. The place of public opinion in national affairs was assured.

Abbreviations

Unless stated otherwise, all manuscript materials referred to in the notes are preserved in the British Library Manuscripts Students' Room.

Add.MS	Additional Manuscript
BIHR	*Bulletin of the Institute of Historical Research*
BL	British Library
Bodl.	Bodleian Library
CJ	*Journals of the House of Commons*
CSPD	*Calendar of State Papers Domestic*
Defoe, Letters	*The Letters of Daniel Defoe*, ed. G. H. Healey (Oxford, 1955)
EHR	*English Historical Review*
Ehrenpreis, Swift	Irvin Ehrenpreis, *Swift: The Man, His Works, and the Age* (London, *1962–*)
HLQ	*Huntington Library Quarterly*
HMC	Reports of the Royal Historical Manuscripts Commission
Loan 29	The Portland Deposit in the British Library (Harley papers).
Luttrell	Narcissus Luttrell, *A Brief Historical Relation of State Affairs from September 1678 to April 1714* (Oxford 1857)
NUL	Nottingham University Library
N & Q	*Notes and Queries*
POAS	*Poems on Affairs of State: Augustan Satirical Verse, 1660–1714*, VII, ed. F. H. Ellis (London, 1975)
PRO	Public Record Office
RES	*Review of English Studies*
Review	*Defoe's 'Review', Reproduced from the Original Editions with an Introduction and Bibliographical Notes by Arthur Wellesley Secord* (22 vols, New York, 1938). References to the *Review* cite the volume number of the original, and not of the reprint
RO	Record Office
Somers Tracts	*A Collection of Scarce and Valuable Tracts on the Most Interesting and Entertaining Subjects*, ed. W. Scott (London, 1809–15)
State Tracts	*A Collection of State Tracts of the Reign of William III* (1706)
Swift, *Prose Works*	*The Prose Writings of Jonathan Swift*, ed. H. Davis (Oxford, 1939–75)

VC   *Letters Illustrative of the Reign of William III from 1696 to 1708 Addressed to the Duke of Shrewsbury by James Vernon*, ed. G. P. R. James (London, 1841)

Notes

INTRODUCTION

1 *Review*, V, 142.

2 Add. MS 28055, fol. 3: Harley to Godolphin, 9 Aug. 1702.

3 Defoe, *Letters*, 115–18: '*Remarks*, etc., sent into the country' [Apr. 1706?]. See also above, pp. 69–71.

4 *Review*, VI, 108, 223.

5 See J. P. Kenyon, *Revolution Principles: The Politics of Party 1689–1720* (Cambridge, 1977), 56–7.

6 *The Life, Unpublished Letters, and Philosophical Regimen of Anthony, Earl of Shaftesbury*, ed. Benjamin Rand (London, 1900), 512: to John Molesworth, Naples, 30 Aug. 1712.

7 [Abel Boyer], *An Address to the Nobility, Gentry, Merchants, and Proprietors of the National Funds. By the Author of the Monthly Political State of Great Britain*, n.d., broadsheet.

8 Geoffrey Holmes's phrase. See *The Electorate and the National Will in the First Age of Party* (Lancaster, 1976), 2.

9 Geoffrey Holmes, 'Introduction: Post-Revolution Britain and the Historian', in *Britain after the Glorious Revolution 1689–1714*, ed. Holmes (London, 1969), 12.

10 W. A. Speck, *Tory and Whig: The Struggle in the Constituencies, 1701–1715* (London, 1970), 17.

11 See Geoffrey Holmes, *British Politics in the Age of Anne* (London, 1967), *passim* for the former, and Speck, *Tory and Whig, passim*, for the latter.

12 Holmes, *Electorate and the National Will*, 4.

13 On this point, see Lee Horsley, '*Vox Populi* in the Political Literature of 1710', *HLQ*, xxxviii (1974–5), 335–53.

14 Holmes, *Electorate and the National Will*, 32.

15 *Vulgus Britannicus* (1710), 120.

16 *The Rehearsal*, I, preface.

17 *Review*, I, preface.

18 *Reasons humbly offered to the Parliament, in behalf of several Persons concerned in Paper-making, Printing and Publishing the halfpenny newspapers, against the bill now depending, for laying a penny stamp upon every whole sheet, and halfpenny stamp upon every half-sheet of all newspapers* [1712], broadsheet.

19 Maximillian E. Novak, 'Fiction and Society in the Early Eighteenth Century', in *England in the Restoration and Early Eighteenth Century: Essays on Culture and Society*, ed. H. T. Swedenberg (University of California, 1972), 60.

20 *An Appeal of the Clergy of the Church of England, to my Lords the Bishops...with some Reflections upon the Presbyterian Eloquence of John Tuchin and Daniel Foe*, in their *Weekly Observators and Reviews* (1706), preface.

21 See Richard I. Cook, ' "Mr *Examiner*" and "Mr *Review*": The Tory Apologetics of Swift and Defoe', *HLQ*, xxix (1965–6), 127–46.

22 For the last two paragraphs, see Kenyon, *Revolution Principles, passim*.

23 PRO, 30/24/22/2: to M. Van Twedde, 17 Jan. 1706.

24 James Sutherland, *Defoe* (London, 1937), 112.

25 Henry L. Snyder, 'The Circulation of Newspapers in the Reign of Queen Anne', *The Library*, fifth series, xxiii (1968), 209.

26 *The Spectator*, ed. D. F. Bond (1965), I, 44: 12 Mar. 1711.

27 Longleat House, MS Thynne xxv, fol. 424.

28 Defoe, *Letters*, 85: Defoe to John Fransham [*c*. 1 May 1705].

29 *Review*, III, 123.

30 PRO, T. 1, 129, fols. 147–8; Loan 29/280, fols. 83, 90–107; NUL, Portland MSS, Pw2 Hy 1042. The first source was originally discussed by James R. Sutherland, 'The Circulation of Newspapers 1700–1730', *The Library*, fourth series, xv (1934), 110–24; the second by J. M. Price, 'A Note on the Circulation of the Press', *BIHR*, xxxi (1958), 215–24; the third by Henry Snyder in *The Library*, fifth series, xxxi (1976), 387–9. Cf. Snyder, 'Circulation of Newspapers', 206–35.

31 For the circulation of the *Review*, see J. A. Downie, 'Mr *Review* and his Scribbling Friends: Defoe and the Critics, 1705–1706', *HLQ*, xli (1977–8), 345–66.

32 James Boswell, *The Life of Samuel Johnson, with a Journal of a Tour to the Hebrides*, ed. G. B. Hill, revised L. F. Powell (6 vols., Oxford, 1934–50), I, 255.

33 Snyder, 'Circulation of Newspapers', 210–12.

34 I am grateful to Dr W. A. Speck for permission to use the MS of his edition of F. F. Madan, *A Critical Bibliography of Dr Henry Sacheverell* (Kansas, 1978).

35 Lois G. Schwoerer, 'Chronology and Authorship of the Standing Army Tracts, 1697–99', *N & Q*, ccxi (1966), 382–90; J. A. Downie, 'Chronology and Authorship of the Standing Army Tracts: A Supplement', *ibid.*, ccxxi (1976), 342–6.

36 Ian Maxted, *The London Book Trades 1775–1800* (London, 1977), xxxi. Maxted's table may give a slightly distorted picture, as no figure is given for 1710. See also above, p. 159.

37 *A True Collection of the Writings of the Author of the True-Born Englishman* (1705), preface.

38 This is W. A. Speck's estimate. See the introduction to The Rota edition (University of Exeter, 1974), and above, p. 116.

39 Swift, *Prose Works*, VI, ix.

40 Swift, *Prose Works*, XVI, 644.

41 Defoe, *Letters*, 424: 31 Oct. 1713.

42 *Review*, II, 37.

43 Add. MS 28094, fols. 165–6: 'A Character of Daniel Defoe, writer of the pamphlet [*sic*] called *The Review*', n.d. [1704].

44 *The Republican Bullies* (1705), 4.

45 HMC *Portland*, VIII, 187–8: Fonvive to Harley, 18 July 1705.

46 Loan 29/38/6: MS notes dated 17 Dec. 1715.

47 Snyder, 'Circulation of Newspapers', 230.

48 Loan 29/162/9: Harley's *Gazette* accounts; as secretary of state he received a 'moiety' of the paper's profits.
49 *The Poems of Alexander Pope: A One-Volume Edition of the Twickenham Text with selected Annotations*, ed. John Butt (London, 1963), 384, 399.
50 HMC *Bath*, I, 105.
51 Pat Rogers, *Grub Street: Studies in a Subculture* (London, 1972).
52 *Poems*, ed. Butt, 354.
53 *Ibid.*, 231.
54 John J. Richetti, *Popular Fiction Before Richardson: Narrative Patterns 1700–1739* (Oxford, 1969), 119–67.
55 Novak, 'Fiction and Society', 62–3.

1. THE PROPAGANDA OF COURT AND COUNTRY

1 Loan 29/141/3: Sir Edward Harley to Robert Harley, 8 June 1691; *ibid.*, 267/5: 'a short breviary' in Harley's hand, 11 Sept. 1723.
2 *Ibid.*, 74/2: Anne, Lady Clinton to Sir E. Harley, 17 Apr. 1690.
3 *Ibid.*, 164/4: 1 June 1689.
4 See J. A. Downie, 'Robert Harley, Sir Rowland Gwynne, and the New Radnor Election of 1690', *Transactions of the Radnorshire Society*, xlvi (1976), 10–20.
5 HMC *Portland*, III, 485: Edward Harley to Sir E. Harley, 23 Dec. 1691; Loan 29/78/3: the same to the same, 10 Jan. 1692.
6 See J. A. Downie, 'The Commission of Public Accounts and the Formation of the Country Party', *EHR*, xci (1976), 33–51.
7 See J. R. Jones, *The First Whigs: the Politics of the Exclusion Crisis 1678–1683* (Durham, 1961); K. H. D. Haley, *The First Earl of Shaftesbury* (Oxford, 1968).
8 J. G. A. Pocock, 'Machiavelli, Harrington, and English Political Ideologies in the Eighteenth Century', *William and Mary Quarterly*, xxii (1965), 571.
9 *Ibid.*, 563.
10 [Simon Clement], *Faults on Both Sides: Or, An Essay upon the Original Cause, Progress, and Mischievous Consequences of the Factions in this Nation* (1710) in *Somers Tracts*, XII, 694. For Harley's part in the publication of this pamphlet, see above, pp. 119–22.
11 Loan 29/165/2; HMC *Portland*, IV, 451; *ibid.*, V, 646.
12 [Pierre Desmaizeaux], *A Collection of several pieces of Mr. John Toland, Now first Published from his Original Manuscripts: with Some Memoirs of his Life and Writings* (1726), II, 340–1.
13 Letters were addressed to him there. Loan 29/185, fols. 149, 159; HMC *Portland*, III, 472.
14 *Ibid.*, IV, 697; Shaftesbury to Harley, 30 May 1711.
15 *The Life, Unpublished Letters, and Philosophical Regimen of Anthony, Earl of Shaftesbury*, ed. Benjamin Rand (London, 1900), 354–5: to William Stephens, 17 July 1706.
16 *Cobbett's Parliamentary History of England* (London, 1806–20), V, 830.
17 Loan 29/164/3: Harley to his wife, 12 Nov. 1689.
18 Dennis Rubini, *Court and Country 1688–1702* (London, 1967), 28; cf. Geoffrey Holmes, *British Politics in the Age of Anne* (London, 1967), 116.

19 *State Tracts*, II, 313.

20 *Ibid.*

21 *Ibid.*, 320, 326.

22 See J. A. Downie, 'Ben Overton: An Alternative Author of *A Dialogue betwixt Whig and Tory*', *Papers of the Bibliographical Society of America*, lxx (1976), 263–71.

23 *State Tracts*, II, 391.

24 NUL, Portland MSS, PwA 1212: Sunderland to Portland, 3 May 1693.

25 For Overton and Sunderland, see *ibid.*, PwA 1238, 1245: the same to the same, 13 July 1694, 29 May 1695.

26 Add. MS 28929, fol. 142: Humphrey Prideaux to John Ellis, 11 Dec. [1693].

27 *State Tracts*, II, 369–71.

28 See Henry Horwitz, *Parliament, Policy and Politics in the Reign of William III* (Manchester, 1977), 211.

29 John Oldmixon, *The History of England during the Reigns of King William and Queen Mary, Queen Anne, King George I* (London, 1735), 89.

30 See HMC *Portland*, III, IV, V, *passim*; Loan 29/149/1; *ibid.*, 314.

31 *State Tracts*, II, 369–71; Add. MS 28929, fol. 142; Luttrell, III, 228: 20 Nov. 1693.

32 HMC *Finch*, IV, 160–1.

33 See *ibid.*, 90–2, 243, 389, 437, 510–12, 515–16, 518.

34 Harleian MS 1243, fols. 129–43. I am grateful to Mark N. Brown for this information. (Another MS copy is to be found in the Harley papers, Loan 29/206/113.) For evidence of Harley's close relations with Halifax, see HMC *Portland*, III, 544–7; HMC *Bath*, I, 51; Loan 29/151/8; *ibid.*, 187, fol. 162; *ibid.*, 142/4. See also Horwitz, *Parliament, Policy and Politics*, 117; and Mark N. Brown, 'The Works of George Savile, Marquis of Halifax: Dates and Circumstances of Composition', *HLQ*, xxxv (1971–2), 153–4.

35 *Halifax: Complete Works*, ed. J. P. Kenyon (Harmondsworth, 1969), 181, 189.

36 *CJ*, XI, 340–5. See Raymond Astbury, 'The Renewal of the Licensing Act in 1693 and its Lapse in 1695', *The Library*, fifth series, xxxiii (1978), 296–322. I am grateful to Mr Astbury for sending me a copy of his article prior to publication.

37 Loan 29/303, unfoliated. Ridpath's 'Reasons against Laying down the *Flying Post*' were sent to Paul Foley as speaker of the house of commons, via Harley.

38 *Ibid.*, 12/7. I should like to thank the librarian and staff of the Goldsmiths' Library for assistance and cooperation in my unsuccessful attempt to trace a printed version of Harley's MS. It is interesting that in *An Account of a Dream at Harwich*, published in 1708, the Junto was also referred to disparagingly as 'five or six jugglers' (p. 8). For the *Dream*, a Harleyite pamphlet, see above, pp. 106–11. Cf. Loan 29/27/1.

39 Loan 29/188, fol. 245: to his father, 23 Nov. 1697.

40 *Ibid.*, fol. 246.

41 *Ibid.*, fol. 251: to his father, 3 Dec. 1697.

42 *A Letter, Balancing the Necessity of keeping a Land-Force in times of Peace: with the Dangers that may follow on it* (1697), 3.

43 Add. MS 30000A, fols. 400, 403–4: Bonet's reports, 14 and 17 Dec. 1697; *ibid.*, 17677SS, fols. 83–4, 87: L'Hermitage's reports, same dates. The broadsheet in question was *A List of King James's Irish and Popish Forces in France*.

44 *A (Second) Dialogue betwixt Jack and Will about a Standing Army* [1697?], 4.

45 *Post Man*, 3 Feb. 1698: 'This day is published'. I owe this reference to Giancarlo Carabelli.

46 *State Tracts*, II, 613.

47 *Ibid.*, 597, 613.

48 *Some Reflections upon a late Paper, entitled, An Argument showing that a Standing Army is Inconsistent with a Free Government, and Absolutely Destructive to the Constitution of the English Monarchy* (1697), 17.

49 Northamptonshire RO, Buccleuch MSS, Vernon letters, I, 177: Vernon to Shrewsbury, 8 Jan. 1698; HMC *Portland*, III, 595.

50 *CSPD*, 1697, 513: Yard's Newsletter, 14 Dec. 1697.

51 *CJ*, XII, 91, 93; cf. *VC*, II, 3: 8 Feb. 1698.

52 Loan 29/189, fol. 4: Harley to his father, 8 Jan. 1698; Northants RO, Buccleuch MSS, Vernon letters, I, 177.

53 Giancarlo Carabelli, *Tolandiana: Materiali bibliografici per lo studio dell' opera e della fortuna di John Toland (1670–1722)* (Florence, 1975), 50.

54 *State Tracts*, II, 594.

55 See Lois Schwoerer, 'The Literature of the Standing Army Controversy, 1697–1699', *HLQ*, xxviii (1965–6), 191n.

56 Schwoerer, 'Chronology and Authorship of the Standing Army Tracts, 1697–9', *N & Q*, ccxi (1966), 384–5, 387.

57 Luttrell, IV, 313: 2 Dec. 1697.

58 Add. MS 30000A, fol. 405: 21 Dec. 1697; *ibid.*, 17677SS, fol. 87: 17 Dec. 1697.

59 Loan 29/282, unfoliated, n.d.

60 *Ibid.*, n.d.

61 *CSPD*, 1698, 377: Sir Miles Cooke to Sir Joseph Williamson, 19 Aug. 1698.

62 Add. MS 30000B, fol. 6: 7 Jan. 1698.

63 *Review*, VII, 570.

64 J. R. Moore, 'Daniel Defoe: King William's Pamphleteer and Intelligence Agent', *HLQ*, xxxiv (1970–1), 251–60.

65 *A Short Defence of the last Parliament, with a Word of Advice to all Electors for the Ensuing* (1701), broadsheet.

66 Carlisle RO, Lowther Correspondence: James Lowther to Sir John Lowther of Whitehaven, 17 Dec. 1698.

67 *A Present taken of England divided in the Election of the Next Parliament* (Loan 29/206/115, printed in HMC *Portland*, VIII, 54).

68 *State Tracts*, II, 595.

69 [John Toland, ed.], *Letters from the Right Honourable the late Earl of Shaftesbury to Robert Molesworth* (1721), xxi; cf. Carabelli, *Tolandiana*, 41–2.

70 *State Tracts*, II, 638.

71 Loan 29/189, fol. 35: George Tollett to Harley, 21 July 1698: 'An Answer is this day come out to a paper entitled *The Danger of Mercenary Parliaments*'.

72 *Considerations on the Nature of Parliaments, and our present Elections* (1698) in *Cobbett's Parliamentary History*, v, appendix, clv.

73 G.W., *A Letter to a Country Gentleman, setting Forth the Cause of the Decay and Ruin of Trade* (1698).

74 *VC*, II, 143: 2 Aug. 1698.

75 See *CSPD*, 1698, 376; Loan 29/25/12; Henry Horwitz, 'Parties, Connections, and Parliamentary Politics, 1689–1714: Review and Revision', *Journal of British Studies*, vi (1966), 45–69; Horwitz, *Parliament, Policy and Politics*, 239–40.

76 Harley to Henry Boyle, 16 Nov. 1698, cited *ibid.*, 240.

77 *State Tracts*, II, 671–3.

78 Loan 29/282, unfoliated: Trenchard to Harley, n.d.

79 See Downie, 'Chronology and Authorship of the Standing Army Tracts: A Supplement', *N & Q*, ccxxi (1976), 345.

80 Bodl. MS Rawlinson, A. 245, fol. 69.

81 See Horwitz, *Parliament, Policy and Politics*, 247–8.

82 See Downie, 'Chronology and Authorship', 345.

83 [Desmaizeaux], *Collection*, II, 227.

84 *Ibid.*, 345.

85 *Ibid.*, 221, 345.

86 Lambeth Palace Library, MS 933, fol. 74: William Simpson to John Toland, 20 Apr. 1697. I owe this reference to G. Carabelli.

87 [Desmaizeaux], *Collection*, I, xxv: John Molyneux to John Locke, 11 Sept. 1697.

88 HMC *Portland*, III, 586: Sir Richard Cox's Newsletter, 14 Sept. 1697.

89 Add. MS 4295, fol. 10.

90 *Ibid.*, 40773, fol. 333: 29 Apr. 1699.

91 See Bodl. MS Rawlinson, A. 245, fol. 85.

92 Loan 29/189, fol. 52: 3 Jan. 1699.

93 HMC *Cowper*, II, 389: Davenant to Thomas Coke, 1 July 1699.

94 Oldmixon, *History*, 198.

95 *A Discourse upon Grants and Resumptions, Showing How our Ancestors Have Proceeded with such Ministers As have Procured to Themselves Grants of the Crown Revenue; And that the Forfeited Estates ought to be applied towards the Payment of the Public Debts* ([1699, but dated] 1700), 357.

96 Carlisle RO, Lowther Corr.: James Lowther to Sir John Lowther, 20 Jan. 1700.

97 *VC*, III, 91–4: 22 June 1700.

98 See Loan 29/165/2; HMC *Portland*, IV, 452.

99 *VC*, III, 91–4: 22 June 1700.

100 *Ibid.*, 132.

101 *Essays* (1700), appendix, preface.

102 Loan 29/190, fol. 17.

2. THE PAPER WAR OF 1701

1 *The Poems of Alexander Pope: A One-Volume Edition of the Twickenham Text with Selected Annotations*, ed. John Butt (London, 1963), 354.

2 *An Appeal to Honour and Justice* (1715) in *Selected Writings of Daniel Defoe*, ed. James T. Boulton (Cambridge, 1975), 168.

3 See Ian Watt, '*Considerations upon Corrupt Elections of Members to Serve in Parliament*, 1701: By Anthony Hammond, not Defoe', *Philological Quarterly*, xxxi (1952), 45–53.

4 See Giancarlo Carabelli, *Tolandiana: Materiali bibliografici per lo studio dell'opera e della fortuna di John Toland (1670–1722)* (Florence, 1975), 42.

5 *The Art of Governing by Parties* (1701), 31–3.

6 [Pierre Desmaizeaux], *A Collection of several pieces of Mr. John Toland, Now first Published from his Original Manuscripts: with Some Memoirs of his Life and Writings* (1726), II, 340–1.

7 *The Wentworth Papers 1705–1739*, ed. J. J. Cartwright (London, 1883), 136–7: Peter Wentworth to Lord Raby, 18 Aug. 1710. Cf. Carabelli, *Tolandiana*, 335.

8 PRO, 30/24/21/231: Shaftesbury to Toland, 21 July [1701].

9 He viewed it as 'a wrong measure, enough to ruin us all', and he referred consistently to 'the new tory ministry'. (*Original Letters of Locke, Sidney and Shaftesbury*, ed. T. Forster (London, 1830), 113–14: Shaftesbury to Benjamin Furly, 11 Jan. 1701.)

10 *Ibid.*, 123

11 *Art of Governing by Parties*, 103, 109–10.

12 Carabelli, *Tolandiana*, 81. Toland's *Propositions for uniting the two East-India Companies* was also published on 3 Mar. 1701, again probably at Harley's instigation (*ibid.*, 83).

13 Burnet of Kemney to Sophia, cited *ibid.*, 79.

14 *Some Queries, which may deserve Consideration* [1701], broadsheet.

15 Bodl. MS Montague, D. 1, fol. 69: to Halifax, 3 Dec. 1701.

16 PRO, 30/24/20/28: J[ohn] T[oland] to Shaftesbury, 19 July 1701.

17 Loan 29/165/2: Harley's 'Large Account: Revolution and Succession'.

18 *Ibid.*

19 *Add. MS 7074, fol. 19: John Ellis to George Stepney, 16 May 1701.*

20 *State Tracts*, III, 260, 285.

21 *VC*, III, 155–6: 2 Sept. 1701.

22 *The Elector's Right Asserted* (1701), [1].

23 Loan 29/7/1.

24 HMC *Downshire*, I, 806: to Sir William Trumbull, 24 Aug. 1701.

25 *VC*, III, 155–6.

26 Clayton Roberts, *The Growth of Responsible Government in Stuart England* (London, 1966), 317–20.

27 J. A. Downie, 'Robert Harley, Charles Davenant, and the Authorship of the *Worcester Queries*', *Literature and History*, no. 3 (March, 1976), 83–99.

28 Jonathan Swift, *A Discourse of the Contests and Dissensions between the Nobles and the Commons in Athens and Rome*, ed. Frank H. Ellis (Oxford, 1967), 44–5.

29 *Post Boy*, 20–2 Mar. 1701; Add. MS 17677WW, fol. 203.

30 PRO, Transcripts 3 (France) 189, fol. 47; Swift, *Discourse*, ed. Ellis, 75n.

31 *Two English Republican Tracts*, ed. Caroline Robbins (London, 1969), 32–3.

32 *True Picture of a Modern Whig* (1701), 32.

33 Swift, *Discourse*, ed. Ellis, 75n.

34 *True Picture of a Modern Whig*, 42.

35 Loan 29/190, fol. 96.

36 *Ibid.*, 7/1 (Bromley's letter is preserved *ibid.*, 128/3). The 'confused materials' in Loan 29/7/1 include a Harley holograph draft of the *Letter from the Grecian Coffee-house*, and a MS transcription in a clerk's hand (or Davenant's at its neatest?). Harley's holograph draft of the *Taunton-Dean Letter* is in Loan 29/12/3.

37 Loan 29/7/1; *ibid.*, 12/3.

38 HMC *Cowper*, II, 436–7.

39 *Letter from the Grecian Coffee-house* (1701), 3.

40 HMC *Cowper*, II, 436–7.

41 Loan 29/190, fol. 131.

42 Lambeth Palace Library, MS 930, fol. 25: 8 Jan. 1702. Cf. *POAS*, VII, 570.

43 *Letter from the Grecian Coffee-house*, 4. A measure of Harley's success in handling mock form may be the fact that this passage has been cited by one historian as a genuine piece of correspondence from Harley 'to a friend, *c.* 1701', and it is viewed as a tirade against the *tory* backbenchers. See A. D. MacLachlan, 'The Road to Peace, 1710–13', in *Britain after the Glorious Revolution 1689–1714*, ed. Geoffrey Holmes (London, 1969), 201–2, and 22n.

44 *True Picture of a Modern Whig*, 7.

45 *Letter from the Grecian Coffee-house*, 5.

46 James O. Richards, *Party Propaganda Under Queen Anne: The General Elections of 1702–1713* (Georgia, 1972), 32.

3. HARLEY AND DEFOE

1 Loan 29/162/5: 'Large Account: Revolution and Succession'.

2 HMC *Bath*, I, 73: to Godolphin, 21 July 1705 (draft).

3 HMC *Portland*, IV, 34: 8 Mar. 1702.

4 See Henry L. Snyder, 'Godolphin and Harley: A Study of their Partnership in Politics', *HLQ*, xxx (1966–7), 241–71; and Angus McInnes, 'The Appointment of Harley in 1704', *Historical Journal*, xi (1968), 255–71.

5 Add. MS 28055, fol. 3.

6 *Review*, I, 1.

7 John Oldmixon, *The History of England during the Reigns of King William and Queen Mary, Queen Anne, King George I* (London, 1735), 456–7.

8 Loan 29/190, fol. 207: 18 Aug. 1702. My italics. This crucial sentence is omitted from the transcription printed in HMC *Portland*, IV, 44.

9 Geoffrey Holmes, *British Politics in the Age of Anne* (London, 1967), 270.

10 J. R. Sutherland, *Daniel Defoe: A Critical Study* (Cambridge, Mass., 1971), 8; see also *Defoe's 'Review'*, ed. A. W. Secord (New York, 1938), introduction, xvi.

11 *Letter from the Grecian Coffee-house*, 5.

12 See HMC *Portland*, IV, 18: Paterson to Harley, 19 and 27 May 1701. 'Proposals for the better restoring of public credit', which Paterson sent to Harley, is extant in MS in Loan 29/190. See also Loan 29/294, unfoliated: James Drake to Harley, 1 Aug. 1702.

13 HMC *Portland*, IV, 43: Paterson to Harley, 6 Aug. 1702.

14 *Ibid.*, 45: Godolphin to the same, 20 Aug. 1702. Cf. *ibid.*, VIII, 104: 7 Sept. 1702: Paterson's 'Things proposed to be done in the ensuing session of parliament', chiefly financial.

15 Defoe, *Letters*, 4–7: Defoe to William Paterson, Apr. 1703.

16 Pat Rogers, 'Defoe in the Fleet Prison', *RES*, n.s. xxii (1971), 451–5.

17 *Defoe's 'Review'*, ed. Secord, xvi.

18 Add. MS 29589, fol. 400, n.d. For support for my dating, see HMC *Portland*, IV, 53–4: Godolphin to Harley, 14 Dec. 1702. Cf. *POAS*, VI, 548.

19 *Cobbett's Parliamentary History of England* (London, 1806–20), VI, 145.

20 Defoe, *Letters*, 4–7. The MS letter is endorsed in Harley's hand: 'Received from Mr William Paterson, Friday 28 May 1703 at one o'clock'. (Loan 29/224, fol. 2.)

21 Defoe, *Letters*, 8: Defoe [to William Penn], 12 July 1703.

22 Add. MS 29589, fols. 28, 43, 45: Godolphin to Nottingham, 17, 21 and 23 July 1703.

23 For Defoe's fanciful account of Harley's intervention, see his *Appeal* in *Selected Writings of Daniel Defoe*, ed. James T. Boulton (Cambridge, 1975), 171. For Defoe's trial, see J. R. Moore, *Defoe in the Pillory and Other Studies* (1939), ch. 1.

24 Longleat House, Portland Misc. MSS, fols. 166–7. See Henry L. Snyder, 'Daniel Defoe, the Duchess of Marlborough, and the *Advice to the Electors of Great Britain*', *HLQ*, xxix (1965–6), 55.

25 HMC *Eighth Report*, 43b. Cf. Snyder, 'Daniel Defoe', 56.

26 HMC *Portland*, iv, 68.

27 *Ibid.*, 75.

28 Add. MS 28055, fols. 13–14. See also Henry L. Snyder, 'The Defeat of the Occasional Conformity Bill and the Tack: A Study in the Techniques of Parliamentary Management in the Reign of Queen Anne', *BIHR*, xli (1968), 174–5; and Loan 29/294, unfoliated: James Drake to Harley, 18 Sept. 1703.

29 Defoe, *Letters*, 9: Defoe to James Stancliffe, Nov. 1703.

30 *A Challenge of Peace, Addressed to the Whole Nation. With an Enquiry into Ways and Means for bringing it to pass* (1703), 23.

31 HMC *Portland*, iv, 155: Godolphin to Harley, n.d.

32 Douglas Coombs, *The Conduct of the Dutch: British Opinion and the Dutch Alliance during the War of the Spanish Succession* (The Hague, 1958), 87.

33 *Review*, i, preface.

34 *Ibid.*, 50, 3.

35 *Ibid.*, 65.

36 See Longleat House, Thynne MSS, xxv, fols. 135, 139.

37 HMC *Bath*, i, 58–9.

38 *Review*, i, 155.

39 Defoe, *Letters*, 26.

40 HMC *Bath*, i, 61: 31 July 1704.

41 Theodore F. M. Newton, 'William Pittis and Queen Anne Journalism', *Modern Philology*, xxxiii (1935–6), 184.

42 Quoted *ibid.*

43 *POAS*, vii, 168n.

44 *Heraclitus Ridens*, ii, 45: 4–8 Jan. 1704; *ibid.*, ii, 59: 26–9 Feb. 1704. Cf. *Observator*, ii, 94, 95.

45 HMC *Portland*, viii, 109, 111.

46 Loan 29/152/2: 20 Oct. 1704.

47 *Ibid.*, 263, 38–9; *ibid.*, 152/2: Northey to Harley, 25 Oct. 1704.

48 See Lee Sonsteng Horsley, 'The Trial of John Tutchin, Author of *The Observator*', *The Yearbook of English Studies*, iii (1973), 124–40.

49 *A Complete Collection of State Trials*, ed. T. B. Howell (London, 1816–26), xiv, 1,131.

50 Daniel Defoe, *An Essay on the Regulation of the Press* (Luttrell Society, 1948), 24.

51 Loan 29/162/5: R.A. to Harley, 1 Apr. [1704].

52 See J. A. Downie, 'An Unknown Defoe Broadsheet on the Regulation of the Press?', *The Library*, fifth series, xxxiii (1978), 51–8.

53 HMC *Portland*, IV, 138: 28 Sept. 1704.

54 Loan 29/155/1: James Rawlins to Harley, 31 Jan. 1705. See also Pat Rogers, 'An Eighteenth-Century Alarm: Defoe, Sir Justinian Isham and the Secretaries of State', *Northamptonshire Past and Present*, iv (1971–2), 383–7, which makes use of papers in the PRO (SP 44/105/90, 135, 152; SP 34/4/42–3, 46–7). Cf. HMC *Portland*, IV, 140: E[rasmus] Lewis to Harley, 28 Sept. 1704.

55 *POAS*, VII, 324.

56 Defoe, *Letters*, 58–62: [Defoe to Harley], 28 Sept. 1704; see also Frank H. Ellis, 'Defoe and *The Master Mercury*', *N & Q*, ccxvii (1972), 28–9.

57 For Defoe's correspondence with Fransham, see Defoe, *Letters*, 64–5, 70–2, 79–81, 83–5, 114–15, 123–4, 184–7, 248–9.

58 *Ibid.*, 87.

59 *Review*, II, 73–6.

60 *Ibid.*, V, 414.

61 Henry L. Snyder, 'Newsletters in England, 1689–1715: With Special Reference to John Dyer – A Byway in the History of England', in *Newsletters to Newspapers: Eighteenth-Century Journalism*, ed. Donovan H. Bond and W. Reynolds McLeod (West Virginia, 1977), 6–7.

62 *Review*, VIII, 708.

63 The itinerary is taken from Defoe, *Letters*, pp. 108–13: 'An Abstract of my Journey with Casual Observations on Public Affairs' [*c.* 6 Nov. 1705].

64 *Ibid.*, 115–18: '*Remarks*, etc., sent into the country'.

65 HMC *Portland*, IV, 110: [Dyer's] Newsletter, 19 Aug. 1704.

66 Defoe, *Letters*, 67: [Defoe to Harley], 2 Nov. 1704.

67 Lansdowne MS 773, fol. 30: Charles Davenant to his son, 21 Apr. 1704. See also McInnes, 'The Appointment of Harley in 1704', 255–71.

68 See Patricia M. Ansell, 'Harley's Parliamentary Management', *BIHR*, xxxiv (1961), 92–7.

69 W. A. Speck, *Tory and Whig: The Struggle in the Constituencies, 1701–1715* (London, 1970), 100–2.

70 *Review*, II, 73–6.

71 *Ibid.*, 99.

72 *Ibid.*, 196.

73 W. A. Speck, 'The Choice of a Speaker in 1705', *BIHR*, xxxvi (1964), 26.

74 See J. A. Downie, 'Mr *Review* and his Scribbling Friends: Defoe and the Critics, 1705–1706', *HLQ*, xli (1978), 345–66.

75 *Moderation, Justice, and Manners of the Review* (1706), 3.

76 *Rehearsal*, I, 87.

77 *Ibid.*, I, 49.

78 HMC *Portland*, IV, 291: [Godolphin to Harley], Good Friday night [22 Mar. 1706]. See also Speck, 'Choice of a Speaker', 20–46.

79 *State Tracts: Containing Many Necessary Observations and Reflections on the State of our Affairs at Home and Abroad; with Some Secret Memoirs. By the Author of the Examiner* (1715), I, 22, 26. I know of no extant, original issues of the *Dialogue between Church and No-Church*, but seven dialogues are reprinted in this edition of *State Tracts* of which the Houghton Library of Harvard University has a copy.

80 Defoe, *Letters*, 119, 122: [Defoe to Harley], 6 May 1706.

81 HMC *Portland*, v, 647: Auditor Harley's 'Memoir'.
82 Loan 29/9/38: memo in Harley's hand, 'Windsor, 22 Sept. 1706'.
83 HMC *Portland*, II, 193: to the duke of Newcastle.
84 *Ibid.*, v, 647.
85 *Review*, III, 244, 278.
86 See William Coxe, *Memoirs of John, Duke of Marlborough* (London, 1847–8), II, 2: Queen Anne to Godolphin, 30 Aug. 1706; HMC *Portland*, II, 196: Harley to Newcastle, 10 Sept. 1706.
87 Defoe, *Letters*, 125: 13 Sept. 1706.
88 For the relations of Defoe and Sunderland, see J. A. Downie, 'Daniel Defoe and the General Election of 1708 in Scotland', *Eighteenth-Century Studies*, viii (1975), 320–1, 326–7.
89 Defoe, *Letters*, 128: 13 Sept. 1706.
90 *Review*, IV, no. 127.
91 *Ibid.*, IV, preface.
92 *The Review Reviewed. In a Letter to the Prophet Daniel in Scotland* (1706), reprinted in Maximillian E. Novak, 'A Whiff of Scandal in the Life of Daniel Defoe', *HLQ*, xxxiv (1970–1), 38–9.
93 See W. Ferguson, 'The Making of the Treaty of 1707', *Scottish Historical Review*, xliii (1964), 89–110. For the assertion that 'Defoe's own share in enacting the union would be difficult to overestimate', see J. R. Moore, *Daniel Defoe: Citizen of the Modern World* (Chicago, 1958), 187. Cf. *POAS*, VII, 210; Downie, 'Defoe and the General Election of 1708', 316–19.
94 Defoe, *Letters*, 202: [13 Feb. 1707].
95 *Ibid.*, 227–9 (copy).
96 *Ibid.*, 202.
97 *Ibid.*, 249.
98 For Harley's fall, see G. S. Holmes and W. A. Speck, 'The Fall of Harley in 1708 Reconsidered', *EHR*, lxxx (1965), 673–98. Cf. Snyder, 'Godolphin and Harley', 263–71.
99 Defoe, *Letters*, 250: [Defoe] to Harley, 10 Feb. 1708; *Appeal* in *Selected Writings of Daniel Defoe*, ed. Boulton, 173.

4. 'THE MEMORIAL OF THE CHURCH OF ENGLAND' (1705):
A CASE STUDY

1 T. Sharp, *The Life of Archbishop Sharp* (London, 1825), I, 366.
2 Loan 29/70/9: Robert Harley to Edward Harley, 22 Apr. 1704.
3 *The Memorial of the Church of England, Humbly Offered to the Consideration of all True Lovers of our Church and Constitution* (1705), 27.
4 See W. A. Speck, 'Choice of a Speaker in 1705', *BIHR*, xxxvi (1964), 20–46, and the same author's unpublished Oxford DPhil thesis, 'The House of Commons 1702–1714: A Study in Political Organization' (1965), I, 142–5.
5 *Remarks and Collections of Thomas Hearne*, ed. C. E. Doble (Oxford, 1884), I, 3.
6 *Memorial*, 4–5.
7 *Ibid.*, 9–10, 27, 43.
8 *Ibid.*, 21.

9 See HMC *Bath*, I, 74–5: Harley to Godolphin, 4 Sept. 1705.

10 HMC *Portland*, IV, 261: to Sir Robert Davers, 6 Oct. 1705. See also Loan 29/171/2: to William Stratford, 10 Oct. 1705.

11 *Remarks*, ed. Doble, I, 3; PRO, SP 44/77/19.

12 Defoe, *Letters*, 91: [10 July 1705].

13 Loan 29/192, fol. 214: 13 July 1705. Cf. HMC *Portland*, IV, 207.

14 Loan 29/130/5. For Clare, see Henry L. Snyder, 'The Reports of a Press Spy for Robert Harley: New Bibliographical Data for the Reign of Queen Anne', *The Library*, fifth series, xxii (1967), 326–45.

15 NUL, Portland MSS, Pw2 Hy 566, 567: David Edwards to Harley, n.d. and 1 Oct. 1705 (endorsed by Harley, 'D. Edwards about the *Memorial*').

16 *Ibid.*, Pw2 Hy 565: 'D. Edwards to Thomas Edwards, at the Right Honourable the Lord Treasurer's in St James's, 29 Dec. 1705'.

17 Defoe, *Letters*, 91–4.

18 Add. MS 4291, fols. 40–1: to his son, 18 Jan. 1706.

19 *Remarks*, ed. Doble, I, 6.

20 HMC *Portland*, IV, 212: to Harley, 23 July 1705.

21 HMC *Bath*, I, 64. This letter is wrongly dated 1704. The original (Longleat, Portland MSS, VII, fol. 23) has no year, but it clearly refers to 1705 and the imminent appointment of Cowper as lord keeper.

22 *The Memorial of the Church of England... To which is added an Introductory Preface, Wherein is contained the Life and Death of the Author, and Reasons for this present Publication* (1711), iii. Interestingly, this edition supplied an account of the enquiry into the authorship of the *Memorial*, and Edwards's pretensions were openly ridiculed, as 'it was impossible to carry on the discovery any farther' (*ibid.*, vi–vii).

23 Loan 29/413. The details of Edwards's story are taken from his deposition before the secretaries of state (*ibid.*, 5/4; cf. NUL, Portland MSS, Pw2 Hy 572). Source materials for the investigation are voluminous. For a full account, and transcriptions of some of the relevant documents, see my PhD thesis, 'Robert Harley and the Press' (University of Newcastle upon Tyne, 1976), 147–88, 390–402.

24 NUL, Portland MSS, Pw2 Hy 568: Edwards to Harley, [20 Jan. 1706]; Loan 29/193, fol. 37: the same to the same, 22 Jan. 1706; *ibid.*, 5/8.

25 *The Private Diary of William, First Earl Cowper*, ed. E. C. Hawtrey (London, 1833), 36–7.

26 G. M. Trevelyan, *England Under Queen Anne* (London, 1965), II, 100.

27 Bodl. Ballard MS 38, fol. 144: to Arthur Charlett, 8 Sept. 1705.

28 *Remarks*, ed. Doble, I, 180.

29 Loan 29/209, fol. 267.

30 NUL, Portland MSS, Pw2 Hy 568.

31 Loan 29/5/9; Luttrell, VI, 57.

32 *Diary*, ed. Hawtrey, 33.

33 *POAS*, VII, 162.

34 Bodl. MS Rawlinson, A. 245, fol. 67.

35 *Review*, III, 166.

36 HMC *Portland*, IV, 292, 294, 303; NUL, Portland MSS, Pw2 Hy 570, 571; Loan 29/163/5–7; *ibid.*, 193, fols. 126, 207; *ibid.*, 194, fol. 147; *ibid.*, 284, unfoliated; *ibid.*, 295, unfoliated.

37 Defoe, *Letters*, 90–1.
38 *Ibid.*, 92–3.
39 *Remarks*, ed. Doble, I, 12.
40 [William Pittis], *The Secret History of the Mitre and Purse* (1714), 29; cf. Theodore F. M. Newton, 'William Pittis and Queen Anne Journalism', *Modern Philology*, xxxiii (1935–6), 184–5.
41 HMC *Portland*, VIII, 200–1: n.d.
42 Harley's phrase, used in a letter of 6 Sept. 1706 to William Stratford, Loan 29/171/2.
43 [Joseph Browne], *A Dialogue between Louis le Petite, and Harlequin le Grand* [1708], 18.
44 Loan 29/192, fol. 221: to Harley, 23 July 1705.
45 Giancarlo Carabelli, *Tolandiana: Materiali bibliografici per lo studio dell'opera e della fortuna di John Toland (1670–1722)* (Florence, 1975), 115–16.
46 [John Toland], *The Memorial of the State of England* (1705), 68–9.
47 PRO, 30/24/20/80–1: Shaftesbury to John Wheelock, n.d. and 27 Nov. 1703.
48 [Pierre Desmaizeaux], *A Collection of several pieces of Mr. John Toland, Now first Published from his Original Manuscripts: with Some Memoirs of his Life and Writings* (1726), II, 337–53: 'Letter to Mr [Penn] London, June 26, 1705'.
49 HMC *Portland*, IV, 230, 235–6: William Penn to Harley, 24 Aug. 1705; anon. [Toland] to the same, 28 Aug. 1705.
50 [Desmaizeaux], *Collection*, II, 228; cf. *ibid.*, I, lix.
51 PRO, 30/24/20/105: 22 Oct. 1705.
52 [Desmaizeaux], *Collection*, II, 354–7. The genuineness of this compilation can be established. See Loan 29/192, fol. 374: John Shower to [John Toland], 27 Oct. 1705. This letter is misaddressed (to Harley) and misdated (24 Oct.) in HMC *Portland*, IV, 268.
53 [Browne], *Dialogue between Louis le Petite, and Harlequin le Grand*, 4.
54 [Desmaizeaux], *Collection*, II, 357: 'Toland to [Harley], 14 Dec. 1705'.
55 *A Letter to the Author of the Memorial of the State of England* (1705), 28–31.
56 Add. MS 4291, fols. 40–1.
57 Loan 29/9/26; Luttrell, VI, 7; *Remarks*, ed. Doble, I, 164.
58 See Douglas Coombs, 'William Stephens and the *Letter to the Author of the Memorial of the State of England* (1706)', *BIHR*, xxxii (1959), 24–37; cf. J. A. Downie, 'William Stephens and the *Letter to the Author of the Memorial of the State of England* Reconsidered', *ibid.*, l (1977), 253–9.
59 Loan 29/155/1: Harley to Thomas Rawlins, 8 Oct. 1706 (copy). See also *The Marlborough–Godolphin Correspondence*, ed. Henry L. Snyder (Oxford, 1975), I, 544, 4n.
60 Longleat, Portland MSS, V, fols. 11, 49: 7 May, 2 July 1706 (copies). The italics are mine.
61 [Desmaizeaux], *Collection*, I, lx.
62 HMC *Portland*, VIII, 279: John Netterville to Harley.
63 *Ibid.*, IV, 408: 16 May 1707.
64 Defoe, *Letters*, 115–18.
65 *Remarks on the Letter to the Author of the State-Memorial* (1706), 3, 30–5.
66 *Review*, III, 169.
67 *POAS*, VII, 15.

68 HMC *Portland*, IV, 283; cf. Loan 29/193, fols. 56–7.

69 *A Letter to the Right Honourable Mr Secretary Harley, by Dr Browne: Occasioned from his late Commitment to Newgate* (1706), 5–8.

70 Loan 29/263, entry under 22 Feb. 1706.

71 *Letter*, 5, 9–10; *Review*, III, 171.

72 HMC *Portland*, IV, 306.

73 Loan 29/193, fols. 172–3.

74 See *POAS*, VII, 642–3.

75 *Dialogue between Louis le Petite, and Harlequin le Grand*, vii–viii. See also *POAS*, VII, 322–9.

76 [Browne], *State Tracts* (1715), I, Preface, sig. A2.

77 Longleat, Portland MSS, V, fol. 253: 30 Oct. 1711.

78 James O. Richards, *Party Propaganda Under Queen Anne: The General Elections of 1702–1713* (Georgia, 1972), 65.

79 PRO, 30/24/20/136, 139, 140; *The Life, Unpublished Letters, and Philosophical Regimen of Anthony, Earl of Shaftesbury*, ed. Benjamin Rand (London, 1900), 384.

80 *POAS*, VII, 161.

81 *Life*, ed. Rand, 354–5: Shaftesbury to Stephens, 17 July 1706.

82 Richards, *Party Propaganda*, 64.

83 See Loan 29/159/11: John Tutchin to Robert Harley, 23 April 1705.

84 Defoe, *Letters*, 85–7: Defoe to Halifax, [*c*. May–June 1705]; Henry L. Snyder, 'Defoe, the Duchess of Marlborough, and the *Advice to the Electors of Great Britain*', *HLQ*, xxix (1965–6), 56–62.

85 John Oldmixon, *The History of England during the Reigns of King William and Queen Mary, Queen Anne, King George I* (1735), 368–9.

86 HMC *Portland*, VIII, 187–8: Fonvive to Harley, 18 July 1705.

87 Calhoun Winton, *Captain Steele* (Baltimore, 1964), 92n. See also *The Correspondence of Richard Steele*, ed. Rae Blanchard (Oxford, 1968), 21–5.

88 Loan 29/158/1: Sunderland to Harley, 20 Jan. 1708. See Henry L. Snyder, 'Godolphin and Harley: A Study of their Partnership in Politics', *HLQ*, xxx (1966–7), 268; Geoffrey Holmes, *British Politics in the Age of Anne* (London, 1967), 115; and Harley's memoranda relating to the Greg case in Loan 29/226.

89 *Cobbett's Parliamentary History of England* (London, 1806–20), VI, 452; *CJ*, XV, 58.

5. THE TORY RESURRECTION, 1708–1710

1 HMC *Portland*, IV, 456; *ibid.*, IX, 289–90.

2 *A Dialogue between Louis le Petite, and Harlequin le Grand; The Welsh-Monster: Or, The Rise and Downfall of that late Upstart, the Right Honourable Innuendo Scribble; POAS*, VII, 297–329. See also HMC *Portland*, IV, 493: Erasmus Lewis to Harley, 19 June 1708.

3 HMC *Bath*, I, 191–2: 11 Oct. 1708.

4 See Henry L. Snyder, 'Defoe, The Duchess of Marlborough, and the *Advice to the Electors of Great Britain*', *HLQ*, xxix (1965–6), 53–62.

5 James O. Richards, *Party Propaganda Under Queen Anne: The General Elections of 1702–1713* (Georgia, 1972), 81.

6 Loan 29/10/22: 14 May 1708.

7   *Ibid.*, 10/1. All quotations from 'Plain English' are from the edition by W. A. Speck and J. A. Downie in *Literature and History*, no. 3 (March 1976), 100–10. Spelling and punctuation have been modernised.

8   On this point, see J. A. Downie, '*The Conduct of the Allies*: The Question of Influence', in *The Art of Jonathan Swift*, ed. Clive T. Probyn (London, 1978), 108–28.

9   Loan 29/171/2.

10 *The Wentworth Papers 1705–1739*, ed. J. J. Cartwright (London, 1833), 74.

11 Loan 29/320: Dyer's Newsletter, 15 Jan. 1709: 'A pamphlet is come out called the *Dream at Harwich*'.

12 HMC *Portland*, IV, 517–18: to his aunt, Abigail Harley; cf. HMC *Bath*, I, 195: [St John to Harley], 26 Jan. 1709.

13 Loan 29/171/3: 12 July 1709.

14 HMC *Portland*, IV, 528: to Harley, 10 Nov. 1709.

15 Loan 29/125/3: n.d. See also HMC *Portland*, IV, 496, 500–1.

16 BL press-mark 3901. b. 22.

17 Bodl. G. Pamph. 820 (10). I quote from this edition.

18 *An Account of a Dream at Harwich* (1708), 2.

19 HMC *Fortescue*, I, 38: Robert Pitt to Thomas Pitt, 15 Nov. 1708.

20 *Wentworth Papers*, 75.

21 *Ibid.*, *Dream at Harwich*, 6–8.

22 *The Interpretation of the Harwich Dream. In a Letter to a Reverend Member of the Convocation, By Don Pedro de la Verdad, the Famous Spanish Interpreter of Cardinal Portocarero's Dream on the Death of King Charles II of Spain* (1709), 2.

23 Loan 29/195, fol. 166: W. Thomas to Edward Harley, 8 Mar. 1709.

24 *Wentworth Papers*, 75.

25 *An Account of a Second Dream at Harwich, Supplying all the Omissions and Defects in the First Dream. In a Letter to the same Member of Parliament, about the Camisars* (1709), 8.

26 *The Speech of Caius Memmius* (1656 [for 1708]), 1. Another edition was sold under the title, *The True Patriot's Speech to the People of Rome. From Sallust* (1656 [for 1708]).

27 *Ibid.*, 4.

28 *Two Speeches for One: Or, Sallust corrected by Livy* [1709], 1.

29 *Cobbett's Parliamentary History of England* (London, 1806–20), VI, 762–6.

30 *Ibid.*, 778–9.

31 *Literature and History*, 107.

32 Loan 29/310, unfoliated: Bromley to Harley, 24 Dec. 1708 and 7 Jan. 1709; cf. *ibid.*, 128/3: the same to the same, 5 Jan. 1709; *ibid.*, 308/2: Haversham to Harley, n.d. [1708–9].

33 John Oldmixon, *The History of England during the Reigns of King William and Queen Mary, Queen Anne, King George I* (1735), 417.

34 Baron Hill MSS, University College of North Wales Library, Bangor.

35 HMC *Portland*, IV, 517: to his aunt, Abigail Harley, 30 Jan. 1709.

36 *Cobbett's Parliamentary History*, VI, 774.

37 *Ibid.*, 775–6.

38 *The Marlborough–Godolphin Correspondence*, ed. Henry L. Snyder (Oxford, 1975), 544: 9 May 1706.

39 Loan 29/171/3.

40 G. M. Trevelyan, *England Under Queen Anne* (London, 1965), III, 62.

41 *POAS*, VII, 319–21.

42 Swift, *Prose Works*, VII, 73.

43 Loan 29/38/1: n.d. Cf. HMC *Portland*, V, 55: 19 July 1711.

44 *New Atalantis* (1709), II, 165; *Letter from the Grecian Coffee-house*, 7.

45 See Gwendolyn B. Needham, 'Mary de la Riviere Manley, Tory Defender', *HLQ*, xii (1948–9), 264–5.

46 HMC *Portland*, IV, 451.

47 Gilbert Burnet, *History of My Own Time* (Oxford, 1833), V, 435.

48 See the introduction to The Rota edition of Henry Sacheverell, *The Perils of False Brethren* (University of Exeter, 1974).

49 HMC *Portland*, IV, 530: to Harley, 21 Dec. 1709.

50 Geoffrey Holmes, *The Trial of Doctor Sacheverell* (London, 1972), 85, 228.

51 Geoffrey Holmes, 'The Sacheverell Riots: The Crowd and the Church in early eighteenth-century London', *Past & Present*, no. 72 (1976), 55–85.

52 *Review*, VI, 542–3.

53 Over 500 titles are to be found in F. F. Madan, *A Critical Bibliography of Dr Henry Sacheverell*, ed. W. A. Speck, (Kansas, 1978).

54 Lee Horsley, '*Vox Populi* in the Political Literature of 1710', *HLQ*, xxxviii (1974–5), 340.

55 HMC *Bath*, III, 437: to Matthew Prior, 15 June 1710.

56 Bodl. Ballard MS 38, fol. 147: to Arthur Charlett, 1 July 1710.

57 See B. W. Hill, 'The Change of Government and the "Loss of the City", 1710–1711', *Economic History Review*, xxiv (1971), 395–411.

58 Loan 29/52/1.

59 HMC *Portland*, IV, 574–5: Robert Monckton to Harley, 23 Aug. 1710.

60 *A Collection of the Addresses which have been presented to the Queen* (1711), 9; *POAS*, VII, 499.

61 *Collection of the Addresses*, 9. My italics.

62 See *The Divided Society: Party Conflict in England 1694–1716*, ed. G. S. Holmes and W. A. Speck (London, 1967), 126–7.

63 Cf. Paul B. Patterson, 'Robert Harley and the Organisation of Political Propaganda' (unpublished PhD thesis, University of Virginia, 1974), 25–30, 138–43, 228–30, 243–51.

64 *The Original Works of William King, LL.D.* (1776), II, 274–9.

65 All quotations from *Faults on Both Sides* are taken from the reprint in *Somers Tracts*, XII.

66 *Ibid.*, 694, 701, 695.

67 *Ibid.*, 696–8.

68 Loan 29/52/1.

69 John Oldmixon, *The Life and Posthumous Works of Arthur Maynwaring* (London, 1715), 171; *Medley*, no. 5; Loan 29/160/9: A. Wilkinson to Harley, 23 Oct. 1710.

70 Burnet, *History*, VI, 12: Onslow's note. See also Henry L. Snyder, 'The Authorship of *Faults on Both Sides*', *Philological Quarterly*, lvi (1977), 266–72.

71 *Medley*, no. 5.

72 HMC *Portland*, VIII, 74. See also *Calendar of Treasury Books*, XII, 184; *ibid.*, XIV,

160; *ibid.*, XVII, 768; *Calendar of Treasury Papers*, LVII, 230; *Catalogue of the Goldsmiths' Library*, I, 3,101, 3,267, 3,487.

73 Loan 29/287, unfoliated: Clement to Harley, 25 Nov. 1704. See also *Calendar of Treasury Books*, XVIII, 267.

74 Loan 29/293, unfoliated (cf. *ibid.*, *passim*); *ibid*, 9/18–19, 35; *ibid.*, 10/23; HMC *Portland*, VIII, 277, 344–5, 377.

75 Loan 29/265, unfoliated: Harley to Churchill, 23 Sept. 1707 (copy); HMC *Portland*, VIII, 296: Churchill to Harley, 24 Sept. 1707.

76 *Calendar of Treasury Books*, XXII, 306.

77 Oldmixon, *History*, 476.

78 *Calendar of Treasury Books*, XXVII, 180; *ibid.*, XXIX, 209.

79 Loan 29/29/22: Dennis Clement to Oxford, n.d.; *ibid.*: Peterborough to Oxford, 13 July 1712. In 1709 Clement saw 'no other way to escape ruin' but through Harley's assistance. *Ibid.*, 39. See also *ibid.*, 45W/2–5.

80 See J. A. Downie, PhD thesis, 267–9.

81 John Oldmixon, *Memoirs of the Press* (London, 1742), 8.

82 *The Management of the War, In a Letter to a Tory Member* (1711), 3. According to Henry Snyder, Arthur Maynwaring and Francis Hare collaborated on this pamphlet, see 'Daniel Defoe, Arthur Maynwaring, Robert Walpole, and Abel Boyer: Some Considerations of Authorship', *HLQ*, xxxiii (1969–70), 148n.

83 HMC *Portland*, IV, 615.

84 *Ibid.*, 94, 111, 141; Loan 29/127/4.

85 *Ibid.*

86 *Somers Tracts*, XIII, 52.

87 White Kennett, *The Wisdom of Looking Backwards* (1715), 77.

88 *Review*, VII, 137.

89 *Ibid.*, 234, 261.

90 Defoe, *Letters*, 270–1.

91 *Ibid.*, 273.

92 *Review*, VII, 234–6.

93 Defoe, *Letters*, 276: 5 Sept. 1710.

94 *An Essay upon Public Credit* (1710), 26–7.

95 *Review*, VII, 254.

96 Defoe, *Letters*, pp. 276–7. See also Oldmixon, *History*, 449; *Medley*, no. 1: 5 Oct. 1710; *The Diary of Sir David Hamilton 1709–1714*, ed. Philip Roberts (1975), 17.

97 This has recently been the subject of a full-length study. See Sheila Biddle, *Bolingbroke and Harley* (London, 1974).

98 Viscount Bolingbroke, *A Letter to Sir William Windham* (1753), 22.

99 See H. T. Dickinson, 'The October Club', *HLQ*, xxxiii (1969–70), 155–73.

100 Swift, *Prose Works*, XV, 86: 8 Nov. 1710. See *POAS*, VII, 475–9.

101 Swift, *Prose Works*, XV, 36.

102 *The Original Works of William King, LL.D.*, I, xxi.

103 Swift, *Prose Works*, VIII, 123.

104 *Ibid.*, XV, 91–2.

105 *Ibid.*, 46; W. A. Speck, 'The *Examiner* Examined: Swift's Tory Pamphleteering', in *Focus: Swift*, ed. Claude Rawson (London, 1971), 145–6.

106 See W. A. Speck, 'From Principles to Practice: Swift and Party Politics', in *The*

World of Jonathan Swift, ed. Brian Vickers (London, 1968), 81.

107 Swift, *Prose Works*, VIII, 123.

108 *Ibid.*, III, 3–4: 2 Nov. 1710.

109 *Ibid.*, 14: 16 Nov. 1710. The italics are mine.

110 *Review*, VII, 383.

111 Pat Rogers, *Grub Street: Studies in a Subculture* (London, 1972), 320.

6. SWIFT, DEFOE, AND THE PEACE CAMPAIGN

1 John Oldmixon, *The Life and Posthumous Works of Arthur Maynwaring* (London, 1715), 276.

2 *Swift, Prose Works*, XVI, 519: 21 Mar. 1712; Ehrenpreis, *Swift*, II, 577.

3 Loan 29/158/9. See also J. A. Downie, 'Dr Swift's Bill', *N & Q*, ccxxiii (1978), 42–3.

4 Swift, *Prose Works*, XVI, 589; 26 Dec. 1712.

5 W. A. Speck, 'From Principles to Practice: Swift and Party Politics', in *The World of Jonathan Swift*, ed. Brian Vickers (London, 1968) 68; cf. Ehrenpreis, *Swift*, II, 608–9.

6 See *The Diary of Sir David Hamilton 1709–1714*, ed. Philip Roberts (Oxford, 1975). In Loan 29/415 there are MS notes in Oxford's hand: 'State of the Case of the deanery of St Patrick's: Qu. Whither it be elective or in the Crown to present? Qu. Whither the Crown is obliged to present one of the Chapter?'

7 See Swift, *Prose Works*, XVI, 446: 26 Dec. 1711; Hamilton's *Diary*, 40; and Philip Roberts, 'Swift, Queen Anne, and *The Windsor Prophecy*', *Philological Quarterly*, xlix (1970), 254–8.

8 See Maurice Quinlan, 'The Prosecution of Swift's *Public Spirit of the Whigs*', *Texas Studies in Literature and Language*, ix (1967), 167–84, and above, pp. 179–80.

9 Richard I. Cook, *Jonathan Swift as a Tory Pamphleteer* (Washington, 1967), 31.

10 Swift, *Prose Works*, XV, 146.

11 *Ibid.*, 159, 178.

12 *Ibid.*, 208.

13 *Ibid*, III, 87–8.

14 HMC *Portland*, v, 464.

15 Swift, *Prose Works*, XV, 194–5.

16 *Ibid.*, VIII, 128. For the *Examiner's* account, see *ibid.*, III, 106–10. See also H. T. Dickinson, 'The Attempt to Assassinate Harley, 1711', *History Today*, xv (1965), 788–95.

17 Loan 29/166/2: in Harley's hand, dated 8 May 1711.

18 Swift, *Prose Works*, XV, 244–5.

19 *Ibid.*, 252–3.

20 *Ibid.*, 272–3.

21 *Ibid.*, 291. For some reason Harold Williams relegates the last part of this quotation (from 'so that if they go on ...') to a footnote in his edition of the *Journal*, without providing any explanation.

22 *Ibid.*, 303.

23 A. D. MacLachlan, 'The Road to Peace', in *Britain after the Glorious Revolution*, ed. Geoffrey Holmes (London, 1969), 210–11.

24 Cook, *Jonathan Swift*, 19–30. See HMC *Portland*, IV, 641: J. Durden to Harley, 5 Dec. 1710.

25 Swfit, *Prose Works*, XV, 322, 340, 343.

26 *Ibid*, 333–4.

27 Defoe, *Letters*, 307: 26 Dec. 1710.

28 *Ibid.*, 331.

29 *Ibid.*, 334.

30 Douglas Coombs, *The Conduct of the Dutch; British Opinion and the Dutch Alliance during the War of the Spanish Succession* (The Hague, 1958), 258.

31 *Review*, VIII, 279.

32 *Reasons why this Nation* (1711), 12, 26–28.

33 *Ibid.*, 33, 37.

34 Defoe, *Letters*, 362: 30 Nov. 1711.

35 Swift, *Prose Works*, XVI, 397.

36 See J. A. Downie, '*The Conduct of the Allies*: The Question of Influence', in *The Art of Jonathan Swift*, ed. Clive T. Probyn (London, 1978), 108–28.

37 Swift, *Prose Works*, VI, 5.

38 *Ibid.*, 15–16.

39 *Ibid.*, 53–4.

40 *Ibid.*, XVI, 441: 18 Dec. 1711. Oxford bought 200. See Loan 29/13/1.

41 *Ibid.*, 431: 6 Dec. 1711.

42 *Ibid.*, 480, 482.

43 *Ibid*, 430.

44 *POAS*, VII, 526–7.

45 Swift, *Prose Works*, VI, 87. Oxford bought 100 copies of the *Remarks*. See Loan 29/13/1.

46 *Review*, VIII, 579–80.

47 *Remarks On a False, Scandalous, and Seditious Libel, Entitled, The Conduct of the Allies* (1711), 2.

48 *A Further Search* (1712), 3–5.

49 *Ibid*.

50 *A Justification of the Dutch* (1712), 31.

51 *Review*, VIII, 461–2. See also Lawrence Postan III, 'Defoe and the Peace Campaign, 1710–1713: A Reconsideration', *HLQ*, XXVII (1963–4), 1–20.

52 *Imperial Gratitude* (1712), 76.

53 Defoe, *Letters*, 376–7: 5 June 1712.

54 Swift, *Prose Works*, XVI, 421–2, 441. Cf. Loan 29/13/1.

7. THE STAMP ACT OF 1712

1 *Journals of the House of Lords*, XV, 545. See Frederick Seaton Siebert, *Freedom of the Press in England 1476–1776: The Rise and Decline of Government Control* (Urbana, Illinois, 1965), 262–3.

2 *CJ*, XIII, 699; *Journals of the House of Lords*, XVII, 22.

3 Defoe, *An Essay on the Regulation of the Press*, 24.

4 *CJ*, XVII, 28.

5 *Ibid.*, 175, 185, 191, 198, 204, 210, 220, 247, 251.

6 *Ibid.*

7 Swift, *Prose Works*, XVI, 499.

8 *Collection of the Addresses*, 9.

9 John Oldmixon, *The History of England during the Reigns of King William and Queen Mary, Queen Anne, King George I* (London, 1735), 476.

10 Staffordshire RO, Chetwynd Diplomatic Correspondence, D. 649/8: George Tilson to John Chetwynd, 16 Oct. 1711. See also Swift, *Prose Works*, XV, 365.

11 *Letters and Correspondence, Public and Private, of The Right Honourable Henry St John, Viscount Bolingbroke; During the Time he was Secretary of State to Queen Anne,* ed. Gilbert Parke (1798), I, 60, 71.

12 Longleat, Portland MSS, IV, fols. 148–9.

13 HMC *Portland*, V, 96: 2 Oct. 1711. See also Swift, *Prose Works*, XVI, 390–1.

14 Longleat, Portland MSS, V, fols. 253–4: 30 Oct. 1711 (copy).

15 Swift, *Prose Works*, VII, 103–4.

16 Ehrenpreis, *Swift*, II, 568.

17 David H. Stevens, *Party Politics and English Journalism 1702–1742* (Menasha, Wisconsin, 1916), 33.

18 Ehrenpreis, *Swift*, II, 568.

19 Swift, *Prose Works*, II, 381. See also *ibid.*, 384–5.

20 *The Political State of Great Britain*, XXXIII [1727], 155–6. Boyer was also prosecuted in 1714 'for handing to the press, at the desire of an Hanoverian gentleman, the late queen's letter to the late Princess Sophia, and the late earl of Oxford's letters to his present majesty and to his royal highness' (*ibid.*). See also HMC *Portland*, V, 470, 473: [Dyer's] Newsletters, 6 and 20 July 1714.

21 Phyllis J. Guskin, 'The Authorship of the *Protestant Post Boy*, 1711–12', *N & Q*, ccxx (1975), 489–90.

22 Swift, *Prose Works*, XV, 365.

23 Oldmixon, *History*, 494–5, 472, 476.

24 Luttrell, VI, 680; *CJ*, XVI, 462.

25 Swift, *Prose Works*, XV, 177–8: 31 Jan. 1711.

26 PRO, T. 1, 129, fols. 147–8. See J. R. Sutherland, 'The Circulation of Newspapers 1700–1730', *The Library*, fourth series, XV (1934), 110–24.

27 Loan 29/280, fol. 80.

28 *Ibid.*, fols. 79, 85, 112. See J. A. Downie, 'A New Steele Letter', *The Scriblerian*, VIII (1976), 78.

29 Loan 29/10/5, n.d.

30 *A Collection of Several Acts of Parliament, Published in the Years 1648, 1649, 1650, and 1651. By Henry Scobell, Esq.* (1651), 44–5.

31 BL press mark 8223. c. 9 (77, 78, 79, 85, 86). See Joseph M. Thomas, 'Swift and the Stamp Act of 1712', *Publications of the Modern Language Association of America*, xxxi (1916), 262.

32 *Review*, VIII, 687, 700.

33 Swift, *Prose Works*, XVI, 553.

34 Ehrenpreis, *Swift*, II, 568–9.

35 Swift, *Prose Works*, VII, 105.

36 *Ibid.*, 103–6.

37 In April 1711, with Harley still out of action after Guiscard's assassination attempt,

St John badly mishandled the Commons over the leather duty. This vital piece of supply was thrown out with the secretary not even present. The following day he blithely introduced a tax on hides and skins in its place. 'I am heartily sorry to find my friend the secretary stand a little ticklish with the rest of the ministry', Swift wrote on 27 April, 'there have been one or two disobliging things that have happened, too long to tell'. *Ibid*, xv, 252.

38 *The History of the Proceedings of the Second Session of this Present Parliament* (1713), 84.

39 *The History and Defence of the Last Parliament* (1713), 183. See also Oldmixon, *History*, 476.

40 *The Miscellaneous Works of Dr William Wagstaffe* (second edition, 1726), 211: *The Plain Dealer*, no. 2, 19 April 1712.

41 *Ibid.*, 212.

42 David H. Stevens, *Party Politics and English Journalism 1702–1742* (Menasha, Wisconsin, 1916), 33.

43 A. Aspinall, 'Statistical Accounts of the London Newspapers in the Eighteenth Century', *EHR*, lxiii (1948), 208–9.

44 *Reasons Humbly offered to the Honourable House of Commons against Laying a farther Duty upon Paper*, n.d., broadsheet.

45 Luttrell, vi, 680–1.

46 Swift, *Prose Works*, xvi, 553–4.

47 J. M. Price, 'A Note on the Circulation of the London Press', *BIHR*, xxxi (1958), 218–19.

48 Siebert, *Freedom of the Press*, 314.

49 Swift, *Prose Works*, xvi, 568–9.

50 W. T. Morgan, *A Bibliography of British History (1700–1715)* (Bloomington, Indiana, 1934–42), ii, 361–443; v, 78–80. Cf. *POAS*, vii, 570–1.

51 Ian Maxted, *The London Book Trades 1775–1800* (London, 1977), xxxi.

52 D. F. Foxon, *English Verse 1701–1750: A Catalogue of Separately Printed Poems with Notes on Contemporary Collected Editions* (Cambridge, 1975), ii, 81–8.

53 W. A. Speck, 'Political Propaganda in Augustan England', *Trans. Royal Historical Society*, fifth series, xxii (1972), 19.

54 *CJ*, xvii, 278. See Swift, *Prose Works*, vi, 202–3; *ibid.*, xvi, 635. For various MS drafts of the speech, see Loan 29/7/9, 14.

8. THE ORGANISATION OF PROPAGANDA, 1710–1714

1 Swift, *Prose Works*, xv, 268–9: 14 May 1711. See also *ibid.*, xvi, 381: 10 Oct. 1711.

2 *Ibid.*, 500–1.

3 Geoffrey Holmes, *British Politics in the Age of Anne* (London, 1967), 30.

4 HMC *Dartmouth*, i, 296.

5 John Oldmixon, *The History of England during the Reigns of King William and Queen Mary, Queen Anne, King George I* (London, 1735), 100.

6 *The Wentworth Papers 1705–1739*, ed. J. J. Cartwright (London, 1833), 212; *POAS*, vii, 499n.

7 *Remarks On a False, Scandalous, and Seditious Libel*, 2.

8 Stowe MS 226, fol. 16: Ridpath to Robethon, 14 Feb. 1714.

9 Swift, *Prose Works*, XVI, 519. Cf. *ibid.*, 446, 572, 574, 579.

10 *Quadriennium Anne Postremum: Or, The Political State of Great Britain* (1718), I, 226.

11 Loan 29/127/4.

12 HMC *Portland*, IV, 615: 17 Oct. 1710.

13 Swift, *Prose Works*, XVI, 384-5.

14 Loan 29/127/4: 19 Nov. 1711. Boyer claimed to have been discharged through Oxford's intervention. *Annals of Queen Anne* (1711), 264-5.

15 Swift, *Prose Works*, XVI, 452. For King, see George C. Williams, 'Dr William King, Humorist', *Sewanee Review*, XXXV (1927), 3-7.

16 HMC *Portland*, V, 55, 95-6; cf. Swift, *Prose Works*, XV, 306.

17 *Ibid.*, XVI, 474.

18 *The Guardian*, 12 May 1713; cf. Ehrenpreis, *Swift*, II, 681.

19 Swift, *Prose Works*, XVI, 430, 637. For the relations of Swift and Oldisworth, see Robert J. Allen, 'William Oldisworth: "The Author of the *Examiner*" ', *Philological Quarterly*, XXVI (1947), 159-73. See also Loan 29/13/1.

20 Swift, *Prose Works*, XVI, 472.

21 *Ibid.*, 454.

22 *Ibid.*, 500-1, 510. For Swift's relations with Arbuthnot, see Ehrenpreis, *Swift*, II, 507-10.

23 See John Arbuthnot, *The History of John Bull*, ed. Alan W. Bower and Robert A. Erickson (Oxford, 1976).

24 *Ibid.*, 168.

25 Swift, *Prose Works*, XVI, 494.

26 Cf. Paul B. Patterson, 'Harley and the Organisation of Political Propaganda' (unpublished PhD thesis, University of Virginia, 1974), 148.

27 *The Miscellaneous Works of Dr William Wagstaffe* (second edition, 1726), 212, 253.

28 *Ibid.*, 247; Arbuthnot, *History of John Bull*, ed. Bower and Erickson, xvii.

29 *POAS*, VII, 572-3.

30 HMC *Portland*, IV, 577.

31 Swift, *Prose Works*, XV, 82-3.

32 *The Diary of Sir David Hamilton 1709-1714*, ed. Philip Roberts (Oxford, 1975), 17.

33 HMC *Portland*, IV, 456.

34 *Ibid.*, 572.

35 *Ibid.*, V, 4.

36 [Pierre Desmaizeaux], *A Collection of several pieces of Mr. John Toland, Now first Published from his Original Manuscripts: with Some Memoirs of his Life and Writings* (1726), II, 222, 237.

37 HMC *Portland*, V, 127: Toland to Oxford, 7 Dec. 1711.

38 Loan 29/162/5: anon. to Oxford, 19 Nov. 1711.

39 *The Private Diary of William, First Earl Cowper*, ed. E. C. Hawtrey (London, 1833), 55.

40 Loan 29/147/1: Hoffman to Oxford, 22 Sept. 1711.

41 HMC *Portland*, V, 94-5; NUL, Portland MSS, Pw2 Hy 956.

42 Loan 29/132/5: Henry Crispe to Oxford, 5 Jan. 1713. See also Loan 29/299: Charles Leslie to Oxford, 10 July 1711 and n.d.

43 Swift, *Prose Works*, XVI, 454.

44 Patterson, 'Harley', 147–8.

45 Swift, *Prose Works*, XVI, 516, 550; see also *ibid.*, XV, 158, 209, 268–9, 340; *ibid.*, XVI, 650–1; *Letters of Swift to Ford*, ed. D. Nichol Smith (Oxford, 1935), 15, 17.

46 Swift, *Prose Works*, XVI, 553.

47 *Ibid.*, 397.

48 See Allen, 'William Oldisworth', 172–3. Cf. Loan 29/13/1.

49 Swift, *Prose Works*, XV, 300, 316, 320–1, 323.

50 *Ibid.*, III, 89.

51 HMC *Portland*, IV, 641: J. Durden to Harley, 5 Dec. 1710.

52 *Review*, I[x], 209–10.

53 Defoe, *Letters*, 414, 441.

54 HMC *Portland*, V, 299–300: June 1713.

55 Geoffrey Holmes, 'Harley, St John and the Death of the Tory Party', in *Britain after the Glorious Revolution 1689–1714* (London, 1969), 224–5. Cf. Ehrenpreis, *Swift*, II, 669.

56 *Correspondence of Jonathan Swift*, ed. H. Williams (Oxford, 1963–5), I, 375.

57 *Mercator*, no. 101: 12–14 Jan. 1714.

58 *Appeal to Honour and Justice* in *Selected Writings of Daniel Defoe*, ed. James T. Boulton (Cambridge, 1975), 183.

59 Defoe, *Letters*, 405–7: 12 Apr. 1713.

60 PRO, SP 34/21/241.

61 Defoe, *Letters*, 411: 19 Apr. 1713.

62 *Review*, I[x], nos. 84, 85, 89, 91.

63 Defoe, *Letters*, 415, 422. The pardon, in PRO, SP 34/37.

64 Roger Coke, *A Detection of the Court and State of England* (1719), 76. See also *Review*, VII, 113.

65 *Whig-Examiner*, 14 Sept. 1710.

66 Henry L. Snyder, 'Arthur Maynwaring and the Whig Press, 1710–1712', in *Literatur als Kritik des Lebens: Festschrift Zum 65. Geburtstag Von Ludwig Borinski*, ed. Rudolf Haas, Heinz-Joachim Müllenbrock and Claus Uhlig (Heidelberg, 1977), 121.

67 Blenheim MSS E 25: Maynwaring to the duchess of Marlborough, n.d. [*c.* 9 July 1711], cited in Snyder, 'Maynwaring and the Whig Press', 127.

68 *Ibid.*, 133.

69 Brampton Bryan, Harley MSS, Box 117: Lord Harley to [Auditor Harley?]

70 Defoe, *Letters*, 424: 31 Oct. 1713.

71 Swift, *Prose Works*, XVI, 644: 23 Mar. 1713.

72 *POAS*, VII, 590–6.

73 Loan 29/7/9, 14; Swift, *Prose Works*, XVI, 635.

74 Oldmixon, *History*, 518–19.

75 Defoe, *Letters*, 418–19.

76 *Ibid.*, 438: [*c.* 10 Mar. 1714]. Buckley's role is difficult to document, and there is no firm evidence of his involvement in the organisation of whig propaganda. His significance, however, can be strongly asserted, especially when he became editor of the *Gazette*.

77 Swift, *Prose Works*, VIII, 31. See also NUL, Portland MSS, Pw2 Hy 956: Francis Hoffman to Oxford, n.d.

78 Defoe, *Letters*, 430: 19 Feb. 1714.

79 Calhoun Winton, 'Steele and the Fall of Harley in 1714', *Philological Quarterly*, xxxvii (1958), 447. See also J. R. Moore, 'Defoe, Steele, and the Demolition of Dunkirk', *HLQ*, xiii (1949–50), 279–302.
80 Ehrenpreis, *Swift*, II, 702.
81 Swift, *Prose Works*, VIII, 31.
82 *CJ*, XVII, 474–5.
83 *Cobbett's Parliamentary History of England* (London, 1806–20), VI, 1263.
84 Swift, *Prose Works*, VIII, 50–1.
85 See Maurice Quinlan, 'The Prosecution of Swift's *Public Spirit of the Whigs*', *Texas Studies in Literature and Language*, ix (1967), 167–84.
86 *Cobbett's Parliamentary History*, VI, 1263.
87 *Political State* (1719), VII, 233–6.
88 *Correspondence of Jonathan Swift*, ed. Williams, II, 38: Swift to the earl of Peterborough, 18 May 1714.
89 Swift, *Prose Works*, VIII, 76.
90 *Correspondence of Jonathan Swift*, ed. Williams, II, 41: 26 June 1714. Oxford was nicknamed the 'dragon' 'by contraries'.
91 *Ibid.*, 12: Oxford to Swift, 4 Mar. 1714.
92 David H. Stevens, *Party Politics and English Journalism 1702–1742* (Menasha, Wisconsin, 1916), 67; Swift, *Prose Works*, XVI, 637.
93 HMC *Portland*, V, 453–4, 458.
94 Defoe, *Letters*, 442: Defoe to Oxford, 26 July 1714; cf. Laurence Hanson, *Government and the Press 1695–1763* (Oxford, 1936), 96.
95 Oldmixon, *History*, 476.
96 J. H. Plumb, *The Growth of Political Stability in England, 1675–1725* (London, 1967), 152.

EPILOGUE: IMPEACHMENT AND AFTER

1 HMC *Portland*, V, 484 (draft).
2 Loan 29/70/10: Oxford to Auditor Harley, 13 Feb. 1717 (copy). His 'Large Account: Revolution and Succession' should also be taken into consideration.
3 Samuel Johnson, *Poems*, ed. E. L. McAdam, Jr, with George Milne (Cambridge, Mass., 1964), 97.
4 HMC *Portland*, V, 491: 30 Aug. 1714.
5 Defoe, *Letters*, 443–4: 3 Aug. 1714.
6 *Ibid.*, 444–5: 26 Aug. 1714. Cf. J. A. Downie, ' "Mistakes On all Sides": A New Defoe Manuscript', *RES*, n.s., xxvii (1976), 431–7.
7 Defoe, *Letters*, 445–7: 31 Aug. 1714.
8 *Selected Writings of Daniel Defoe*, ed. James T. Boulton (Cambridge, 1975), 194. The last extant letter between the two men is dated 28 Sept. 1714 (Defoe, *Letters*, 447–8).
9 *The Secret History of the White Staff, Being an Account of Affairs under the Conduct of the Late Ministers, and of What Might Probably Have Happened if Her Majesty Had Not Died* (1714), 19–20.
10 *The Secret History ... Part III* (1715), 76.
11 John Oldmixon, *The History of England during the Reigns of King William and Queen Mary, Queen Anne, King George I* (London, 1735), 537.

12 Loan 29/171/4; cf. *ibid*.: the same to the same, 12 Mar. 1715.

13 HMC *Portland*, V, 501.

14 A MS copy of this notice is extant in the Harley papers at Brampton Bryan, Box 117.

15 See W. L. Purves, *The Authorship of Robinson Crusoe* (London, 1903), and James Means, 'Lord Oxford and the Authorship of *Robinson Crusoe*', *The Scriblerian*, ix (1977), 139–40.

16 Loan 29/38/6: 17 Dec. 1715.

17 'Epistle to Robert Earl of Oxford, and Earl Mortimer', in *The Poems of Alexander Pope: A One-Volume Edition of the Twickenham Text with Selected Annotations*, ed. John Butt (London, 1963), 313–14. See Geoffrey Tillotson, 'Pope's "Epistle to Harley": An Introduction and analysis', in *Pope and his Contemporaries: Essays presented to George Sherburn*, ed. James L. Clifford and Louis A. Landa (Oxford, 1949), 58–77.

18 He has also been identified as Lord Munodi in *A Voyage to Laputa*, but see J. A. Downie, 'Political Characterization in *Gulliver's Travels*', *The Yearbook of English Studies*, vii (1977), 108–21.

19 *A Continuation of the Review of a Late Treatise* (1742), 56–61.

20 T. B. Macaulay, *A History of England to the Death of William III*, ed. C. H. Firth (London, 1916), VI, 2409.

21 Winston Churchill, *Marlborough, His Life and Times* (London, 1933–8), II, 311; [W. A. Shaw], *Calendar of Treasury Books. Introduction to Vols. XI–XVII*, 1.

22 Keith Feiling, *A History of the Tory Party 1640–1714* (Oxford, 1924); Henry L. Snyder, 'Godolphin and Harley: A Study of their Partnership in Politics', *HLQ*, xxx (1966–7), 241–71; Elizabeth Hamilton *The Backstairs Dragon: A Life of Robert Harley, Earl of Oxford* (London, 1969); Angus McInnes, *Robert Harley: Puritan Politician* (London, 1970); Sheila Biddle, *Bolingbroke and Harley* (London, 1974).

23 *The Life, Unpublished Letters, and Philosophical Regimen of Anthony, Earl of Shaftesbury*, ed. Benjamin Rand (London, 1900), 512.

24 [Sir Humphry Mackworth?], *A Word of Advice* (1705), 6.

25 *Collection of Addresses* (1711).

26 Paul Langford, *The Excise Crisis: Society and Politics in the Age of Walpole* (Oxford, 1975), 151.

27 Loan 29/171/4: to Stratford, 22 Mar. 1715.

28 Swift, *Prose Works*, XVI, 430–1: 5 Dec. 1711.

29 *POAS*, VII, 521.

30 Cf. Michael Foot, *The Pen and the Sword* (London, 1957).

31 James Boswell, *The Life of Samuel Johnson, with a Journal of a Tour to the Hebrides*, ed. G. B. Hill, revised L. F. Powell (6 vols. 1934–50), I, 115–16.

32 Langford, *Excise Crisis*, 21–3; Bertrand A. Goldgar, *Walpole and the Wits: The Relation of Politics to Literature, 1722–1742* (Lincoln, Nebraska, 1977).

Index

Campbell, Mr, 123
censorship, *see* press
Charles II, 19, 20, 30, 32, 35, 43, 119
Charles II of Spain, 39, 48, 166
Church of England, 7–8, 63, 72–3, 80, 81–3, 88–9, 105–6, 116, 118–19, 120, 127–8; 'Church in Danger', 11, 72–3, 81–3, 99, 106, 108, 119; 'Church party', 12, 103
Churchill, George, 122, 215
Churchill, John, *see* Marlborough, John Churchill, 1st duke of
Churchill, Winston, 190
circulation: of newspapers, 6–7, 8–10; of pamphlets, 10–11, 159
Clare, Robert, 84, 86, 210
Clarges, Sir Thomas, 19–20, 24
Clarke, Edward, 27, 36, 42, 50
Clement, Dennis, 122
Clement, Simon, 43, 121–2, 125, 134, 168, 214–15; 'Case of Prohibitions of Commerce and Correspondence with our Enemies Truly Represented, The', 121; *Faults on Both Sides*, 21, 43, 106, 119–22, 128, 214; *Short Discourse Concerning the Coin, A*, 121
Clements, Henry, 116
coffee-houses, 6, 8–9, 15, 67, 70, 93, 143 (*see also* Grecian Coffee-house)
Coke, Thomas, 52–3, 204
Conduct of the Allies and the Late Ministry, The, *see* Swift, Jonathan
Cook, Richard, I., 133
Coombs, Douglas, 64, 139
country party, 20–4, 33–5, 38–40, 41, 44, 47, 50, 53, 54, 56; organisation of propaganda, 22, 23–5, 26–7, 29–33, 34–5, 36–9, 42–5, 48–56, 104–15, 178; 'country theory', 20–3, 82–3, 104–5, 126, 128
court party, 21, 28, 31, 33–5, 38, 41, 43, 82, 104; organisation of propaganda, 25–7, 30, 31, 33–4, 57–79, 88–90, 92–3, 98–100, 104, 110–12, 119–48, 162–72, 176, 178–83, 191–5
Cowper, William, 1st earl, 86–7, 100, 118, 122, 125, 168, 174, 210; *Letter to Isaac Bickerstaff, A*, 122, 174
Craftsman, The, 194
Crispe, Henry, 169, 220

Daily Courant, The, 3, 7, 9–10, 97, 150, 174, 178, 182
Danger of Mercenary Parliaments, The, 34–5, 37, 43, 203
Dartmouth, William Legge, 1st earl of, 117, 144
Davenant, Charles, 2, 37–9, 46, 48–56, 60–1, 63–4, 69, 75, 84, 91, 103, 132, 167–8, 171, 208; organisation of propaganda, 2, 41, 52–5; *Discourse upon Grants and Resumptions, A*, 37–8, 46; *Essays on Peace at Home and War Abroad*, 63–4, 69, 75; *Essays upon I. The Balance of Power*, 39, 48–9; *Essay upon Trade*, 37; *Mercator, The*, 168, 171; *Sir Thomas Double at Court*, 54, 167; *Tom Double Returned Out of the Country*, 54; *True Picture of a Modern Whig, A*, 49–50, 54, 56
Davenant, Henry, 91, 132, 208, 210
Defoe, Daniel, 1, 2, 3, 5, 6, 9, 11–12, 13, 14, 15, 33–4, 46, 54, 56, 59–79, 80, 81, 83, 84, 88, 89, 92–3, 94, 96, 97, 98, 99, 103, 104, 116, 119, 121, 124–5, 128–30, 131, 132, 133–4, 139–41, 145–8, 150, 151, 155, 156, 158–9, 162, 169, 170, 171–3, 174, 175–6, 177, 178, 179, 180, 182, 186–8, 191, 192, 193, 194, 195; audience, 6–8; 'King William's pamphleteer', 33–4, 42, 46; in prison, 13, 60, 61–3, 172–3; in Scotland, 71, 76–7, 98, 104, 139, 209; intelligence network, 2, 69–71; peace campaign, 139–41, 145–8; propaganda in 1705, 72–3, 81, 97; relations with Harley, 59–66, 67–71, 72–9, 124–5, 139–41, 145–8, 162, 171–3, 182, 186–8; style, 6, 14, 129–30; under the Oxford ministry, 129–34, 139–41, 145–8, 162, 171–3, 192; *Account of the Conduct of Robert, Earl of Oxford, An*, 186, 188; *And what if the Pretender should come?*, 172–3; *Answer to a Question that Nobody Thinks of, An*, 172–3; *Appeal to Honour and Justice, An*, 42, 186, 207; *Argument showing that a Standing Army, with Consent of Parliament, is not Inconsistent with a Free Government, An*, 33; *Atalantis Major*, 139; *Challenge of Peace, A*, 64; *Collection of Dyer's Letters, A*, 70; *Defence of the Allies and the Late Ministry, A*, 146; *Dyet of Poland, The*, 89; *Essay on the Regulation of the Press, An*, 68, 150, 155; *Essay on the Treaty of Commerce, An*, 171; *Essay upon Public Credit, An*, 125, 167; *Further Search into the Conduct of the Allies, A*, 146–7; *High Church Legion, The*, 88, 89; *History of the Kentish Petition, A*, 46, 60, 67; *Honour and Prerogative of the Queen's Majesty Vindicated, The*, 179; *Imperial Gratitude*, 141; *Justice and Necessity of a War with Holland, The*, 147; *Justification of the Dutch, A*, 146; 'Legion-Letter, The', 46, 47, 50, 60, 75, 190; *Legion's Humble Address to the House of Lords*, 68; *Little Review, The*, 65; *London Post, The*, 6; *Master-Mercury, The*, 68–9; *Mercator, The*, 1, 168, 170, 171–2, 177, 181–2; *Minutes of the Negotiations of Monsieur Mesnager*, 186; *Reasons against Fighting*, 147; *Reasons against the Succession of the House of Honover*, 172–3; *Reasons why this Nation Ought to put a Speedy End to this Expensive War*, 140–1; *Remarks on the Letter to the Author of the State-Memorial*, 2, 69, 70, 92–3, 96; *Review, The*, 1, 2, 6, 7,